FROM JACOBIN TO LIBERAL

FROM JACOBIN TO LIBERAL

MARC-ANTOINE JULLIEN, 1775–1848

Edited and Translated by R. R. Palmer

PRINCETON UNIVERSITY PRESS

PRINCETON, NEW JERSEY

COPYRIGHT © 1993 BY PRINCETON UNIVERSITY PRESS

PUBLISHED BY PRINCETON UNIVERSITY PRESS, 41 WILLIAM STREET,

PRINCETON, NEW JERSEY 08540

IN THE UNITED KINGDOM: PRINCETON UNIVERSITY PRESS, CHICHESTER, WEST SUSSEX

LIBRARY OF CONGRESS CATALOGING-IN-PUBLICATION DATA

JULLIEN, MARC-ANTOINE, 1775–1848.

[SELECTIONS, ENGLISH. 1993]

FROM JACOBIN TO LIBERAL: MARC-ANTOINE JULLIEN,

1775–1848 / EDITED AND TRANSLATED BY ROBERT R. PALMER.

P.   CM.

A SELECTION OF WRITINGS BY MARC-ANTOINE JULLIEN

TRANSLATED FROM THE FRENCH.

INCLUDES BIBLIOGRAPHICAL REFERENCES AND INDEX.

ISBN 0-691-03299-8

1. JULLIEN, MARC-ANTOINE, 1775–1848. 2. REVOLUTIONARIES—

FRANCE—BIOGRAPHY. 3. AUTHORS, FRENCH—19TH CENTURY—BIOGRAPHY.

4. FRANCE—HISTORY—REVOLUTION, 1789–1799—SOURCES.

5. FRANCE—INDUSTRY—HISTORY—19TH CENTURY—SOURCES. 6. LIBERALISM—

FRANCE—HISTORY—19TH CENTURY—SOURCES. I. PALMER, R. R. (ROBERT

ROSWELL), 1909–. II. TITLE.

DC255.J8A3   1993

944.06'092—dc20   [B]   92-46872   CIP

THIS BOOK HAS BEEN COMPOSED IN ADOBE PALATINO

PRINCETON UNIVERSITY PRESS BOOKS ARE PRINTED
ON ACID-FREE PAPER, AND MEET THE GUIDELINES FOR
PERMANENCE AND DURABILITY OF THE COMMITTEE ON
PRODUCTION GUIDELINES FOR BOOK LONGEVITY
OF THE COUNCIL ON LIBRARY RESOURCES

PRINTED IN THE UNITED STATES OF AMERICA

1 3 5 7 9 10 8 6 4 2

CONTENTS

PREFACE ix

ONE

A Boy and His Parents in the French Revolution 3

Schoolboy in Paris
Letters from His Mother
Radicalization
A Jacobin Family
Sojourn in England
A Regicide Father

TWO

Young Agent of the Terror 31

Serving the Committee of Public Safety
Mission to the West
Letters to Robespierre and Others
Horrors in the Vendée
Terror at Bordeaux

THREE

Democrat among the "Anarchists" 63

Acceptance of Thermidor
Imprisoned with Babeuf
Rejection of "Communism"
Editing the Orateur Plébéien
Revolution beyond France

FOUR

Bonaparte—Italy—Egypt—Naples 76

Serving General Bonaparte
Editing the Courrier de l'Armée d'Italie
Fructidor
Revolution in Italy
The Cisalpine and Neapolitan Republics

FIVE

For and Against Napoleon 93

Self-Appointed Adviser to Bonaparte
Hopes for Consolidation of the Revolution
Serving the Empire

Growing Doubts
Disillusionment
Writings to Overthrow Napoleon

SIX

The Hundred Days   119

Acceptance of Napoleon's Return from Elba
For a Liberal Empire
Waterloo
Defiance of Allied Invaders

SEVEN

Constitutional Monarchist   133

Acceptance of the Monarchy
Liberal Pamphleteering
Self-Justification
Attempts at Election to Chamber of Deputies
Revolution of 1830
Advice against the Republic

EIGHT

Theorist of Education   151

Education and Politics
Schooling and Political Economy
And for Social Classes
And for Prevention of Revolution
Pestalozzi
Fellenberg
Comparative Education

NINE

Apostle of Civilization   175

Classification of the Sciences
Editing the Revue Encyclopédique
International Scope
America
Steamships and Railroads
Frankenstein
German Idealism
Robert Owen's New Lanark

TEN

The Later Years   200

Persistence of the Past
Memories of His Mother

More Disappointments
Learned Societies
The American Philosophical Society
Electoral Reform
Fortification of Paris
The Amazon
1848: Vive la République!

REFERENCES 227

INDEX 241

PREFACE

THIS IS A BOOK of selected translations, although about a third of it is of my own writing. The person translated is Marc-Antoine Jullien, whose life in France coincided with the whole era of revolution in Europe and the Americas from 1775 to 1848. He may be taken as typical of many in France who had their hopes raised and dashed by so many rapid changes.

Born in the year when armed rebellion against Britain began in America, he witnessed the fall of the Bastille as a schoolboy in Paris, joined the Jacobin club, took part in the Reign of Terror, advocated democracy, put his hopes in Napoleon Bonaparte, turned against him, welcomed his return from Elba, became an outspoken liberal under the restored Bourbons, rejoiced in the revolution of 1830, had doubts about the July monarchy, welcomed the revolution of 1848, and died a few weeks before the election of Louis-Napoleon Bonaparte as president of the Second Republic.

Beyond France he was aware of revolutionary movements of similar purport on both sides of the Atlantic; he worked for revolution in Italy in 1797, admired the United States as a new creation, and favored the Latin American revolutions against Spain. In addition, he became a writer of some importance on education, and an alert observer of the contemporaneous Industrial Revolution. The schoolboy of 1789 lived to be excited by steamships and railroads. He also became a foreign member of the American Philosophical Society.

His writings on these subjects were abundant. They consist of books, pamphlets, reports, letters, book reviews, magazine articles, poems, and private notes and memoranda. Hence the excerpts selected here for translation are only a small fraction of the whole. In the present volume they are supplemented in the first chapter by letters from his mother in the early years of the French Revolution, and in the ninth chapter by articles by his collaborators in the *Revue Encyclopédique*, of which he was editor in the 1820s.

We have here a career that may shed light on the meaning of Jacobinism, liberalism, and the "bourgeois revolution." Readers can judge these elusive matters for themselves. Marc-Antoine Jullien was certainly a bourgeois in the sense of the word current in his own time. He went through many twists and turns, adapting to many political systems, yet always with a preference for what he would call the principles of 1789, a dislike of their adversaries, and a hope that constitutional and representative government, with assurance for human rights, would ultimately prevail.

Jullien clearly enjoyed writing, and indeed his mother tells us, in one of her letters to him, that when he was a boy she had often wished that he would go to bed earlier, and not sit up so late at his desk with his candle still lighted. His written style is easy to translate, but is rather verbose and often repetitious, and occasionally marked by un-usually long but well-constructed sentences, and by a habit of using words in pairs, such as two adjectives or two verbs where one would suffice. He often put words in italics or small capitals, duly repro-duced in the present translations. Though long-winded, his style could be forceful and emphatic.

None of Jullien's work has ever been translated. All the materials presented here are in print. Collections of papers exist in Paris and Moscow, as explained in the appended references, but I have felt no need of them for the present purpose, nor any inclination to travel to see them under my present circumstances, including age.

R.R.P.
Princeton, N.J.
May, 1993

FROM JACOBIN TO LIBERAL

ONE

A BOY AND HIS PARENTS IN THE

FRENCH REVOLUTION

MARC-ANTOINE JULLIEN, as a young boy, lived comfortably with his family in a small town in southern France, at Romans near the Rhône River, in the old province of Dauphiny in what would be the department of the Drôme in and after the Revolution. He had one younger brother, a mother who was well educated and articulate, and a father who had the leisure to think and talk about recent books and public matters, since he had no business or profession to consume his time. They enjoyed an annual income of about 5,000 *livres* from their property, which consisted partly of small pieces of rural land from which they shared the income with their tenants, and partly of income, or *rentes*, from funds that they had placed with others. They had a house in town and a home in the country, and kept a servant. Their property was inherited. Marc-Antoine's mother's father had been a merchant near Paris, and his father's father a country surgeon in a village near Romans, a "surgeon" at that time needing no medical degree and having only a modest social status. The Julliens were very middle class, well above skilled artisans and wage workers, and with the kind of education and manners that let them occasionally have amicable contact with more aristocratic persons. Marc-Antoine's father had once been a tutor in the house of a duchess, and was acquainted with the Abbé de Mably, who though a *philosophe* was also a minor cleric and a noble. The Julliens were Catholic in background, but more inclined to natural religion in their actual feelings. They had read Rousseau as well as others, and were, withal, products of the Enlightenment.

When Marc-Antoine was ten years old his parents decided to send him to school in Paris, that is, to a "college," which was the word for a place where boys from about ten to sixteen or eighteen received what we would call a secondary education. He would go to Navarre College, one of the colleges in the faculty of arts of the University of Paris. Most students lived within the college walls, but some lived in nearby boarding houses, and some with relatives in the city to whom parents in the provinces entrusted their children. For Marc-Antoine these were thought to be undesirable arrangements. His father would accompany him to the big city. Father and son took lodgings in the Latin Quarter, next to the newly built church of Sainte-Geneviève, now the Panthéon, and within a short walk of Navarre College and all other establishments in the ancient university. Jullien *père* busied himself with developing his literary and other acquaintance in the city, which later proved useful to him—and to Mme Jullien—during the Revolution. Mme Jullien meanwhile, in 1785, remained at home in Dauphiny with their younger son and a domestic servant.

She felt her isolation, and wrote a good many letters to both her son and her husband. She expected frequent letters from Marc-Antoine. He dutifully wrote a great many, which have not been preserved, but to which his mother often refers. In her letters to him she shows the concern for feeling and sensibility, the unblushing insistence on "virtue," and the preoccupation with self-improvement that it was the fashion for both men and women to declare openly. We can see in her also a rather overwhelming and possessive mother, freely giving salutary advice, with a touch of self-pity and a need to hear a word of appreciation for her efforts.

Hardly was the ten-year-old Marc-Antoine settled in Paris when he received the following communications from his mother, written at the country home of the Julliens, called Les Délices. She always called him Jules as he was known in the family, since he had the same given names as his father.

Aux Délices, Thursday, 29 September 1785

... My good Jules, only one thing consoles me in my low spirits, and that is your application to your studies. Work hard, my boy, and remember the tender advice of your mother to practice the lovable virtues that we have always tried to instill in you. Make yourself liked by everyone; there is nothing more pleasant than to be liked. Remember too, my good Jules, what you owe to the Supreme Being that gave you existence, provided you with good parents, and has already showered so many favors upon you.

Be good and be virtuous! I shall repeat that in all my letters. ...

Your good papa is to stay with you while you are at college. Think of the sacrifices that we are making for you, dear Jules, and may your affection for your papa be redoubled by thinking of all the proofs of his affection for you! What happy auspices for the beginning of a career! Be never the last in any competition, and think of the joy that your successes will bring to your mother. ...

Aux Délices, 8 November 1785

... My dear Jules, my poor Jules, it is now two months and three days since I spoke to you and embraced you. And haven't your papa and I been separated since the same date? But I must suppress a little all such ideas and keep my feelings within the bounds of moderation.

Take advantage of your new position, dear boy, to acquire wisdom and knowledge, and then my sacrifices will be less cruel.

You tell me of your activities, but you don't say whether you are enjoying them or are happy in your new order of things. What does your teacher think of you? Try to respond to his attentions and be grateful to him. Win him over by your diligence, and win over your schoolmates by your gentle and obliging ways.

Let everyone see in my Jules the child of a virtuous father and a tender and sensitive mother. My dear boy, how heaven has favored you in your father! Love and imitate him, and you will be and do all that your mother could wish. Write to me often about your papa. How is he? What is he doing? What does he say? Am I always in your thoughts, as you are in mine? Are you concerned about me, as I am about you? . . .

Some time later Mme Jullien moved to Paris and the family was reunited in an apartment in the Latin Quarter. There was therefore no occasion for her to write to Marc-Antoine except during brief and infrequent periods of temporary separation. We can only surmise that the whole family watched the mounting crisis in public events with keen attention. After 1785 the affairs of the French government went from bad to worse, as impending bankruptcy forced the royal ministers into altercations with bodies claiming to represent the public interest. The result was the assembly of the Estates General in May 1789, a gathering of the three "orders" of the clergy, nobility, and Third Estate, which in defiance of the king, and against obstruction by the nobility, converted itself into a National Assembly to embrace the three orders. Those of the Third Estate, or bourgeoisie, took an oath never to disband until they had written a constitution for the kingdom. The king assembled troops in the neighborhood of Paris with the intention of dissolving the Assembly. The people of Paris suffered from the soaring price of bread, the consequence of a poor harvest in the autumn of 1788. Economic and political discontents came together. It was feared that "aristocrats" were trying to starve the people into submission and frighten the Assembly into inaction. On 14 July rioters stormed and captured the Bastille. Insurrection also broke out in much of rural France, motivated by food shortage, belief in an aristocratic conspiracy, and false rumors and contrived misinformation. On 4 August, in a tumultuous evening session, the Assembly suppressed all legal privileges and declared the "abolition of feudalism." It then promulgated its famous Declaration of the Rights of Man and the Citizen. The Marquis de Lafayette became head of a new citizen militia or national guard in Paris, and attempted to keep order as the agitation continued.

On these events we have only general comments from Mme Jullien. Her next letter was written at Romans in Dauphiny to her son Marc-Antoine still at school.

Romans, 6 September 1789

You have written me two charming letters, my dear boy, and I thank you for the pleasure they have given me. I have shared them with all our friends, who love you tenderly and wish me to tell you so.

The troubles in Paris and the embarrassment they cause for the National Assembly are truly frightening. Yet I remain hopeful. All that formerly threatened us with the greatest evils has brought the greatest good, and I flatter myself that the same will now be the case. Our courageous representatives, after braving the thunders of despotism, will not let themselves be intimidated by the clamors of an excited populace; and if the disorderly elements should go to dangerous excesses the hero who now heads the Parisian militia will know how to control them.

Everything is quite calm now in our province and wherever I have passed in coming here, but many chateaux have been burned, and what is even more cruel, many peasants have been massacred by soldiers of the bourgeois militia, or died at the executioner's hands. These unfortunates, deceived by false orders that were read to them, thought they were obeying the king by burning chateaux and the legal papers of their seigneurs. If any guilty persons ever deserved clemency it would certainly be these poor souls. Yet they have been treated most barbarously. It is all very deplorable, but anyone who knows men, their passions and prejudices, will feel more sorrow than surprise.

It is understandable that Mme Jullien, as a small-town *bourgeoise* owning rural property and employing rural workers, should at first feel more sympathy for distressed peasants than for the "excited populace" in the city. She soon returned to Paris, so that in the absence of letters we have little evidence of her changing views until the correspondence resumes more regularly in May 1792. There is enough, however, to reveal how she became increasingly suspicious of some of the leaders of the Revolution, including her hero Lafayette, and so more inclined to look with favor on popular disturbances in the city.

In June 1791 the king tried to escape from Paris, traveling incognito with Marie-Antoinette to join military units in eastern France whose commanders sympathized with their difficult situation. The king intended to make another attempt at dissolving the Assembly and checking the course of the Revolution. He was stopped at Varennes in Lorraine and escorted back to the capital. Demands were heard for the establishment of a republic. A majority in the Assembly, and even at the Paris Jacobin club, were alarmed by the popular turmoil and hoped to maintain the king in office, however unwillingly, under the new constitution which they had almost completed. A crowd of people in the Champ-de-Mars, petitioning for a republic in July, was forcibly dispersed; it was Lafayette who ordered the national guard to fire, and fifty of the demonstrators were killed. In September the Assembly promulgated the new constitution, providing for a constitutional monarchy under these unpromising conditions.

During this summer of 1791 Marc-Antoine Jullien was on vacation at the family home in Romans. Now sixteen years old, he was approaching the end of the usual college program of study. He wrote to his parents announcing his desire to leave college and remain at Romans, where, he said, he would continue his education by private reading and reflection. We may surmise that he was rebelling against his situation in Paris, where, unlike his classmates at the college, he was obliged to live in an apartment with his mother and father, and listen to their moral lectures and exhortations. He had also become interested in the local Jacobin club at Romans. In any case, he was dissuaded from this course by a long letter from his father and by the following from his mother:

Paris, 20 October 1791

Your cries are not unheard, my son, and your father, who wants nothing in this world more than the happiness of his children, and whose enlightened philosophy is free from prejudice, leaves you the liberty of choosing the vocation that suits you. Good conduct in any occupation, and strict practice of the virtues of which he sets you the example, are all that he asks of you, and more for your own happiness than for his own. As for me, my son, I am less accommodating, and I will give you some reasons.

First, I am hurt by the criticism that you make of the upbringing we have given you. Your quotations from Jean-Jacques [Rousseau] are in fact not relevant to the subject, for you have seen us live in such a way that even visits to the royal palace make no more impression on you than they do on us. Anyone who has sound principles on what is of true worth cannot be dazzled by such tinsel. Either these principles must be written on your heart in ineffaceable characters, or you will never acquire them at all. In the meanest provincial setting you will find obstacles to virtues whose base is so weak that it needs support of many kinds.

My son, you are a man and made to live among men. There are vices and virtues in Paris, Peru and Japan, in the provinces and in the villages. You must know men and study them deeply before finding the ground on which some men are good and some bad, and on which you yourself want to stand. All things considered, the provinces are perhaps more dangerous than the capital. A young man who wants to isolate himself here in Paris is a thousand times more free, and more protected from dangers of the passions, than if shut up in a small town where he cannot escape them. There is corruption here, but it is so low and abject that I think it poses no danger to anyone with any elevation of mind or who has received an honest heart from nature.

Examine yourself seriously, my son, and be honest with yourself. Perhaps the three months you have spent at Romans have been worse for your moral being than the six years you have spent here in the capital in exercises which you now in your wisdom regard as futile. And in this crazy wisdom you rebut your father with an argument from Rousseau, that "a wise preceptor must begin with physical education." Is this a reproach? Or a lesson?

Poor young man! Don't you know that from the moment of your birth we have tried to have you grow up sound in both mind and body? Don't you know that we lived in the country from your childhood so as to give you physical strength? Or that we left our simple pleasures to come here to Paris with you to till a field that you alone will harvest? Or that other parents entrust their children to strangers, and send them to gain knowledge at the risk of virtue? Your father and mother followed you here to shield you under their wings. So you have not been happy in the paternal nest and the usual life of young people? The peace of our domestic pleasures, the comrade given you for emulation in your work and as a companion in your amusements—has all that meant nothing for your happiness? Your good conduct and success in your studies gave me pleasant illusions. I thought you happy until the moment when you told me you had not been so. . . .

Marc-Antoine returned to college for the school year 1791–1792, but like everyone else he was soon caught up in political controversy. His father had been elected in the newly formed *département* of the Drôme as an alternate delegate to the incoming Legislative Assembly, which first met in October 1791 when the new constitution went into effect. The elder Jullien was also a member of the Paris Jacobin club. Young

Marc-Antoine also spoke several times at the club, and became acquainted there with such friends of the family as Brissot and Condorcet, who were members of the Assembly, Pétion, the new mayor of Paris, and Dumouriez, who became minister of war in March 1792. All these were militant Jacobins who would be called Girondins and branded as moderates a year later. They reacted strongly to the threats of émigré royalists who appealed to the Austrian emperor for armed intervention against the Revolution. In November the Assembly enacted two decrees to control the activities of French émigrés in Germany and refractory priests in France. Louis XVI vetoed these decrees, as was his right under the new constitution. He thus confirmed his opposition to the course taken by the Revolution, as he had done in his attempt to leave the country the preceding June. The probability of war was enhanced. Sympathizers with the king believed that a war would strengthen the royal executive power. Zealous revolutionaries hoped that war would expose traitors. Among the most vociferous were these friends of the Julliens. Brissot and others called for a war of all peoples against all kings, expecting that the French would be welcomed as liberators. Only a handful among the Jacobins, including Robespierre, spoke out against the war spirit. They believed that if war came the French generals would dominate the government and destroy all the gains that the Revolution had made.

In January 1792 Marc-Antoine ventured to deliver a speech at the Jacobin club in which he argued against war unless France was actually attacked. His speech turned into an attack on the king and the royalists as the ones most eager for war. It is curious to observe that at this late date the term of address at the Jacobins was *Messieurs*; it would be *Citoyens* a few months later.

Messieurs:

Everyone's mind is now occupied with a great political question on which depends the destiny of France and perhaps of Europe.

Shall we go to war, or not?

Shall we initiate the attack, or await it?

Such are the two points of view taken by most publicists. But in both cases the question seems to me poorly framed. It is not a question of war or not, nor of initiating or waiting for an attack. It is a question of protecting ourselves, if it is still possible, from the terrible scourges that threaten liberty and the people; it is a question of preventing or averting war, of stopping the incursion of our enemies into French territory.

I shall therefore examine the measures we should have taken to crush at their birth the evils that now weigh upon us. . . .

He went on to say that if stronger and more outspoken measures had been taken sooner against the king, the royalists, and the émigrés, the foreign powers would not have supported them, so that there would be no danger of war. That is, the Revolution had been too tame.

> Let someone tell me of a single instance, since the date of our liberty, in which Louis XVI has deserved the least bit of confidence from the French people. He took an oath to uphold the constitution. Yes, but the oath was forced on him by public opinion. He protested, and made a cowardly attempt at flight; he has violated his promises, ignored his duties, betrayed his fellow citizens. Remember the days of 28 February and 21 June [the flight to Varennes]; remember the *vetoes* of the decree against émigrés and the decree against priests. . . .The royal court is not and cannot be favorable to your interests, yet it is this court that now proposes war. War is useful to its projects, and hence contrary to yours, and you should reject it.
>
> Let me summarize, and I say: We have neglected the measures that might have preserved peace, so that war is now almost inevitable; but in the interest of humanity, the interest of liberty, and the supreme interest of the people we should make a final effort to save us from this dreadful scourge. If we can save a single drop of blood and prevent a single private grief, while at the same time preserving the advantage of our liberty, we would have too much to reproach ourselves with if we go off instead like tyrants into an unnecessary war that might have been easily avoided. After this effort, which need not last long, we shall have rendered our cause more just than it already is, we shall have neglected nothing that might have saved us and others from the calamities inseparable from combat, and we will fly to the colors of our country, to death or to victory, and honor the sacred engagement of all friends of the constitution: *to live free or die.*
>
> M.-A.J.F.

Jullien's speech was printed and circulated. It was also signed, for the "F" in M.-A.J.F. is to be read as *fils*, to distinguish the speaker from his better known Jacobin father, who had the same initials as his son.

Such a speech by a sixteen-year-old could hardly sway opinion, or even offend the bellicose friends of the Julliens, but it probably called the youthful speaker to the attention of Robespierre, whose ideas it echoed. A few weeks later the emperor Leopold II died and was succeeded by Francis I, a youth only seven years older than Marc-Antoine but in his sympathies at the opposite end of the political spectrum. The new emperor was the nephew of the French queen Marie-Antoinette. War seemed inevitable, and the French Assembly almost unanimously voted to declare it. The revolutionaries intended to consolidate and advance the revolution; the king, and especially the queen, the "Austrian woman," hoped that armies from Germany would prove victorious, invade France, and rescue them from their captors. So was laid the way for the coming great crisis of the Revolution. A week after hostilities began a few untested units of the French army broke and ran, even murdering one of their generals.

At this moment it was decided, by whom is unknown, that Marc-Antoine should go to England, ostensibly to continue his studies there. In reality he was to be a secret agent of the French government. He would be too young to be suspected as such in England, from which he was to report on the state of public opinion and the attitude of the British government. He was liberally supplied with letters of introduction to important persons. We learn much from a letter written by his mother to his father.

Paris, 16 May 1792

MM. Dumouriez, Condorcet, La Rochefoucauld, Brissot, etc. have approved the plan for Jules to go to London. The poor boy is so loaded with letters of introduction that he will be kept only too busy. He has letters to Dr. Priestley, Lord Stanhope, Talleyrand, the younger Garat, our ambassador Chauvelin, and others. The one I like best is from Mme Le Roux to her brother M. de Meuse, asking him to give Jules lodgings for the first few days, and treat him as his own child.

I saw him off this morning. Mesdames Dejean and Perrond went with me, and our good Jules was overwhelmed by our caresses and regrets. I looked over his traveling companions. There was a Dutchman, a good patriot, with the honest rustic frankness of a thinking man, who said that he would give my son advice and assistance in case of need.

The political storm gets worse here, and there is talk only of conspiracies, assassinations and a Saint Bartholomew of patriots. It makes one tremble. In truth, things go badly. . . .

Saint Bartholomew is a reference, proverbial in France, to the slaughter of Protestants during the religious wars, on Saint Bartholomew's Eve, August 1572.

She wrote to her son Marc-Antoine in London, a few days later:

Paris, 19 May 1792

. . . I have received a long letter from your father, who is in Grenoble. He says that the city is to be put on a war footing, with a camp located in the neighborhood, and that the mountain people are afire with patriotism.

I went with Mlle. C— to hear a sermon at Saint-Eustache. Never has the pulpit of truth been so worthily occupied. The preacher delivered a discourse sparkling with eloquence on ways to prevent civil war and turn the foreign war to our advantage. Holding up the Gospel and the Constitution, he preached Liberty, Equality and Fraternity with the thunders of genius. The pictures he drew of the perversity of tyrants, and of the degradation or sufferings of peoples, were so striking and truthful that I have heard nothing so fine or forceful since the Revolution. It was touching and ironic to hear the contrasting picture that he drew, very artfully, of a citizen-king loyal to his oath who would march with a firm step in the path of virtue and rise with the Nation to the height of glory.

People talk here of the victories of the English over Tippoo-Saïb, which put them in possession of all the wealth of Hindustan. Tell me if this is true. I follow anything concerning that nation with interest. I have read with admiration their debates on the slave trade. I want to follow the progress of that cause, which is the cause of humanity.

Don't forget to tell me of their general opinion on our Revolution. . . .

From a letter of Mme Jullien to her husband we learn that Marc-Antoine's letters of introduction produced results. He had met the Earl of Stanhope, one of several members of the House of Lords who sympathized openly with the French Revolution.

6 June 1792

Jules was unable to see Lord Stanhope when he called. But his lordship obtained his address and went in person to see him at M. de Meuse's house in Soho Square. Jules was not at home. His lordship very courteously requested Mme de Meuse to ask the young foreigner to come to him. They then had a conversation in French that lasted for two hours, and the philosophical lord overwhelmed the poor child with his friendship. M. the bishop of Autun [Talleyrand] has offered his services. M. Chauvelin [the French ambassador] was so considerate as to invite him to come often, and in a second visit gave him the right to dispatch his letters with his own, and even offered him a place in the ambassador's box at all the theaters.

Mme Jullien remained alone in Paris with her younger son during the hectic summer of 1792, writing to Marc-Antoine in London and to her husband in Dauphiny. As the military and political crisis unfolded she became thoroughly disenchanted with her former hero, Lafayette, and more willing than in September 1789 to favor the "excited populace" in the city.

While the Austrian and Prussian armies prepared to move toward Paris the French king, queen, and court eagerly awaited their prompt arrival. Royalists exulted and issued threats, while partisans of the Revolution were gripped by a fear that was by no means paranoid. On 20 June an angry mob invaded the royal palace, the Tuileries, confronted the king, and obliged him to put on a cap of liberty and drink a toast to the "people." Royalists saw in this incident an outrageous insult to Louis XVI, while for revolutionaries Louis XVI's action was another piece of royal hypocrisy. Lafayette, then commanding one of the armies at the front, rushed back to Paris, appeared before the Legislative Assembly, and denounced the Jacobin club and the popular militants. He returned to his army, having created a fear of counterrevolutionary military dictatorship. On 11 July the Assembly proclaimed *la patrie en danger*. Thousands of volunteers enrolled in hastily formed battalions throughout the country. On 28 July the Brunswick Manifesto became known in Paris, an ultimatum signed by the commander of the Austro-Prussian forces, threatening Paris with "military execution and total subversion" unless the Parisians submitted "immediately and unconditionally to their king." On the next day at the Jacobin club Robespierre called for the deposition of Louis XVI. Mme Jullien wrote to her husband on 5 August:

5 August 1792

. . . As for poor Louis XVI, it is to relieve him of a burden too heavy for his shoulders that I wish for his deposition. This unfortunate king has been pushed to the abyss by false friends.

Tomorrow I go to the National Assembly. This week I went to the Jacobins, which I left only by an effort of reason at half-past nine so as to be home at a convenient hour. I had not been there for three months. . .but I want to tell your provincials that these Jacobins are real men, true soldiers, not sansculottes, but the flower of the Paris bourgeoisie, to judge by the jackets they wear. There were also two or three hundred women present, dressed as if for the theater, who made an impression by their proud attitude and forceful speech. I might have thought myself in the Roman forum.

I heard the former deputy Antoine speak, and also Robespierre. But I was sorry to hear them denounce Brissot and Vergniaud.

I am tired of people who judge only by words. These Jacobins are nothing but the strongest pillars of liberty and the terror of tyrants. Without them, without their energy and active oversight of what happens, and without the publicity of their discussions, which enlighten and energize the people and arouse their patriotism, the counterrevolution would already have brought joy to our enemies. If the Jacobins should be paralyzed, good-bye to the Constitution.

... All these enlistments that are taking fifteen or twenty thousand young men from Paris, to serve under a general who may be working for the counterrevolution, make me think them already dead while yet alive, so that I thank divine Providence for exiling my son from a country whose supreme head finds it in his interest to mow down the young, since the young are the warmest friends of liberty. But heaven will not allow such an outcome, and our salvation is written in the book of destiny.

She also described the ominous political situation to her son, remembering to conclude with motherly admonitions:

Paris, 8 August 1792

At this moment the horizon is clouded with vapors portending a terrible explosion. There is lightning in these clouds; where will it strike?

The National Assembly seems too weak to support the will of the people, and the people too strong to be subdued by the Assembly. The outcome of this conflict, this struggle, will be liberty or slavery for twenty-five million human beings. My feelings and my need of activity take me often to the National Assembly, to the Jacobins, and to the public promenades where there is so much talk of our present affairs.

In all these places I hear such pertinent observations that I see and foresee the future with a prescience that I believe prophetic. The patriot party will win; but it is unfortunately impossible for its laurels not to be stained with blood very soon.

The dethronement of the king, demanded by the majority but opposed by the minority that controls the Assembly, will be the occasion for a frightful collision now being prepared. The Assembly will not have the courage to pronounce it, and the people will not have the cowardice to see public opinion scorned. Our armies, in the hands of traitors, give pride and hope to our enemies, but it is from the armies that salvation will come. The soldiers of liberty can no longer be the satellites and avengers of despots.

... Would you believe that the stupid royalists pretend that it is the British government that pays the Jacobins to work for social disorganization, so as to bring matters to such an extreme that everything can be destroyed? There is no madness that anyone cannot invent to alienate the French from the English. ...

To relax my head let us talk of you. What are you doing? You have been slow in telling me what progress you make in the English language and whether you are getting used to the customs of that country. Be observant; learn to know your fellow men, to accord them the indulgent affection that comes from a study of the human heart. . . .

If you have the opportunity learn to ride a horse and to swim. I recommend that you develop your strength and the habit of frugality that is the best preservative. Excesses of any kind enervate both body and mind. My good friend, for your mother's happiness and your own, which concerns me deeply, live always under the aegis of Minerva. I don't want to be always the doting mother exhausting all the commonplaces of morality. I write to you as a friend, one that nature has formed within me from the most precious elements of my own being, sensibility and love of virtue; with this I have nothing to prescribe and everything to hope.

There is an alarming agitation among the people. Yesterday some deputies were roughly manhandled. Don't worry about me, but think of the very real troubles by which the country is menaced.

The expected violence took the form of the vast insurrection of 10 August, a popular assault on the Tuileries palace, prepared and openly announced in advance in the "sections" of Paris, the subordinate districts under the city government. It was carried out with the support of armed men from the provinces, called *fédérés*, who were mostly volunteers enlisted for the war. The most in view were those from Marseilles, who brought with them a marching song (actually written in Strasbourg), ever since known as the *Marseillaise*. The uprising revolutionized the municipal government (the Commune) and forced the Assembly to suspend the king (not yet dethrone him) and dissolve itself by holding elections to a new National Convention within the following weeks. Historians have called these events the "second revolution," an expression used by Mme Jullien on the very day of 10 August.

The palace was defended only by the Swiss Guard and a few national guards from the affluent quarters of Paris. It was attacked by sectionnaires and fédérés.

10 August 1792

My dear Jules, amazing news! A second revolution as miraculous as the one that took the Bastille, but it is costing us blood and has kept us for twenty-four hours in a state of frenzy mixed with joy, despair, pain and rage.

Last night all through Paris we heard the dreadful sound of the tocsin, the general alarm and cries to arms that raise all the horrors of incipient civil war. With daylight the evils seemed to abate and our

fears were calmed. The people had so far done nothing except to surround the chateau and set guards at the Assembly. The Assembly had
been debating the question of dethronement, and seemed inclined to
deal gently with the illustrious criminal, as it had done with his protector, Lafayette. This morning as the debate resumed the people,
milling about as spectators, pressed for a decision. Preparations to
assassinate liberty were made at the Louvre, and the Henry IV battalion was at the ready. At six in the morning Louis XVI reviewed his
Swiss in the Tuileries garden, and the Swiss then left the garden and
took their posts in the chateau. Cannon had been placed inside, facing
the great gates. While national guards occupied the garden the men
from Marseilles and other fédérés, along with some armed Parisians,
filled the place du Carrousel. The Assembly had a triple guard. The
people were scattered here and there, as usual.

About six in the morning the royal family slipped furtively into
the hall of the Assembly. The king appeared there. The details of this
important scene will reach you through M. Euvy and the newspapers. I know nothing except that the royal family were seated in the
stenographer's booth.

To come back to the chateau, surrounded by the people as I have
said, the windows and doors were suddenly flung open; they were
full of Swiss, who, *without provocation*, discharged cannon and mus-
kets, killing some and putting others to flight. After only a moment of
surprise and fright the assailants fired on the Swiss, but the national
guards had almost no lethal weapons, and the aggressors, who were
well supplied, replied with several discharges from their advantageous positions. The tocsin rang for the deaths, and brought all the
fire-eaters of the capital to the field of battle. The Tuileries were
forced as quickly as the Bastille had been, and the unfortunate Swiss,
the criminal instruments of a vindictive court, met death in a thousand different ways. The furniture of the palace was broken up, the
royal luxury was trampled underfoot, and immense riches were
thrown from the windows. The Swiss barracks was put to the torch,
and the flames devoured that nest of perfidy. . . .

There have been some popular executions that show the awak-
ening of the lion. I draw a veil over these horrors, which are more
than my too sensitive heart can bear to look on. Yet my reason tells
me emphatically that humanity has lost fewer men by the gross barbarity of the people than by the civilized rascality of kings and their
ministers. . . .

It may be called a day of dupes, for the counterrevolution was
ready to go, with collusion in part of the Assembly, and it is now
decidedly put off for a long time. We were so close to being thrown

back into chains that I consider this unexpected event to be a miracle wrought by the Supreme Being as protector of his people. It lets us defeat Austria and Prussia here in Paris, strengthens the neutrality of England, and gives new encouragement to the Belgians, Liégeois, and my good friends the Dutch patriots. . . .

My dear Jules, I have wept many tears in these last twenty-four hours. This evening, at eleven o'clock, the sound of drums made me shiver again, but this time it was to announce a long reading of a decree or proclamation of the National Assembly. I could not hear the words, except that everyone listening at the windows applauded and cried *Vive la Nation!*

Writing to Marc-Antoine about a week later, Mme Jullien describes the mood in Paris as one of troubled calm. She is relieved by the success of the uprising of 10 August, but she is also radicalized by the continuing menace of invasion, royalist intrigues, and a belief that the French army command cannot be trusted. In this radicalization, insurrectionists become the "people," and the "people" take on the virtues attributed to them in literary circles since Rousseau. She also reflects a change in language that was taking place among committed revolutionaries, with the word "bourgeois" now conveying a bad sense and the term "sansculottes" coming into use. Originally coined insultingly to mean someone "without knee breeches," and hence of the lower class, the word sansculottes was soon adopted with pride and defiance by activists in the cause of the Revolution, both working-class men and women and middle-class persons eager to work with them and obtain their support. The term Feuillant had a brief vogue to mean a revolutionary in the style of 1791 who feared the populace but still believed in the possibility of a constitutional monarchy.

18 August 1792

I am not worried about anything personal. My spirits have risen, dear boy, and my feelings are absorbed by the public interest. Yet the present tranquillity has something terrible in it, because we are kept in a state of apprehension and watchfulness, on the defensive, but prudent and alert. . . .

No one of our acquaintance has perished in the memorable day of the 10th, and the number who died is still estimated at three thousand. But if the counterrevolutionary party had won millions of patriots would have been buried along with liberty everywhere in the country. . . .

The Rights of Man have replaced the royal effigy in the hall of the Assembly. I have seen all the images erected to the pride of kings overturned, calmly and deliberately. Even the statue of Henry IV has disappeared from the Pont-Neuf. The good often pay the penalty for the faults of the bad and the foolish.

Never have I done so much walking as since last Friday. I go along slowly with eyes and ears open, with your younger brother at my side. I note in the language of the people a nobility and pride that arouse my admiration for mankind when it is close to nature and not corrupted by wealth. The stupid Feuillant bourgeois are surprised not to be pillaged or murdered now that the people are masters. Indeed the people are giving many lessons in generosity. My friend, if there are virtues in this earth, they are to be found under the ragged clothes of those that some try to degrade by calling them sansculottes. . . .

A few days later she reports the coming elections to a new National Convention, which is to produce a revised constitution. On the eve of the September Massacres she finds Paris surprisingly peaceful. She calls the assembly a Senate, to evoke Roman grandeur and dignity, perhaps with a touch of irony.

21 August 1792

. . . My dear boy, we are to have a new Senate, which will only have to lop off a few branches, without touching the trunk, to make the constitution perfect.

Things are calm since the 10th, as if nothing had happened. Interregnums are times of repose. Trade flourishes here, foreigners pour into Paris, and no one is leaving, so that the population is greater than ever. Everyone is armed. The Commune, the sections and the Senate are in perfect harmony. . . .

My dear boy, if you could see Paris and hear the story of the 10th, you would not believe it possible, such is the apparent cordiality that prevails everywhere. The crowds come and go and bustle about with all the activity and liveliness of the French. Men carry their heads higher and seem pensive, especially among the common people. There are no more special patrols, and there is no sign of agitation. There have never been so few gatherings in the streets. Indeed, you can address your next letter to me in the street, for I take such pleasure in observing the public spirit that I am running the whole day. Tell Mme P- that I went to the Assembly and the Arsenal by way of the quays, in leisurely fashion, taking with me your little brother, who is amazed by everything and is marvelously useful to me. He makes me look like a silly mother with a spoiled child. . . .

For this moment we have a letter written by Marc-Antoine himself. Found in the archives of the French Foreign Office, it was addressed to Condorcet, who had written to Marc-Antoine in London sending him extracts from the Paris press. Several things are to be noted in Marc-Antoine's letter. He honors the Tenth of August by dating his message the Year I of Equality. (It had become usual to call 1789 the Year I of Liberty, but the actual Revolutionary calendar was not adopted until October 1793.) He thinks that a latent or potential revolutionary spirit existed throughout Europe, a belief that he shared with his Girondin friends and which he continued to express, on various occasions, until the end of his life. Although he fails to mention the prime minister, William Pitt, who was attempting to keep England out of war, and although his picture of George III as a principal warmonger only reflects an inflamed republican ideology, his portrayal of the division of opinion in England was by no means false. Gillray's cartoons were in fact presenting the French as bloodthirsty cannibals, Edmund Burke and others were urging the need of war against the Revolution, and others in all social classes preferred to remain neutral.

London, 28 August,
Year I of Equality

Monsieur,

I have received the letter that you so kindly wrote to me, and I hasten to thank you both for the letter and for the papers that you so considerately enclosed. Your explanations and the public proofs in the printed materials that you sent should open the eyes of the blind if they are honest, and shut the mouths of scoundrels. I am using these powerful weapons to combat those who think that Louis XVI was guilty of no more than weakness, and that his suspension was a useless act. Several persons have been obliged to agree.

I am taking care also to refute allegations that represent the French nation as a horde of cannibals. They have gone so far as to say that the skulls of the Swiss were cooked over open flames in preparation for eating. The pen recoils from repeating such atrocious statements. Newspapers in the pay of the government publish such calumnies. It is said in print that Pétion has been hanged, the king and queen massacred, M. d'Affry roasted over a slow fire, etc., etc. In this way it is hoped to win support for the war which some are eager to declare on France, but the saner elements, the friends of truth and liberty, are at great pains to disabuse the people. It is only by deceiving the people that despots can achieve their ends, and the ruses they employ are themselves an homage to the people's virtues. Let us hope that all eyes will see the light, and that the Austrians, Prussians, Uhlans, and all others will embrace and throw down their arms, or only take them up to exterminate their own despots. For today it is not a particular war of the French nation against other nations but a general war of all peoples against all tyrants. . . .

I should not close this letter, Monsieur, without speaking of the attitudes that I observe in England. There is a great debate going on here, of which the outcome is uncertain, between public opinion and the royal will. George is eager to declare war on the French to avenge the majesty of an outraged throne. He thinks his dignity requires him to join the holy crusade against infidels and rebels. The English people think differently, and believe it highly unnecessary to mix in matters that do not concern them. They are not in a mood to sacrifice, by war, their commercial interests, tranquillity and happiness in the supposed interests of their monarch, and they think it unworthy of them, as a free people, to trouble another people in the establishment of its liberty. Yet George so wills it, and a king rarely wills in vain, but he is afraid of public opinion. So he tries to influence and change it; hence all those pamphlets that spread lies and slanders. However that may be, opinion here is more favorable than might be thought. If the king dared, in defiance of opinion, to declare war on the French nation I think the British nation mature enough to seize the occasion to recover its liberty. I beg you to accept, Monsieur, the sentiments of respect and gratitude that I owe to your patriotism, and, if I may say so, to your friendship for myself.

The delusive calm in Paris was shattered by the September Massacres, which went on for four days from September second through the fifth. About 1,300 persons were dragged from the prisons and killed in the streets after pretended trials by popular activists. The occupation of Longwy and siege of Verdun by the Prussian army, as it moved seemingly irresistibly toward Paris, had created something like a panic in the city. The indomitable Rosalie Jullien wrote to her husband on the very day the massacres began. Expressing horror, she explained them by the argument used later by historians: that with the departure of so many young men for the front the prisoners might break out and wreak vengeance on the unprotected population. It must be remembered that these prisons were not places of maximum security; mostly they were only large buildings such as convents and schools in which both wrongdoers and political suspects were confined. To her husband:

2 September 1792

Who wills the end must will the means; humanity is not barbarous. The people have risen, terrible in their fury, to avenge the crimes and vile treachery of the last three years. Oh my friend! I take refuge in your arms to shed a torrent of tears, but above all I cry to you, "France is saved!" The tears are for the fate of our unfortunate patriot brothers who have fallen in battle with the Prussians. Verdun is besieged, and can only hold out for two days. The joy of our ferocious aristocrats contrasts with our deep affliction. Listen and tremble: the alarm cannon thunders toward noon, the tocsin sounds. There is a scurrying about in the streets. It is a violent crisis. The excited proclamations of the municipal government grip attention and touch every heart; "Rush to help your brothers! To arms! To arms!" Everyone hastens to comply. By evening forty thousand men are on their way to fall on the Prussians at Verdun, or sooner if the enemy keeps advancing. A prodigy of martial frenzy seizes the Parisians—fathers of families, bourgeois, soldiers, sansculottes, all depart. The people speak: "we leave our wives and children at home in the midst of our enemies. Let us purge the earth of them."

My friend, with a trembling hand I draw a veil over the crimes the people have been forced to commit by those who have victimized them for three years. The dark plots that are discovered everywhere throw a frightful light, with positive evidence, on the fate that was awaiting the patriots. It was kill or be killed! An atrocious necessity, the appalling work of our enemies. Heads cut off, priests massacred. . . . I cannot tell you all, but my enlightened reason cries out: "The Prussians and the kings would have done as much or a thousand times worse." If the people. . . . Oh, the unhappy people. . . . be careful not to malign them! . . .

Here is a detail that I heard from six masons returning from their work. A battalion of the populace, seeing the imminent danger of our being attacked by malefactors from all the prisons, in consequence of some plot or the approach of the Prussians, got some judges to go with them, and all visited each prison in turn. Thieves were killed, counterfeiters were killed, counterrevolutionaries were killed; prisoners for debt were released; ordinary brawlers were let go; and young men confined for some youthful indiscretion were allowed to join the band. Thus all the prisons were emptied, even Bicêtre. The national gendarmerie and other troops, on departing, had said to the citizens: "Comrades, we leave our wives and children to you; protect them from enemies of the interior that might kill them while we are away fighting the external foe."

These latest executions, with a terrible and barbaric justice, were, it is said, very coolly carried out. Several priests have been sacrificed to the popular vengeance. These masons saw heaps of corpses at the doors of prisons. My profound humanity makes me weep over the fate of the guilty and innocent mixed together. Good God! Have pity on a people provoked and forced into such carnage; do not hold it against them. . . .

The month of September saw a turning point in the fortunes both of the Revolution and of the Jullien family. At Valmy, on the 20th, a cannonade by the French artillery persuaded the Prussian commander to give up his march on Paris and turn back toward Germany. Meanwhile elections throughout the country brought the National Convention into being. The elder Jullien was chosen as a deputy from the department of the Drôme. The Convention first met on the very day of Valmy, and by declaring the abolition of royalty it indirectly proclaimed the French Republic. Young Jullien returned to France. The family was thus reunited, but only briefly, for although Mme Jullien now had her husband with her in Paris, her son was now dispatched on a new mission. A friend of the family, Joseph Servan, who back in 1781 had published a book prophetically entitled *The Citizen-Soldier*, served for a few weeks as minister of war. He appointed Marc-Antoine as an assistant war commissioner and sent him to southern France to help in the recruitment and supply of the Army of the Eastern Pyrenees.

The Prussian retreat relieved Paris of its fear of invasion, but the Convention was soon racked by internal dissent. All deplored the September Massacres, but some made known their distaste and contempt for the Paris mobs, while others, like Mme Jullien, thought it best in the circumstances to "draw a veil" over the recent horrors and not be too critical of the "people." The former group were called, by their opponents, Brissotins, Rolandists, or Girondins, since many of them came from the Gironde and other departments distant from Paris. The latter, with Robespierre as their chief spokesman, called themselves the Mountain, since when sitting in the Convention they took the highest seats. Many Montagnards represented Paris constituencies. The two groups were fluid and hard to identify, and each was a minority, but for several months the ministries and political initiative were in the hands of the Girondins.

All had been Jacobins not long before, joined in support of the Revolution. Now the friends of the Julliens—Brissot, Servan, Condorcet, Dumouriez—became associated with the Gironde, while all three Julliens became Montagnards. In the following letter, written to Marc-

Antoine while he was in the South, we can see Mme Jullien turning into a Montagnard before our eyes—and offering a paradigm of what happened to many others. Her former friends are now "Brissotins"; they form a faction in the Convention, favor the rich, and propose to bring an armed force "from the departments," that is from the provinces, to protect the Convention against the radicals of Paris. She thinks that the admitted horrors of the September Massacres had forestalled a "Saint Bartholomew" or equally gruesome massacre of patriots.

Paris, 24 October 1792

I am going to talk politics, and the very thought of it withers my soul. I see a Republic without republicans, and I shall see none to my taste except in the future generation, which is now only in the germ or the bud.

The intrigues and artifices of the Brissotins, sustained and propagated by Gorsas and the *Patriote français*, are devastating to the friends of justice and liberty. Don't let yourself be taken in. As for me, with the tact and subtlety of my sex and four years of observations, I think I have the touchstone for patriotism in my hands. I have rubbed Brissot, Buzot, Guadet, etc., on it, and I see how "pure gold has changed to base lead." I find that Robespierre, Panis, and Robert pass the test, for they show marks of the purest gold despite their detractors.

My idea is that some want a republic for themselves and for the rich, and others want a popular republic for the poor; and that that, along with human passions, is what so scandalously divides our Senate. The Brissotins make all the noise, for the others dare not speak, thanks to the Medusa's head [the September Massacres] that their opponents cleverly hold up to dominate imbeciles and fools. Our commune, though slyly calumniated, is giving a good account of itself.

The day of September 2, over which I draw a veil moistened by my tears, is the primary cause of the vilification of Paris, the Commune, and the Parisian deputies to the Convention. It was indeed an atrocity, but it was caused by their enemies. This bloody day saved the patriots from a new Saint Bartholomew, and anyone who finds fault with it would have been a first victim. All the political circumstances of that moment have faded from superficial minds. . . .

The provinces have the roses of the Revolution. We have all the thorns and dangers. The generous devotion of the Parisians and the sublime elevation of their views are concealed from our brothers in the departments. The pygmies who ask for giants to defend them are entirely mistaken. Their proposed armed guard is the hope of Lilliputians; real men need only two sentinels to guard the Senate—love and justice.

Mme Jullien continued to express her sentiments privately, in her letters and in conversations with friends that her letters reveal. Jullien *père* declared his openly. He was one of the first to speak in the Convention when the trial of the king began. Agreeing with Robespierre, he excitedly insisted that Louis XVI was a "monster" who deserved no constitutional protection, that he himself would have put him to death immediately on 10 August, and that France should set an example to Europe of how kings should be dealt with. Meanwhile Marc-Antoine, on his tour of the South, gave speeches in Jacobin clubs and soldiers' clubs, excoriating the selfish rich and denouncing all who would stir up the rest of France against Paris in time of war. It is curious to see both these highly radicalized parents urging their seventeen-year-old son to be more careful. His father, only a few days after his speech against Louis XVI, wrote to Marc-Antoine in language that anticipated the Babeuf of 1796 and the socialism of the nineteenth century, as well as the Montagnard social programs of 1793 and 1794, and indeed the welfare state of later times.

15 December 1792

I have received your letter and your speech, my friend, and am pleased with them both. . . . But I hope too much for your happiness to wish you so much celebrity, which is never obtained except at too high a price. . . . Your eagerness to win proselytes for the system of equality is no doubt commendable, but it will be your ruin unless you moderate it. Too much zeal in working for humanity often brings only misfortune to oneself. Don't move forward too fast, judge the strength of prejudices before combatting them, and make only indirect attacks when you cannot count on a full victory.

The great vice of our social system (and it is probably irremediable) comes from the monstrous inequality of fortunes. The rich realize that this could not long endure in a democratic republic, and so are selfishly aroused against a system of government that sooner or later would despoil them of part of their fortune. . . .This is the rock on which modern philosophy founders. It has indeed established the equality of rights, but it wants to maintain that prodigious inequality of fortunes that puts the poor at the mercy of the rich, and makes the rich the arbiters of the poor man's rights by not granting him the right to subsistence. This must not happen; it would lead to tyranny.

For the Republic to last, it is absolutely necessary that the poorest citizens be assured of a modest living by their labor, and that those who cannot work be maintained at public expense. . . .

The Brissot faction does not dare to justify the king, but it clearly wants to save him. It obstructs the proceedings in the Convention every day by denunciation and incidents that cause trouble and make scandalous scenes. I do not know where it will end, but we are obviously surrounded by dangers, and we are doing nothing to strengthen ourselves in the love and confidence of the people, which is our only possible guarantee.

Good-bye for now, my friend, and hold fast to your principles, but the first principle should be to act with prudence. Study the minds and hearts of others before giving free rein to your own ideas and feelings.

And from his mother:

Paris, 24 December 1792

Your papa is very dissatisfied, like all the good patriots in the Convention. It is shameful. Imbeciles and intriguers are in the majority. The Brissotins are very devils. Roland [minister of the Interior] has managed to corrupt public opinion in the departments by paying money to some of the patriotic writers. He takes two thousand copies a day of Gorsas's journal. Gorsas, Brissot, Carra, who used to shed light, now spread darkness. Their authority is so well established by three years of civic reliability that no one can believe in such a horrible change, without looking under the table. . . .

I would rather live in the woods and forests than in this present society. The denizens of those regions are less tigerish and fierce than our politicians—Brissotins, Girondins, etc.

The Revolution has aroused such passions that it is impossible to see the truth about anybody. You must be prudent to avoid the traps of designing men. You must keep a lock on your lips and a key to your mouth, and not let a word escape that can be held against you. . . . My good friend, I shiver from head to foot when I see the dangers that surround your youthful candor and firmness of mind. . . . Your speech to the Jacobins at Toulouse gave me gooseflesh. I fear that you are making enemies. But that is natural; I am a woman and a mother and don't claim to be anything else.

During this struggle between Girondins and Montagnards, Mme Jullien wrote to Marc-Antoine every few days. For example:

Paris, 5 January 1793
Year I of the Republic

The Roland faction triumphs in the Convention, and the volcanic eruptions of the Mountain produce only ineffectual noise. The Girondins are unbelievably malicious. It is as clear as day that they want trouble, and even if they don't want civil war they may come to regret the bloody dissensions that they have excited. Just yesterday they demanded and obtained the printing and sending to all the departments of a disgraceful diatribe against Paris. . . . The faction has not abandoned its project for filling the capital with troops from the departments so as to produce a partial insurrection and have the Convention move to another city. Their purpose is so obvious that anyone who does not see it must be blind.

14 January 1793

. . . I will not speak of the National Convention; it is overwhelmed by the weight of its own ignominy. There has never been such a well-matched combination of talents and vices, to the shame and sorrow of humanity. Your papa, who has remained pure as heaven, is among the Spartans of the Mountain, or I should say those who fought at Thermopylae. There are about twenty like him, men of straightforward purpose and truly republican souls. They are called factious. They must speak, yet when they try to, the floor is denied to them. . . .

Poor humanity? Poor people! Your father is in such a state of painful depression that the evils around us make us the saddest and unhappiest people in the world.

Write to us often. It is only your letters that give us pleasure. Save time on your other correspondence to give more to us. You write too much and stay up too late at night. I wish I could be at the door of your room in the evening, as I used to be, to persuade you to snuff out that cursed candle that deprived you of sleep. Take care of your eyes, your health and your mind; they all wear out like an old coat unless they are kept in good condition.

My friend, don't talk so much in the clubs. Those who like to favor young talents may get tired of hearing you, or become envious. . . .

On 15 January the Convention voted unanimously, 707 to 0, that Louis XVI was guilty as charged. On the next day it voted on the penalty to be inflicted. Each member stood up publicly to declare his sentence. The barest possible majority, 361 to 360, in a public roll call, voted for death. The elder Jullien was one of this majority. After further parliamentary maneuvers, in which proposals for a reprieve or popular referendum were defeated, Louis XVI was put to death on the guillotine on 21 January, 1793. Jullien *père* was now marked for life as a regicide.

Mme Jullien reports calm in Paris, but also fears of assassination. These were not unfounded; one of those voting for the king's death, Le Peletier de Saint-Fargeau, was in fact assassinated by a royalist on the very day of the vote.

Paris, 26 January 1793

. . . The death of the king has passed in Paris like the banishment of the Tarquins from Rome. The people show a calm and a majesty that would do honor to the finest days of the Roman republic. Our enemies stab in the back like cowards and threaten all the deputies who voted for the death of their chief, so that I share in the terrors of all who are most gravely concerned. Your father is very brave, and gives the matter no thought. As for me, my heart is divided between you two, and I am in a continual state of worry. I don't feel well, and that contributes not a little to the phantoms of my imagination and makes my days sad and dreary.

With French victories and occupation of Belgium (the Austrian Netherlands) it could be foreseen that the British and Dutch would become involved in the war, which the international outrage at the execution of Louis XVI made more likely. It was the French who declared war on these two powers on 1 February. The French Republic now faced an alliance known retrospectively as the First Coalition: Austria, Prussia, Great Britain, the United Provinces of the Netherlands, the Kingdom of Sardinia, and Spain.

In the following letters, Mme Jullien mentions the war, and expresses her belief in the existence of antiwar sentiment in the enemy countries (exaggerated but not mistaken), but their main interest for present purposes is in her portrait of Robespierre, whom she had admired at a distance but not yet known personally.

2 February 1793

Our political horizon has never been less stormy nor Paris more tranquil. Our Convention regains its vigor; the Montagnards are winning, and drawing so many of the plain [the "center"] to them that I have no doubt that we shall have a good majority when the circumstances require it. You can see as I do what now concerns us—war with the Dutch and British. In that there is not much to be afraid of, for we have friends among these enemies who will give problems to their cabinets. . . .

Robespierre, his brother and his sister are to dine with us today. I shall get acquainted with this patriotic family whose head has made so many friends and enemies. I am most curious to see him close up. . . .

Paris, 10 February 1793

. . . I was very pleased with the Robespierre family. His sister is naive and natural like your aunts. She came two hours before her brothers and we had some women's talk. I got her to speak about their home life; it is all openness and simplicity, as with us. Her brother had as little to do with the events of August 10th as with those of September 2. He is about as suited to be a party chief as to clench the moon with his teeth. He is abstracted, like a thinker; dry, like a man of affairs; but gentle as a lamb; and as gloomy as the English poet, Young. I see that he lacks our tenderness of feeling, but I like to think that he wishes well to the human race, more from justice than from affection. . . .

In March the war again took a bad turn for the Republic. Losing the battle of Neerwinden, the French army withdrew from Belgium; its commander, Dumouriez, attempted to turn the army against Paris, dissolve the Convention, and thus crush the Montagnards; the army refused to follow him, and Dumouriez defected and fled to the Austrians. This "treason of Dumouriez" stigmatized the Girondins. Peasant insurrections against the Convention broke out in western France, and there was much disaffection against Paris in the leading provincial cities.

Writing to her son in May, Mme Jullien expresses both hope and desperation. She is disillusioned by both Girondins and Montagnards. She thinks that instead of quarreling they should unite to uphold the Republic. Disenchanted with politicians, she still believes in the goodness of the people, Rousseau, the Greeks and Romans, the Revolution, and divine providence.

Paris, . . . May 1793

The ship is beaten by the most awful storms, and our pilots, driven by human passions, far from struggling against the winds, far from joining forces to bring the ship into port, divide against each other and present the crazy spectacle of sailors who fight each other at the very moment when the waves are about to engulf them. . . . Our legislature, the executive power, and the Commune of Paris, though all composed of friends of the Revolution, collide so scandalously that the aristocrats and imbecilic friends of royalty are greedily counting the profit to themselves in such fortunate discords. . . .

The salvation of the people is the supreme law, and it has required, in the most terrible circumstances that a nation can be in, some sacrifices not clothed in legal forms. The Commune has called for such sacrifices, and made enemies among false or feeble friends of humanity. I appeal to you, Roland and Servan, because I know that you have honest hearts. . . .

The salvation of twenty-five million is at stake, and perhaps the happiness of the world. But patriots form factions to fight each other, and so divide a party which with all its combined strength is hardly enough to overthrow the hydra of counterrevolution. Among a strong and virtuous people Robespierre and Brissot would have sacrificed their private differences and embraced the general interest. Themistocles and Aristides, as well as two famous Romans, offer them a magnificent example. . . .

Brissot and Robespierre, if you carry your hatreds and actions into the assembly that is to decide our destinies, can we consider you to be among the sincere defenders of the people? Save us, and save yourselves! There is only one open and certain way; it is in the union of patriots in a generous oblivion of all personalities. . . . Rousseau said that it would take gods to govern men. I say that we need only men to govern the French, because this magnanimous people, taught by its woes and proud of having shaken off the fetters of a degrading slavery, needs only wise laws to live happily. Justice, Liberty, Equality and everything else built on these sacred bases will be immortal as the deity from which they come.

Here ends the series of Rosalie Jullien's letters to her son. It is unfortunate that none survive for the following months, which saw Marc-Antoine's active participation in the climax of the Revolution.

During May, as Mme Jullien wrote the letter above, the militants of Paris organized another massive insurrection reminiscent of the one of the preceding 10 August that had overthrown the monarchy, the Legislative Assembly, and the first revolutionary constitution. On 31 May they invaded the Convention, to which they returned on 2 June reinforced by national guards from the popular quarters of the city, who brought cannon with them. Aiming the cannon, they threatened to prevent the members from leaving the hall until their demands were met. These demands included the arrest of members disliked by the sansculottes, more stringent price controls, forcible distribution of food, more severe pursuit and punishment of suspects, a purge of army officers, and the promulgation of a new democratic constitution to include universal male suffrage and popular referendums.

To evade or postpone action on these demands, and hoping to preserve the dignity or even the existence of the Convention, or simply out of fear for their lives, moderates joined with Montagnards in voting the arrest of twenty-nine members, all branded as Girondins. In the following months the Convention remained vulnerable to radical and popular pressures, which were repeated in another invasion of its hall on 5 September. Meanwhile the Convention proceeded to create a more effective executive arm, reorganizing and strengthening its Committee of Public Safety that it had authorized in April—the *Comité de salut public*, the word *salut* actually meaning the "salvation" which Mme Jullien had begged for in her letter of May. Robespierre entered this committee on 27 July. The link joining Marc-Antoine Jullien to Robespierre and the Terror was about to be forged.

TWO

YOUNG AGENT OF THE TERROR

NOW EIGHTEEN YEARS OLD, Marc-Antoine Jullien served as a kind of special agent, or traveling inspector, for the Committee of Public Safety from September 1793 to July 1794, with one brief interruption. The Committee of Public Safety consisted of twelve members of the National Convention, which reelected them every month. After suspending the newly written democratic constitution, the Convention proclaimed the government of France to be "revolutionary until the peace," that is, an extra-constitutional and presumably temporary apparatus designed to prosecute the war and advance the Revolution. In this apparatus the Committee of Public Safety was the coordinating head, and it gradually built up what was in effect a war cabinet and a collective revolutionary dictatorship. Its most prominent member was Maximilien Robespierre.

Robespierre joined the Committee on 27 July, and shortly thereafter the Committee summoned Jullien to Paris. It may therefore have been Robespierre who suggested Jullien's name, for we know that Jullien's mother had had Robespierre to dinner, that his father had voted for the death of the king, and that he himself had spoken in the Paris Jacobin club and in the clubs of southern France. Jullien was later accused of having been a secret agent or private spy for Robespierre, but it is evident that he regarded himself as an agent of the whole Committee, and was so regarded by the Committee itself. Of his known letters written at this time twenty-one were addressed to Robespierre, but eighteen were addressed to the Committee as a whole, and twenty-nine to four other members of the Committee. These included eleven to Barere in Paris, one to Saint-Just, and seventeen to two members of the Committee operating in Brittany while Jullien was there: Jeanbon Saint-André and Prieur of the Marne. There was nothing that Jullien said to Robespierre that he did not say to the others. In his own letters he often refers to letters received by him from Robespierre and from the Committee, none of which seems to have survived.

The reader of the following pages may benefit from a glossary of terms then in common use. The "representatives of the people" were members of the Convention dispatched to various parts of France and to the armies at the front; they often acted independently, and it was a problem for the Committee of Public Safety to control them. Some became "ultras," or what historians have called Hébertists; their revolutionary violence went beyond what Robespierre and the Committee approved. The "constituted authorities" were the local governments or "communes" in towns and villages, or in some cases the regional "departments." The "popular societies" were local Jacobin clubs, of which there were hundreds throughout the country. The "sansculottes" were popular militants who were or were said to be of the working class, but middle-class revolutionaries might also adopt the term. They were to be "electrified" by agents of the national government, electricity then being a recently discovered wonder of science. The "revolutionary armies" were not armies but bands of armed and roughly organized activists who patrolled the country in search of food and hunting suspects. The Committee of Public Safety eventually dissolved them. "Muscadin" (the word normally meant a dandy or fop) was a term used by revolutionaries in 1793–1794 to designate their opponents. "Fanatics" were those Catholics who most firmly resisted interference with their religion. "Federalists" were those, usually of the upper strata in the provincial cities, who might be republicans but who objected to the radicalism of Paris and the centralization of power under the Committee of Public Safety; they were accused of wanting to decentralize or "federate" and hence weaken the country in time of war.

In late August the British fleet occupied the Mediterranean port of Toulon in collusion with royalists in that city. It was feared in Paris that the Atlantic ports might also fall into enemy hands, especially since that region was disturbed by federalists, and even more troubled by a peasant insurrection loosely called the Vendée, which was penetrated by clandestine agents of the French émigrés and the British government.

Into this dangerous and chaotic situation the Committee of Public Safety decided to send young Marc-Antoine Jullien, along with two of its own members, Prieur of the Marne and Jeanbon Saint-André, to impose its authority in the West. Its orders to Jullien were drafted on 10 September 1793:

> The war commissioner Marc-Antoine Jullien, called to Paris by the Committee of Public Safety, will proceed as agent of the Committee successively to Le Havre, Cherbourg, Saint-Malo, Brest, Nantes, La Rochelle, Rochefort and Bordeaux, and will return by way of Avignon, Marseille and Lyon, to gather information and reanimate the public spirit in these different towns, enlighten the people, support the popular societies, watch over enemies of the interior, break up their conspiracies, and correspond faithfully with the Committee of

Public Safety. He will present himself to the representatives of the people who find themselves in the localities that he visits, explain the purpose of his mission, and follow their instructions. He may call when needed on the constituted authorities for assistance, and for use of the public force, but only after formal authorization by the representatives of the people, except where there is positive ground for the arrest of conspirators in places where there is no representative of the people, and except for cases where it is urgent to act for the good of the Republic. He will present himself also to the popular societies in places where he arrives in the exercise of his mission.

Signed: C. A. Prieur, Barère, Carnot

And on the same day:

The Committee of Public Safety directs the National Treasury to transmit to Citizen Marc-Antoine Jullien the sum of 12,000 livres, to be taken from the 50 millions at the disposal of the Committee of Public Safety.

Signed: Carnot, C. A. Prieur, Prieur (of the Marne),
Hérault, Billaud-Varenne

Jullien was at Le Havre as early as 14 September, and he began immediately to report. His letters make clear that the government in Paris, under the pressure of war and invasion, the need of raising a mass army, and the appalling internal divisions within France, appealed to the "poor" against the "rich." He especially worked to develop a network of Jacobin clubs. He wrote to Barère:

Le Havre
18 September 1793

No doubt you have seen, my good friend, my last letter to Robespierre and the one I sent to the Committee of Public Safety, with information on Le Havre and accompanying notes. It would be well to put my proposals into effect, and here are some new ones that I offer.

The popular society at Le Havre, which is animated by the best principles, stands alone in maintaining public spirit here, and although not numerous it is successfully opposing the insolence of Muscadins and aristocrats. But this society, consisting only of poor sansculottes, is absolutely without resources. It needs a hall suitable for its meetings. I propose to put the hall of the ex-Capucins at its disposal and to advance funds to it for the necessary arrangements, or even to compel the rich merchant gentry to contribute to this expense. I beg you not to lose sight of this goal. It is urgent also to arm the sansculottes with pikes, since in this town it is only the former active citizens who are armed.

Another urgent need in the present circumstances is to establish surveillance committees in all the maritime towns, to watch over all suspects and arrest the most dangerous of them, observe the conduct of the constituted authorities, uphold and encourage the popular societies and rearouse the energy of the patriots. I have seen the good that these societies can do. We need them in all the ports, and especially at Cherbourg, where the situation is very bad. If the Committee so wishes, I will have a society set up in each port, and will act only along the lines indicated by the Committee.

I have been present several times at meetings of the society here, and have had it appoint a commission to go out and establish affiliated societies in the neighborhood, which will watch over enemies of the country, instruct the people, and propagate public spirit. One of the causes that has led public spirit astray is the lack of clubs; I am trying to multiply them to carry out my mission. I beg you, dear Barère, to communicate my letter to the Committee, press for the measures that I propose, and send me word at Cherbourg on the result.

A few days later he wrote to Robespierre:

> *Saint-Malo*
> *1 October*

> I have already, my good friend, expressed to the Committee of Public Safety all my joy and acknowledgment, shared by the sansculottes of Le Havre, that the Committee has so quickly decreed the measures that I proposed in conjunction with the popular society. My last letter to Barère gives details on the good effects these measures have produced. I await impatiently your reply to the letter I wrote to you, in which I raised several general questions in my desire to make my mission still more useful. I think myself fortunate to be entrusted by the Committee with this patriotic tour of inspection, which enables me to judge every day, more than I would have thought possible, the excellence of public spirit if only it is enlightened and electrified, for it shows the unanimous will of the French for a triumph of the Republic One and Indivisible.

> I preach everywhere to the popular societies that they should rally round the National Convention and establish patriotic associations in all the communes of the Republic. I urge them everywhere to occupy themselves with popular instruction, surveillance of enemies of the people, and distrust of merchants, Muscadins and rich people

who favor aristocracy as obviously as the priesthood and nobility do. I work at raising up the people, showing that the Revolution is made for them; that it is time for the poor and the sansculottes to rule, since they are the majority on this earth and the majority ought to dominate; that the general will is the sole source of law and the good of the greatest number the purpose of the social contract. I insist repeatedly on strict execution of the decrees, inviolable obedience to the laws, full confidence in the national representation, eternal hatred of the enemies of liberty, firm resolve to perish rather than capitulate. . . . I evoke the horrors of tyranny by the hideous image of the crimes of despots. . . . I associate the popular societies in a common responsibility with the representatives of the people. . . .

Everywhere I see these speeches received with enthusiasm, patriotism electrified and filled with new energy, suspects arrested, and the measures authorized by the National Convention enforced.

The popular societies are multiplying, and the countryside is enlightened and aroused passionately for the Revolution. The republicans understand the extent of their duties and pledge themselves to repulse the enemy, especially the British, whose very name is held in horror in these regions. The British occupation of Toulon with the aid of traitors in that place has aroused public indignation. Wherever I go the patriots promise me to be responsible for the territory where they live and where invasion would expose them to frightful calamities. . . .

I must now give the Committee a succinct account of my travels since Le Havre, from which I reported details on that town, to Saint-Malo, where I now am. . . . The republicans at Cherbourg have pledged themselves, like those at Le Havre, to be responsible to the Republic for the part of the frontier that they occupy. These solemn engagements are not much in themselves, but they rekindle enthusiasm in a revolutionary crisis, and enthusiasm in a revolutionary crisis is the most powerful of incentives and the best guarantee of success.

Since I had noticed in my visit to Caen, and had been told by the deputies Lindet and Oudot, that the public spirit in that town was greatly in need of stimulation, I caused the popular societies at Cherbourg and Coutances each to send a committee of six to Caen to rally the sansculottes there, wipe out the traces left by the likes of Buzot and Barbaroux [two Girondins or federalists], inspire the people and establish a good popular club to purge a place soiled by Muscadins. I also caused these two societies, as well as those at Granville and Dol, to scatter patriots through the countryside to set up popular societies, since the misleading of public spirit is the primary and almost the sole cause of our troubles. . . .

I am impatient to receive my certificate of membership from the Jacobins of Paris, which I asked you to obtain for me, and which you can address to me, if it is not sent already, to general delivery at Lorient, where I shall be pleased to receive one of your letters in reply to mine.

Jullien moved on into Brittany, reaching Lorient, then one of the most important French ports for the Atlantic trade. Here he met with some of the worst disorders of the Revolution and the climax of his mission in the West. The peasant insurrection, spilling over from the Vendée into the neighboring department of the Morbihan, merged into a host known as the Catholic and Royal Army. It was opposed by a confused medley of representatives of the people, constituted authorities, popular societies, a few hastily recruited republican soldiers, and a nondescript revolutionary army led by zealots from Paris. Anarchy prevailed. Some revolutionaries thought others not revolutionary enough. The representatives of the people took contrary initiatives, quarreled with each other, and arrested each other's agents, while the revolutionary army frightened everyone with whom it came in contact. The program of the Committee at this time was to make the representatives work together and accept orders from Paris, and to replace the local revolutionary armies with a single national one, until such time as these paramilitary formations could be simply abolished.

Jullien's instructions were to make himself useful to the representatives of the people, but since they disagreed he cooperated with some, in this case J. B. Tréhouard and Prieur of the Marne, and he ran into serious trouble with others, especially J. B. Carrier. At first Jullien was willing to give Carrier the benefit of the doubt, but within a few weeks he felt obliged to denounce him. And indeed Carrier acquired one of the most sinister reputations of the French Revolution, as instigator of the famous *noyades* at Nantes, in which two thousand persons or more were deliberately drowned in the Loire.

Jullien was invited by Tréhouard to join him at Vannes, a town not far from Lorient in the department of the Morbihan. From there he wrote to the Committee of Public Safety on 19 December, using the republican calendar adopted in the preceding October.

> *29 Frimaire*
> *[19 December 1793]*

I recently wrote to you, citizens, informing you of the measures that seemed useful to take in the Morbihan and also of the actions of one of Carrier's agents, who well deserves the title of ultra-revolutionary, because he has brought terror into the hearts of the patriots themselves instead of using it against the aristocracy. No doubt Carrier was mistaken in trusting such a man. I hurry now also to tell you of the dissolution of the revolutionary army by virtue of the law, and of our inquiry into the actions of the civilian and military leaders of this army. . . .

As soon as we learned at Lorient that a revolutionary army was occupying the Morbihan, and that several men there had been shot without any prior interrogation, and as soon as we received though not yet officially the decree suppressing such armies, so that there should be only one such army for the whole Republic, the representative of the people Tréhouard invited me to come to Vannes to enforce the law and gather information on the illegal and arbitrary acts that might have been committed there. The departmental administration joined me in collecting detailed evidence, and the violation of sacred rights and ignoring of the laws will receive the punishment that is due. . . .

We need in the Morbihan a section of the [reformed and legitimate] revolutionary army to enforce the recovery of requisitioned grain, which is being hidden away by selfish and ignorant men [peasant farmers] who have been induced to turn against the towns. Otherwise the difficulty in the food supply will be extreme. We need a section of the revolutionary army to lay hands on former nobles and priests who are distributed through the countryside, where almost daily disturbances give a picture of a partial counterrevolution. We need men to translate into the Breton language the laws of which the country people are left in ignorance, or which are represented to them in a way to make the Republic hated. And finally, we need funds specifically assigned to the popular societies for holding their meetings in large and convenient rooms, and money for reprinting useful material and for republican festivals of the *décadi* [in the republican calendar], which should electrify the people and make them forget the old Sunday and the dreary Catholic festivals. I beg you to reply concerning these measures, which are almost a short summary of the plan I have submitted to you.

p.s. The departmental administration has sent me all the papers relative to the conduct of Lebatteux, a commissioner to the revolutionary army holding unlimited powers. I was shocked to find that he had arrested a large number of patriots whom the public outcry forced him to release; that he had municipal officers snatched from the town hall itself with no explanation for their arbitrary removal; that he had men shot, with no prior questioning, simply because they had been called uncivic, and by a refinement of barbarity had the ditches dug

before their eyes that were to receive them after death; that he subjected the guilty and innocent alike to these cruelties, aroused fanaticism by his atrocious persecution of fanatics, extorted taxes from the
unfortunate country people, and in general exercised an appalling
despotism and committed every abuse of authority of which anyone
can be guilty. Judge after all that whether Lebatteux should not be
brought before the courts. . . .

He wrote also to the Committee of Public Safety:

5 Nivôse
[25 December]

. . . I must inform you again about the port of Lorient, where every
day I am the more convinced of the need for the actions that I proposed in my last letter. Since I wrote them two events that I should
report have justified our well-grounded fears. It was announced that
on a certain night the storage depots at the port would be set on fire,
and on the night indicated traces of powder were found in different
places, which leave no doubt of the attempt to execute this horrible
project. After that, fire broke out in a small quarter of the port, and
only our zeal and activity prevented a general conflagration. . . .

Although the republican forces had now driven the British from
Toulon (with a young officer named Bonaparte commanding the artillery), the Committee of Public Safety still had reason to fear a British
occupation of Lorient. We find recorded in its minutes:

7 Nivôse
[27 December]

The Committee of Public Safety approves the measures taken and
the expenses paid for improvement of the public spirit in the department of the Morbihan by citizen Jullien, its agent sent to the maritime
departments.

[Signed] Couthon, B. Barère, Billaud-Varenne

And on the same day it wrote to Prieur of the Marne, its absent member:

Citizen Colleague:

The Republic in its triumphs must still expose new plots and beat
back enemies that constantly revive with greater audacity. We have
information that a plot exists to surrender the port of Lorient and
burn the stores there. There are accomplices in Lorient.

Suspicion falls on the ministry of marine. The minister is now taking steps to make the necessary changes in his administration.

Jullien, agent of the Committee in the maritime departments, will give you all details on this matter. You will know how to take vigorous measures to correct the evils caused by Tréhouard's weakness. Only by energetic action and active surveillance, in concert with Jullien, will you be able to undo these machinations.

The British prowl our coasts, waiting to see the effects of their intelligence in our ports. You must go instantly to Lorient.

Signed: B. Barère, Carnot

In his letter of 5 Nivôse quoted above, after noting a royalist conspiracy, Jullien went on to report the dangers produced at the other extreme of the political spectrum, by the ultra-revolutionaries and the revolutionary army. Here too he saw the hand of British spies.

... The conduct of the so-called revolutionary army and its pretended civil and military commissioners, commanding it in the Morbihan with supposedly unlimited powers, has fully justified the expression "patriotically counterrevolutionary" by which Robespierre has described the agents of Pitt. It is by revolution itself that they want to kill the Revolution. We have seen men coming from I know not where—one a monk's lackey and the other an intriguer appointed by Beurnonville—suddenly charged with an important mission by a representative of the people whose confidence they had usurped; and these so-called revolutionaries have perpetuated pillage, arson and murder. By burning churches they have reawakened the fanaticism that they persecuted. They have won new friends for the priests and the aristocracy. What do the peasants, as victims of these atrocities, say to each other? "We would rather have the Catholic and Royal Army than a republican army that no longer respects our property, our lives, or our churches, and knows no law or restraint."

I have turned over to your colleague Tréhouard all the evidence of brigandage, fires, murders and abuses of authority of which the main leaders of this army have been guilty. He should have sent you copies and taken steps to bring these criminals before the Revolutionary Tribunal. They must be agents of Pitt, these people who have tried to implicate the national representation in their liberticide projects by giving themselves powers of which they were unworthy....
At Quimper they have arrested patriots, put federalists back into public office, and stirred up an atrocious persecution of fanatics by burning churches and saints, so that Quimper is a victim of counterrevolution because of the so-called revolutionary actions that have been taken....

And to Barère:

12 Nivôse
[1 January 1794]

I have just received, my good friend, your letter and one from Robespierre by special messenger from the Committee of Public Safety.

Agents of Carrier in the Morbihan have aroused complaints from the patriots and constituted bodies, which after being regenerated embodied the will of the people. Tréhouard, representative of the people in the department of the Morbihan, is also a depository of this will. When the decree of the Convention suppressing local revolutionary armies arrived Tréhouard ordered me to come to Vannes to help enforce it and collect information on violations of the law and arbitrary acts. I took exact notes. I saw evidence of pillage, arson and murder under pretext of revolution, and in their perpetrators I saw rather the agents of Pitt than deputies of a sound Montagnard representative of the people. Tréhouard, seeing the authentic materials I had collected, decided to arrest Lebatteux. On learning this Carrier wrote a lot of silly things about Tréhouard and seemed to call Lebatteux inviolable. You will see the evidence herewith. He is now doing more; he is sending new agents to arrest the patriotic administrators and make the trouble worse. Some people complain of the despotic acts of Carrier's envoys and the way he supports them against everyone else. Others think Tréhouard too weak, uncertain and indecisive when faced with these just complaints. Carrier should seem to you far more guilty of discrediting the national representation. . . .

It seems to me urgent to recall both Carrier and Tréhouard, the former especially. . . . Knowing something of the sea, Tréhouard might be useful at Brest with Jeanbon Saint-André, who could give him direction. I forgot to tell you that among Carrier's agents are several known aristocrats, although he calls them and perhaps thinks them to be pronounced republicans, and among them are some big merchants of Nantes, where there is indeed a mercantile aristocracy.

Jullien wrote to Robespierre on the same day:

12 Nivôse
[1 January 1794]

The arrival of Prieur of the Marne gives hope and joy to all patriots. The letter from the Committee of Public Safety gives great pleasure to the popular society.

I am sending to you, as also to Barère, the four most important papers relative to the conduct of Carrier. . . . It is revolting. . . . Tyrannical acts are committed. There is an indecent struggle between two representatives, one of whom (Carrier) threatens to arrest the other. You will see the details in my letter to Barère and the adjoining pieces. They require prompt attention.

Frustrated as he was by the course of the Revolution in western France, the young Jullien entertained somewhat contrary ideas, on the one hand that the only true revolutionaries were in Paris, and on the other that revolution might spread far beyond France. As for Paris, he wrote to Robespierre:

> *Nantes*
> *10 Pluviôse*
> *[29 January]*

. . . Let us send from Paris into these remote regions some revolutionaries qualified to guide opinion and instruct the people, and let us bring to Paris patriots from this region and give them temporary employment, which can keep them for a while at the central point of the Republic. It is only in Paris, the fireplace of the Revolution, that ardent apostles of the Revolution can be found. Electrified there, they will then return to their respective communes to electrify their fellow citizens. The progress of public spirit would be advanced by several years by this exchange of patriots called to Paris and patriots of Paris sent to the departments.

But he also shared in the dream of a far-spreading revolution, such as the now discredited Girondins had believed in. Doubtless remembering his own sojourn in England almost two years before, he eagerly looked forward to the liberation of that island. There were those in Paris, even in the Committee of Public Safety, who were tempted by similar ideas.

He wrote with boyish excitement to Prieur of the Marne:

> *Décadi, 10 Pluviôse*
> *[29 January]*

I have arrived at Nantes, my good friend, and hasten to send you the gist of a very official letter that I have received from Paris. England is aflame. There are outcries in London that kings are no longer needed. George and Pitt can make the most of it! The Committee of Public Safety intends to give strong support to the inhabitants of the banks of the Thames. The mission of representative of the French people to the English nation is destined for you. Very likely I shall go also, and make the same tour in Great Britain as I have done in the Little Britain of Brittany. Hurry up and finish with the Morbihan. I now move on rapidly to Bordeaux and Port-la-Montagne [Toulon]; and as I said to you at the meeting of the popular society before my departure from Lorient, our next rendezvous will be in England.

Meanwhile the horrors of the present had to be faced, with the Revolution, as Jullien said, being killed by revolution itself. He saw Carrier at Nantes, and then, following his original instructions, turned south toward Bordeaux, with stops at Angers, Tours, and La Rochelle. Immediately after leaving Nantes he wrote to his father, to Barère, and to Robespierre giving further details on Carrier's extravagant ultra-revolutionism and the need of recalling him. To his father:

> *Angers*
> *15 Pluviôse*
> *[3 February]*

On receiving this letter please hurry to Robespierre, taking with you the brave sansculottes whom I am sending to you. The Vendée is reviving and must be crushed. Carrier is killing liberty and must be recalled. . . . Read this letter to Robespierre, and also read the one that I am writing to him. I shall send more details from Tours. Write to me promptly at La Rochelle.

And to Barère:

We must save Nantes and the Republic. I have seen the Old Regime there. I have just come from Nantes and seen the Vendée coming back to life. Charette is rallying the remains of the Catholic and Royal Army, which grows larger every day. I have seen generals prolonging the war on purpose. "Don't worry," they say; "we will end it when we want to." Yet it never ends. At Nantes I saw Carrier acting like a satrap, a despot, an assassin of public spirit and liberty. I do not exaggerate. Listen to the details from the patriots of Nantes who bring this letter. The Committee must recall Carrier and replace him. . . .

And to Robespierre, at more length:

> *Tours*
> *16 Pluviôse*
> *[4 February]*

I promised you some details, my good friend, on Carrier and Nantes. I shall also inform the Committee of what I have seen. The Committee should make haste to find a remedy.

Nantes is menaced by the three scourges of pestilence, famine, and war. A great number of royalist soldiers were shot not far from the city, and the air was corrupted by the great mass of their bodies and by pestilential exhalation from the bloodstained Loire. National guards were sent by Carrier on labor service to bury the dead, and two thousand persons died of contagion in less than two months. The blockage of the Loire has prevented the arrival of provisions to replace those used by our armies, and the town is a prey to frightful shortage. It is said that the Vendée is finished, yet Charette at four leagues from Nantes throws back the Republican battalions, which are sent one after another as if to sacrifice them on purpose. The generals make no secret of their desire to perpetuate the war. "We will end it when we want to," they say; and yet it does not end. When our cannon are captured, a general answers, "We have the time to get them back."

. . . Our army is at Nantes without discipline or order, while scattered units are sent out to be butchered. The Republic is pillaged and done to death. A crew of generals, taking pride in their epaulettes and the gold braid on their collars, rich with what they have stolen, run over in their carriages the sansculottes on foot; they are always with women, or at the theater, or at sumptuous meals that insult the public misery. They openly disdain the popular society, which they and Carrier rarely attend. Carrier makes himself invisible to the constituted bodies, club members and patriots. He gives out that he is ill, or away in the country, so as to avoid the exertions that circumstances require. No one is deceived by these lies; he is known to be well and in town, in a seraglio surrounded by insolent sultanesses and epauletted flunkeys who serve as eunuchs. . . .

Yet a certain justice should be rendered to Carrier, for at one time he crushed the business interest and thundered against the mercantile and federalist aristocracy, but since then he has made terror the order of the day against the patriots themselves, by whom he wants to be feared. He has very bad men around him. He rewards a few courtiers with jobs, rebuffs the patriots, rejects their advice, and suppresses their enthusiasm. By an unheard of act he closed the meetings of a Montagnard society for three days. . . .

I am assured that he had all the prisoners at Nantes taken out indiscriminately, put on boats, and drowned in the Loire. He told me to my face that one could run a revolution only by using such measures. He called Prieur of the Marne an imbecile for not knowing what to do with suspects except incarcerate them. My conference with him was too long for me to give details. It was also Carrier who publicly refused to recognize one of his colleagues as a representative of the people. This action, of which I sent you word, was, in the full force of the word, counterrevolutionary. It is necessary to recall Carrier with-

out delay, and send someone to Nantes who can revive the energy of
the people. . . .

Reply to me at La Rochelle. I have given details on our generals,
Carrier, and Nantes. The patriots who bring you this will tell the rest.

On the next day, Jullien wrote to the Committee, informing it of his
letters to Barère and Robespierre which he had asked them to communicate to the Committee. On 8 February it recalled Carrier. On the
same day it wrote to Prieur of the Marne, ordering him again to proceed to Nantes and take charge of the matters there. The Committee
added: "To conclude with what concerns Carrier, you will learn with
surprise that he has abused Jullien, our agent, whose mild manner
and republican energy are well known to you. Jullien had to leave the
city with precautions that an agent of the Committee should not have
to take."

It is clear that Jullien had confronted Carrier personally. Over forty
years later he made public a fuller account of this stormy interview. By
this account, at their meeting, Carrier accused Jullien of falsely and
secretly denouncing him to the Committee of Public Safety; he ordered Jullien to be put instantly to death; Jullien boldly reasserted his
authority from the Committee and boasted that his father was an important Montagnard; Carrier, impressed and afraid, countermanded
his order for Jullien's execution, lamely declaring that there had been
a confusion of names. It is always a question what credence to give to
memories recorded forty-five years later. If the scene as described in
1839 really happened in 1794, there is no written evidence that Jullien
mentioned it at that time to Robespierre, the Committee, or his father.
Yet the Committee knew that its agent had been "abused." It is easy to
believe that Jullien in defying Carrier face to face had risked his life,
and that he departed abruptly from Nantes. He reported to Paris only
after arriving safely at Angers. The youth had escaped from the
"ogre's den."

In the West he had reported the dangers of excessive revolutionary
zeal, but as he moved South he found too much that was lukewarm
and half-hearted. He now began to denounce moderation, or *modérantisme* as it was called in the language of 1794. But he was consistent
in warning against both extremism and moderation, for in both cases
he was attempting to enforce the policy of the ruling Committee. He
had read Robespierre's two great speeches in the Convention with
approval, one on the Principles of the Revolutionary Government in
December, and the other on the Principles of Political Morality in February. In the latter Robespierre had explained what he meant by virtue, and what he meant by democracy. He had said that the basis of

popular government in time of peace was virtue, and that in time of war and revolution it was both virtue and terror—"virtue without which terror is murderous, terror without which virtue is powerless." Marc-Antoine Jullien fully agreed. Moderates, in this view, in deploring terror only revealed their indifference to virtue. The significance of moderation of course depends on the speaker and on the questions at issue. It was a conservative United States senator who once said that moderation in the cause of freedom is not a virtue. And if extremism also is relative, Jullien was surely becoming more extreme.

At La Rochelle he favored the Jacobin club with a discourse on "moderatism," which the club later ordered to be printed and circulated. A few selections will suggest its tone:

Discourse on the Dangers of the Contagion of Moderatism and the Means of Shaping the Public Spirit

... From observations each year since the beginning of the Revolution, I may almost say in all parts of France, I have gained a certain experience of men and things. What have I seen? Everywhere an involuntary tendency by which the purest patriot is led on to moderation and weakness. That is why our enemies have all the advantages. That is why the popular societies, though repeatedly purged, still need regeneration. That is why the belated justice done to Capet [Louis XVI] and his accomplices, to Custine and other conspiring generals, to Brissot and his adherents, has not stopped the continuing existence of treason or prevented the agents of Pitt and the allied powers from penetrating our ranks and even holding public offices granted by the people.

Let me give you some details on the petty intrigues that propagate moderatism, for we owe it to ourselves to instruct one another. The class of moderates see with trepidation the line that divides them from the class of republicans. The revolutionary austerity of the latter, their unvarying commitment to principles, arouses the fears of these moderates. But do not suppose that they attack our sternness of character directly. If they did, they would be like a wave breaking impotently on a rock. Do not think that they make open war on the patriots. They lack the manly courage for such a conflict. They kill us with caresses. In pompous banquets marked by honeyed politeness, with much affectation of words like "fraternity," "sansculottes" and "republicanism," in meetings whose true purpose is kept hidden, in melodious voices, games, festivals, pleasures and evening parties, in all such things there lurk the perfidious plots of an ingenious moderatism that undermines republican austerity. And what happens to this austerity? Who can tell the influence of a private conversation, a familiar exchange, a smile, a look? Who can be firm enough to take action against a person whose hospitality he has received, to whose table he has been admitted, to whose soul he has bared his own? No, the sternest energy melts like ice before fire. An old proverb has it, "Tell me who you see and I will tell you who you are." So! I say it openly, woe to the republican who lacks the strength to shun the society of a moderate.

I know that there are estimable men, patriots, who are far from wishing to do harm to the Revolution, but whose love of tranquillity leads them to a self-indulgent moderatism. I know that there are estimable and virtuous women, of pleasing airs, whose grace and spirit can be seductive, and whose only fault is a lack of humanity. You must flee from them as you flee from roses that cannot be touched without exposure to the thorns. You must fear an agreeable contagion, the more dangerous because it is hidden. The serpent glides among the flowers. The moderate, even without meaning to, conveys a vice of temperament to anyone who associates with him. If you let a child drink from the glass of a child who has been inoculated, you will inoculate him without doing so purposely. If a republican eats at table with a moderate, even though neither intends it, the evil spreads and the republican is enfeebled. . . .

I invite you to reread every *décadi* the excellent report of Saint-Just on the recent arrests and the two reports of Robespierre on our foreign and domestic policy. In them you will find the lessons that should guide you, and when you have absorbed them you will have a sure antidote against moderation and weakness. . . .

. . . There is a true saying: Liberty has no bed except mattresses for corpses, or, as has also been said, to the shame of nations, blood is the milk of liberty at its birth. But let only the impure blood inundate our land, and the pure blood be spared. . . .

This phrase about liberty lying on mattresses for corpses was later recalled by Jullien's enemies to prove his bloodthirsty fanaticism in 1794. He never denied it, but in his later explanations he gave a different wording and said he had been quoting Mirabeau and Raynal. Such expressions were within the common language of the Terror and of the Revolution itself. As for blood, no less an authority than the *Marseillaise* announced that the *sang impur* of foreign invaders would irrigate the fields of France.

More immediately, in February 1794, these blasts against moderation raised trouble for Jullien with the "district" of La Rochelle, the administrative level above the town and below the department. Officials of the districts and departments were often, on the average, of a more comfortable social position than the majority in the Jacobin clubs and the town offices. Probably the district authorities thought of themselves as good republicans, and saw Jullien as an itinerant whippersnapper suddenly appearing in their midst. They put him under arrest, and gave him a taste of his own medicine by subjecting him to the suspicion and interrogation that he meted out to others. He wrote indignantly to Barère, in a letter revealing both ideological conflict and bureaucratic rivalry among the local constituted authorities. It is not known what the illness was to which he refers; perhaps it was bronchitis, a common ailment of the time.

La Rochelle
29 Pluviôse
[17 February]

Is it necessary today, my good friend, for patriotism to be persecuted in the persons of those who come to propagate the lessons of patriotism, and are honored by the confidence of the Committee of Public Safety? I will recount to you briefly and simply the facts as they happened to me. Please be so kind as to inform the Committee.

On arriving at La Rochelle I showed my passport and made known my mission to the municipality and to the popular society, to which, as my mission required, I spoke much as I had done elsewhere. Both men and women republicans were enthusiastic on hearing an expression of the principles by which they were animated themselves, and which needed only the lightest stimulation. I flatter myself on having electrified the public spirit. . . .

On my ninth day at La Rochelle, and the third day of a cruel illness which kept me in my bed, I received a letter form the district authorities, of which I enclose a copy. Since I could not read the letter myself I was told what was in it. It ordered me, giving no reason, as you can see, to present myself to the district office before noon. . . .

The district, in this order, did not even regard me as a citizen; it simply called me "a certain Jullien, a stranger." Since when am I deprived of the title of French citizen, which even accused persons cannot lose since the law presumes them innocent until found guilty? Where is the principle of the unity and indivisibility of the Republic if in a French town a French citizen, performing a mission, is designated as a stranger?

I was conducted to the district office. The meeting was secret; I saw none of the people. My papers were examined. The district could easily have learned my credentials from the municipality. I was interrogated. My crime was in not having paid a visit to the district office. . . .

My crime also was to have sown dissension by speaking out against moderatism, and distinguishing the class of patriots from the class of the thoughtless and the selfish. I was questioned on minor details of my public and private statements, which apparently had been carefully spied on. Finally I was released. I was free after two hours of an arbitrary and inquisitorial interrogation.

My first step, on leaving this long session, was to inform myself on public opinion concerning the district officials. Several patriots told me that the district did not enjoy their complete confidence, and that two of its members had not been judged worthy of the popular society. I assure you that if this constituted body had been composed of republicans and enjoyed the esteem of the people I would have overlooked the gross error, or rather the atrocious injustice, to which I was subjected, and I would have been the first to fraternize with them. But it is not myself, it is my patriotism, that they attacked.

Jullien moved on to Bordeaux, one of the great cities of France. Before the Revolution it had been one of the most prosperous, enriched by trade with the colonies and northern Europe, but its shipping was idled by the war and the British blockade. While its general population suffered from unemployment and food shortage its merchants still lived in fine houses with opulent furnishings, and mixed with former royal officials and resident gentry. Important in its own right, Bordeaux resisted subordination to Paris. It was in fact a nursery of federalism, and as the capital of the department of the Gironde it had given its name to the outlawed Girondins.

It was at Bordeaux that Jullien became most extreme, sharing resolutely in the mounting crescendo of the Terror. He joined the Club National, the most fiery of the political clubs in Bordeaux, and repeated there the speech on the "dangers of moderatism" that he had delivered at La Rochelle, and which the Club National reprinted as a second edition. But he continued also to denounce the "ultras." His purpose in either case, whether warning against moderates or ultras, was to insist on the authority of the Committee of Public Safety as the only possible and legitimate government of France at the moment. His position, like that of the Committee and of Robespierre himself, became more ambiguous and untenable. He sometimes reported the public spirit at Bordeaux as excellent, sometimes as very bad; the Club National sometimes as influential and sometimes as very weak; the best revolutionaries sometimes as expressing a majority will, and sometimes as only a saving remnant. He made lifelong enemies on all sides.

In his first report to the Committee of Public Safety from Bordeaux he was reminded of what had happened at Lyon, another great busi-

ness center, where the ruling merchants had rebelled against the radicalism of Paris; the Convention had sent an army that besieged and
conquered the city, after which two thousand persons were executed
by firing squad, encouraged by representatives of the people that
Robespierre came to regard as ultras. Lyon was devastated by the Terror more than any other city of France. Jullien favored a more discriminating use of the Terror at Bordeaux as elsewhere, but he thought that
the main danger at Bordeaux came from federalism and moderatism.
His change of attitude is shown in his relations to two representatives
of the people. At Nantes he had denounced Carrier as an ultra. At
Bordeaux he came to suspect Ysabeau, the representative there and
even a member of the Club National, of moderatism.

He wrote to the Committee of Public Safety:

> *Bordeaux*
> *24 Germinal*
> *[13 April]*

It might have been natural for Bordeaux to meet the fate of Lyon,
and for both cities to be destroyed by civil war, except that a different
course was followed here, since a skillful and restrained use of terror
made a siege unnecessary. The people rallied to the good cause, and
the party of merchants and federalists, seeing itself the weaker, re-
sorted to dissimulation. . . .

Then those who had some influence on opinion, and who had
shown themselves to be patriots when they saw the fall of the clergy
and nobility, became aristocrats on learning that the town bourgeois
would be only the equal of the country person, and the rich merchant
or ship-owner would not be above the shopkeeper and artisan. What
should the representatives of the people have done? What they did
do: they began by punishing the guilty. . . .

But the spirit at Bordeaux is good, because at Bordeaux as everywhere else the sansculottes form the mass of the people. While the
rich and the merchants show a certain disdain for the sansculotte, and
by a sarcastic smile insult the modest contribution of the poor man,
they think that a reputation for patriotism goes to those who offer the
most, as if republican principles were measured by weight of gold,
and so they make overwhelming patriotic gifts, which they loudly
enumerate in the hope that the evil they have wanted to do to liberty
will be forgotten. I know that among those who give there are many
excellent patriots of commendable dedication, and that even in the
merchant class there are citizens of the purest intentions who form an
exception to the general rule, but I must speak frankly and give you
a true idea of this businesslike mentality at Bordeaux. We should
make use of this very recent inclination to generosity, but mistrust it

as long as revolutionary crises are upon us. We should be thankful that Bordeaux is now as it is, that the Mountain triumphs, the Muscadins and aristocrats are reduced to silence, and the temple of Reason is full of people every *décadi*. . . .

Other systems are used to assassinate public spirit. The Vincents and Hébert [the deceased and discredited "ultras"] have their agents here, faithful sectaries of their doctrine and imitators of their examples. Some of them, by atrocities that are revolting to humanity, nature, and virtue, have tried to make the Revolution odious in the eyes of decent people. They called themselves revolutionaries when they were only oppressive tyrants. . . .

After much else, this letter goes on to describe a festival at which a tree of liberty was planted in honor of the late Marat, and scenes of vengeance and edification were depicted:

Dumouriez has no country in which to lay his head; Brissot and Danton die on the scaffold; images of Marat are presented to the eyes of patriots through the vast extent of France, and the ashes of Marat sleep in the Panthéon. Ysabeau, representative of the people, and Jullien, commissioner of the Committee of Public Safety, stand on a mountain, dominate an immense assembly, and address the people. . . . Cries of *Vive la Montagne* resound, hats are thrown in the air. Ysabeau and Jullien drink to the prosperity of the arms of the Republic, and all the people respond with enthusiasm.

But soon Jullien began to have his doubts about Ysabeau. And in fact it seems that Ysabeau, who a few months before with his colleague Tallien (now departed) had been firmly repressive, had been softened by contact with the Bordeaux bourgeoisie, or perhaps was concerned that continued repression of the merchants would only bring further ruin on the city. Jullien's distrust of Ysabeau was perhaps motivated by jealousy of his prominence at Bordeaux, but also by a fear that Ysabeau was succumbing to "moderatism." He reflects also the fear, felt by many, that the Revolution would end up in the hands of a personal dictator. He wrote the following to Robespierre, discreetly mentioning Ysabeau only once, while clearly referring to him throughout:

Bordeaux
1ᵉʳ Floréal
[20 April]

I have not written to you for a long time, my good friend, since I supposed that you were too busy, and I had little of interest to say, while nevertheless keeping up my regular correspondence with the

Committee of Public Safety. Today I want to submit to you, with complete candor, a few observations on Bordeaux that I have already communicated in detail to the Committee.

The spirit here is generally good, and the Republic is sincerely loved. Even the rich, who do not love it, are prodigal in their sacrifices, and their self-interest is seemingly subdued. But the Club National has no stability, influence, or energy. It is hardly known to exist, and my plan to give it the preponderance it should have is hard to carry out.

One great reproach I would make to the Bordelais is that they treat the representative of the people as if he were an intendant of the old regime. When he passes in the street with his gendarmes some even cry, "Long live the saviour of Bordeaux!" If he appears at the theater, the club, or at any assembly the same cries are heard. Enthusiasm and idolatry are carried to an extreme, and I have noticed that even the aristocrats, to give themselves an air of patriotism, clap their hands in a way, I think, that dishonors free men. Applause should go not to the presence of a man but to the principles that he expresses. Lately, on a rumor that the representatives sent to Bordeaux would be replaced, it was said that Bordeaux was lost. It was even blasphemously proposed, in a well-attended gathering, that the people should go in large numbers to oppose the departure of their friend.

These facts and others have led me to the thought, which I think to be true, that a representative clothed with unlimited powers should never remain in the same place very long, since if he does badly he should not have the time to victimize the people by his bad conduct, and if he does well we should fear the all too easy tendency of the people to feel a kind of gratitude and idolatry that becomes the death of liberty. It is to be feared that the people may form the habit of needing a man with whom they feel so identified as to think they cannot do without him.

Yet I must say in justice to Ysabeau that he has worked constantly to discharge his mission, and deserves praise for his services. He himself has said that he would like to be transferred to the Army of the Eastern Pyrenees and have a month of rest after thirteen months' absence from Paris on his mission, and then resume his seat in the Convention.

I will now give a few words about myself. My letters to the Committee will have told you what I have said and done to regenerate the public spirit. I took the occasion of discovery of the last conspiracy [of the Dantonists] to electrify a bit the popular societies at La Rochelle and Nantes when I was there, and I have done the same at Bordeaux. I have reported in detail on the shortages in this department and their causes, and on the infamous war in the Vendée and the most effective ways to end it, from my knowledge of facts and localities. In my mission I have always followed the same system, that to make the Revolution lovable we must make it loved by publicizing acts of virtue, republican marriages and adoptions [as of orphans of those killed in the war], and by associating women with the love of country and binding them by solemn engagements. This system has been very successful. The influence of one sex on the other is a powerful incentive for warming up republican feeling in private and in public. I have given the Committee details on our festival where a tree was planted in honor of Marat. I did much the same at Port-Malo [Saint-Malo, the word "saint" being proscribed], Lorient, La Rochelle, Rochefort and Nantes. The women of Bordeaux, by their public promises with the commune to witness, have rekindled enthusiasm and pressed their husbands, sons and whole families into following the path of virtue.

Having seen the incalculable effects of festivals of this kind, I have thought it well to offer all France, at least on the stage, a little patriotic diversion that I have composed, entitled "les engagements des citoyennes." I shall offer it respectfully to the Committee of Public Safety, and, if it be thought good, will have it printed with details of the republican ballet with which it ends, to be enacted in Paris and other communes. I have not thought this effort irrelevant to my mission of forming the public spirit, and in any case it has taken me only three days to compose it. I embrace you, and please write to me at Bordeaux.

While the status of Ysabeau remained temporarily unsettled, Jullien was unexpectedly recalled to Paris, to become a member of the newly created Executive Commission on Public Instruction. The words "public instruction" referred to plans for the ordinary schools, but even more urgently to the propagation of attitudes favorable to the Revolution. For this activity Jullien was well qualified by the "instruction" he had been disseminating on his travels. He had shown initiative in organizing patriotic festivals, urged the town Jacobins to send missionaries into the country, and personally written the "diversion" mentioned in the preceding letter. He remained in Paris for about four weeks, through the month of Floréal, or from mid-April to mid-May.

While in Paris he attended the Jacobin club and spoke there on several occasions. Some of the Jacobins had their doubts on a decree of the National Convention, enacted on 7 May, declaring that "the French people recognize the Supreme Being and the immortality of the soul." Robespierre favored the decree, which would eventuate in the famous festival of the Supreme Being a few weeks later. As the Jacobins hesitated, Jullien in a speech of 15 May urged them to come forward with a strong statement in support of the decree, which, he said, only conspirators and hypocrites could oppose. He went on:

> . . . I have traveled in several departments of France and seen all eyes fixed on the Convention and the Jacobins. Your deliberations have been perceived with joy by all good citizens of the Republic. . . . Let the Jacobins speak out in these circumstances that are so fortunate for liberty, and let republicans be consoled to hear the tyrants cry in despair, "We are lost because the Jacobins have risen against us!"
>
> . . . There are men so bold as to make immorality into a dogma and atheism into a system. It is against such wretches that the Jacobins have directed and will still direct their efforts.
>
> Recall the unhappy time of the war in the Vendée. Remember how old men, women and children encouraged those nearest to them to take arms in defense of the country. It would have been no great encouragement to say to them: "Go and fight for liberty. If you survive you will enjoy its triumphs, but if you succumb you will find only nothingness in the grave." They said instead: "Go and if you perish as victims of your zeal you will live forever in the hearts of your brothers and bring yourselves into the bosom of the Deity." After these comforting words our defenders rushed into the cannon's mouth, and in the height of danger they saw not death but immortality. It would be a guilty offense for anyone not believing in immortality to propagate his doctrine. Those who would deprive man of the most potent germ of virtues should be proclaimed as traitors to their country. It is important that the Jacobins, as the living body of public opinion, should make a pronouncement. Aristocrats in the departments are saying that the Jacobins are silent, that they disagree with what the Convention has done. Such calumnies must be destroyed and their authors confounded. I propose that the Society present at the bar of the Convention the address that I am about to read.

The record states that Jullien then read the proposed address to unanimous applause. One member, however, raised an objection, saying that it would create an unfavorable impression to adopt a measure "proposed by a commissioner of the Committee of Public Safety." It must be recalled that the Executive Commission on Public Instruction, to which Jullien belonged, was a creation of the Committee of Public Safety, not a committee of the Convention.

Robespierre, sensing an attack not only on virtue and the Supreme Being but on the government, the Committee of Public Safety, and himself, sprang to his feet to support the proposal for which Jullien had acted as spokesman. The proposal was adopted. Jullien had again identified himself with Robespierre and the ruling Committee, at a time when opposition to them, even among the Jacobins, was beginning to develop.

The festival of the Supreme Being took place in the garden of the Tuileries on the following 8 June. Its purpose, in Robespierre's view, was to institute a common ground on which deists and law-abiding Catholics could stand together. Jullien would have enjoyed the occasion if he had been there. But only three days after his speech at the Jacobins the ruling Committee, obviously pleased with him, ordered him back to Bordeaux. Since it also ordered Ysabeau to return to Paris, Jullien on this second mission to Bordeaux would have a freer hand. His new orders were as follows:

> *Paris*
> *29 Floréal*
> *[18 May]*

The Committee of Public Safety orders that Marc-Antoine Jullien, sent as agent of the Committee to the maritime departments, and now adjunct commissioner in the Executive Committee on Public Instruction, shall proceed immediately to Bordeaux to enforce and oversee the execution of the revolutionary laws and revive and maintain the energy of the constituted authorities. Citizen Jullien should also concern himself with matters relative to the Executive Commission of which he is a member [i.e., public instruction or republican propaganda].

> *[Signed] Carnot, Robespierre, Billaud-Varenne, Barère*

And on the same day the Committee also ordered:

that the surveillance committee at Bordeaux is to be renewed, and that citizen Jullien, its envoy at Bordeaux, shall obtain information on the patriots suited to compose the new surveillance committee and revolutionary commission.

> *[Signed] Billaud-Varenne, Robespierre, Carnot, Barère*

Having suppressed federalism with death sentences at Toulon, Marseille, and Lyon, the Committee was determined to exterminate its remaining refuge at Bordeaux. In this attempt it had in Jullien a willing and zealous agent. As the Terror reached its deadly climax in May and June of 1794, with over a thousand persons condemned to death in Paris alone, much the same happened at Bordeaux, on a smaller scale but with equal ferocity. About two hundred victims died on the guillotine at Bordeaux in these next few weeks.

Ysabeau, though ordered to leave, remained obstinately in Bordeaux, claiming direct authority from the National Convention, to which Jullien opposed his direct authority from the ruling Committee. The duel between them reflected the larger conflict that raged in Paris. For a while he wrote to Robespierre almost every day. To Robespierre:

Bordeaux
11 Prairial
[30 May]

I promised to write to you about Bordeaux, my dear friend, and I shall keep my word. It was urgent that Ysabeau should depart, and yet he is still here, despite the order of the Committee of Public Safety dated 25 Floréal. . . .

Last night he came again to the club, and his affectation of attending assiduously and remaining until the end of the session, which he had never done before, makes all the more suspicious the contrast between his public speeches and his private conversations. He even occupied the chair, though he was not the president, receiving the acclamations of the people and reiterating his farewells to awaken a pernicious idolatry and expressions of regret. Hardly had he spoken when we saw one of his secretaries mount the tribune and repeat, almost in tears, that Bordeaux was losing its friend, and demand that the Club National should urge him to return to Bordeaux after his leave in the Hautes-Pyrénées. . . .

My mission here faces great obstacles. My coming just as Ysabeau departs is enough to make me a bugbear. The constituted bodies are hardly open to me. . . .

Public spirit is still moderate and selfish; and enthusiasm is less for liberty and country than for individuals. Ysabeau, flattering the people so as to gain their flattery, keeps saying that Bordeaux is the most revolutionary commune in France, and the merchants echo his words. We are called alarmists when we try to show, however tactfully, that the maximum of energy has not been attained. . . .

With a good surveillance committee, which I am now trying to organize, I hope that matters will go better at Bordeaux. Act quickly to send a representative to Bordeaux to replace Ysabeau, someone who is reliable, firm, and willing to follow the advice of the Montagnards with whom I will surround him. My position here is painful and delicate. . . . I need support by the Committee of Public Safety. Except for nine or ten pronounced republicans everyone turns his back on me. The moment has come to revolutionize this commune, and whoever undertakes this work, especially after such a sweet-talking and moderate man as Ysabeau, will not be loved. When I spoke out yesterday against fanaticism, which is still all powerful, he claimed that it was dead and that there were only five or six priests in the department, which I know positively to be false. Thus he deceives and flatters the people.

On the next day:

I must give you my thoughts: we are going to revolutionize Bordeaux, and I now have a good surveillance committee, but this is not enough, for the other constituted bodies are not in a mood to support it. They must be entirely renewed, purged of suspects and dangerous men who block the good that others might do. See whether the Committee of Public Safety has enough confidence in me to charge me with this operation, which I think useful. . . .

P.S. Hurry to send a representative here to replace Ysabeau, someone who is reliable, firm and revolutionary. There are intrigues here to obtain signatures to a petition for Ysabeau's return.

And on the following day, 1 June:

My friend, the time of crisis has come for Bordeaux. The patriots depend for everything on the Committee of Public Safety. . . . Ysabeau has not yet left. . . . He intends to create a party. . . . His conduct tends to discredit the Committee publicly. . . .

The Terror should not fall only on the federalists, some of whom are of good faith . . . , but on aristocrats, moderates, intriguers, and federalists who know what they are doing and of whom several are still unpunished. It would be useful for a firm and reliable representative to arrive immediately. Otherwise I shall need the means of acting myself.

And on 3 June, still to Robespierre:

Ysabeau left last night. . . . There is a cabal of merchants here, and liberty is up for sale. . . . Bordeaux will be regenerated by the punishment of intriguers, some of whom like Chabot had only their own interest in mind, others served Hebert and Danton, and all of whom aspired to destroy the Committee of Public Safety, so as to destroy liberty.

It is clear that Jullien, as terrorist at Bordeaux, acted as the agent of the Committee. But he was no passive agent; he positively asked for and solicited the powers that he wanted. He modestly urged that a new representative of the people should be sent, who would outrank him. But as agent of a Committee which by now was feared even by many members of the Convention, Jullien possessed an intimidating influence among the revolutionaries at Bordeaux.

At this time he also wrote his only letter to Saint-Just, Robespierre's fiery younger colleague on the Committee. Jullien had recently talked with him in Paris, while Saint-Just was there on a brief absence from the Belgian front. Jullien wrote him a long letter giving him a history of his mission. In the course of it he revealed how liberty in his mind had been obsessively preempted by equality. It may be remembered that his father had warned him, in December 1792, that his enthusiasm for equality would lead him to grief; and his father was soon proved to have been an accurate prophet.

To Saint-Just:

> *Bordeaux*
> *25 Prairial Year II of the Republic*
> *[13 June 1794]*

You asked me recently in Paris, my good friend, for some details on Bordeaux, from which I had then just arrived. Little did I think that I would so soon be back. Your return to the Committee has made me want to write, and I now fulfill the promise I gave you.

Bordeaux is a hotbed of commercialism and selfishness. There were many big merchants and many scoundrels, and liberty could not extend its empire, of which virtue is the base. There were many rich; the poor were pressured by them; and equality was unknown. Where there was a thirst for gold it was impossible to arouse a love of country. The human ego absorbed everything; various private interests stifled the public interest. At the beginning of the Revolution the merchants with brilliant fortunes, with their gilded palaces, lackeys and coaches, were only envious of the parchments of the nobles and privileged caste; they wanted no more than to take their places, and called themselves patriots. Bordeaux then provided rich offerings and numerous battalions. But when the federalist crisis came, the lawyers, whose talents and influence were put to use by the moneyed men, in a coalition to supplant the defunct parlements and nobility, wanted to destroy a republic whose emerging principles frightened their ambitions. They hoped to form the departments into several principalities, which they would share among themselves, and of which they thought they ought to be the peaceful and happy possessors. But equality arose to put all at the same level, and the federalists, sectarians of a new tyranny, saw their hopes extinguished.

He goes on to tell Saint-Just of Ysabeau's consorting with merchants, his pretensions, ostentation and popular acclaim, and to conclude by dwelling in sharp contrast on his own republican virtue.

I avoided the gross trap of flattery. The example before my eyes was too recent and too terrible. I had seen a man that I had long believed to be patriotic and virtuous corrupted by eulogy and flattery. I had seen the people duped and victimized, deceived and unhappy. I rejected the acclamations, dinners, caresses, praises, gifts and honors. I spoke of the principles of equality, the sacred rights of the people, the stern duty of those honored by its confidence; and I tried to unite precept and example and be consistent in theory and practice. This conduct seemed to gain me esteem; the national festivals have revived the energy of the people, and the revolution by becoming more lovable is more loved. The intriguers have fled from me; the republicans have surrounded me. . . . Bordeaux is purified and regenerated. I am glad to have come here, since I have done some good, but am impatient to leave, since after three years of labor my health is exhausted. My eyesight and chest are affected. Soon I shall be unable to write or speak. I am condemned to remedies worse than the diseases, and yearn ardently for rest.

This letter invites a psychological analysis, for which adequate evidence is lacking, but there is enough to show faith in a simple class analysis of the Revolution, in which the bourgeoisie overthrow the nobility and are in turn overthrown by the common people, and the poor defeat the rich in a triumph of virtue—all as seen by a young man complacent in his own sterling qualities, believing in a republican consensus that did not exist, and feeling sorry for himself because of poor health, which in fact was not poor enough to keep him from writing at length for the next fifty years.

But still not enough had been done at Bordeaux. The surveillance committee learned that several fugitive Girondins were in hiding at Saint-Emilion, about twenty miles east of the city. They were former members of the Convention, expelled and outlawed in the great insurrection of 31 May 1793, and wandering through France since that time. It was thought that one of them was Condorcet, to whom Jullien had written a respectful letter from England in August 1792. Jullien ordered that they be pursued and brought to justice. Condorcet was in fact secretly in refuge near Paris, where he soon met his death, but five others were discovered in a manhunt through the woods and vineyards near Saint-Emilion. The first two to be found were Guadet and Salle, who were captured in the house of Guadet's father, taken to Bordeaux, and executed as outlaws on mere verification of their identity. Guadet's father, aunt, and brother were put to death as guilty by association. Next came Barbaroux, who attempted suicide on being detected, was carried on a stretcher to Bordeaux, and hastily guillotined to affirm revolutionary justice before he could die of his wounds. Then, on 26 June, the mangled bodies of Pétion and Buzot were found in the woods, "half devoured by wolves." Apparently they were suicides.

The Committee of Public Safety, though not yet knowing all these details, approved of Jullien's actions.

> 7 Messidor Year II
> [25 June 1794]

The Committee of Public Safety approves of the conduct of Citizen Jullien, sent by the Committee to Bordeaux, and of the expenses he has incurred on this mission.

> [Signed] Barère, Robespierre, Billaud-Varenne

And Jullien wrote back, urging the continuation of harsh repression. To Robespierre:

> Bordeaux
> 12 Messidor Year II
> [30 June 1794]

I have received by special messenger from the Committee, my good friend, the letters and various decrees that it has sent to me. I will work more than ever to justify its confidence. Since my health is failing, I think from what Barère writes that I may be permitted to take a little rest in the Pyrenees.

I am writing to the Committee in detail on my operations. I beg you to obtain a reply to me on the following matters. . . .

1. Extend to the whole district of Bec d'Ambès the powers of the surveillance committee at Bordeaux, add nine new associate members, and authorize for the members, who work night and day, the payment of the hundred louis that their predecessors enjoyed.

2. Have the houses destroyed in which Guadet, Salle, Pétion, Buzot, and Barbaroux were found; transfer the military commission to Saint-Emilion to judge and put to death on the spot those who concealed them or were accomplices in their concealment. . . .

6. Should I not immediately replace the constituted bodies at Saint-Emilion and Libourne, which have been dismissed by order of the Committee for having protected, if only by negligence, the hiding places of the outlawed counterrevolutionaries?. . .

I beg you, my good friend, to obtain for me a prompt reply on these matters. I shall neglect nothing to fulfill my mission, in conformity with the wishes of the Committee and with the public good, but I am often held back by fear of deviating from the powers entrusted to me, so that I need to consult frequently.

In extenuation of this ruthlessness it can only be said that Jullien believed that he was punishing dangerous counterrevolutionaries and faithfully executing the policy of the Committee of Public Safety. No letter of his later than 30 June, either to Robespierre or to the Committee, is known to exist. He stayed on at Bordeaux for about a month, during which Garnier de Saintes arrived to replace Ysabeau as representative of the people. The death sentences at Bordeaux went on unchecked. Garnier proved to be as fiercely determined as Jullien to expose and punish the guilty, and especially "the intriguers and the rich," as he put it in his report to the Committee of Public Safety.

Jullien left Bordeaux on 13 Thermidor (31 July), heading for Paris—he would get no rest in the Pyrenees. He did not know that, four days before, the Convention had revolted against the Committee of Public Safety. On 9 Thermidor, which soon became a memorable date, a small group within the Convention had denounced Robespierre, Saint-Just, and Couthon as a triumvirate of conspirators aiming at dictatorship, and the Convention had expelled and outlawed them. They were guillotined the next day. Jullien heard the news at his first stop, Rochefort.

The startling fact is that he immediately thought that Robespierre might indeed be guilty. It was at Rochefort on 15 Thermidor that he began a career of personal exculpation that lasted the rest of his life. Stigmatized as Robespierre's spy, creature, or toady, he insisted and continued to insist that he had been the faithful agent of the Committee of Public Safety at a time of extreme national peril, but never the associate, friend, agent, or dupe of Robespierre himself. In the course of these exculpations he would sometimes say things that were dubious or untrue. Yet the evidence supports the general truth of his defense. He had worked for the Committee, not for Robespierre. It was later held against him that he had called Robespierre his friend, *mon bon ami*, in his letters. But he had addressed other members of the Committee in the same way. He had written also to Saint-Just the long friendly letter that has been quoted. But the tone of this letter, also, is of a report to a member of the ruling Committee.

Patriots everywhere were bewildered on hearing of Robespierre's fall. They could not know what to think, since the event was sudden and secret, but even if they had known they might be confused, since Robespierre had been overthrown by an unlikely combination. It included some extremists, whom Robespierre had called ultra-revolutionaries, as well as others who had simply accepted the Terror so long as civil discord and foreign war seemed to require it. It was not yet clear whether Thermidor signified a relaxation or an intensification of the Revolution.

Jullien lingered at Rochefort long enough to write to the Jacobin clubs of several neighboring towns to reassure them. The one to La Rochelle has survived, since the club there ordered it printed. It shows that Jullien was not surprised by the new turn of events. Rumors of dissension in the Convention had probably reached him in Bordeaux. He fitted this latest news into his general understanding of the dangers that beset the Revolution, one of which was the possibility of a dictatorship or a relapse into monarchy. In an atmosphere of universal distrust, and hence of hypocrisy, any man might, like Ysabeau, contrive deviously to profit from personal adulation. Conceivably even Robespierre had done so. Jullien therefore urged the good patriots of La Rochelle to rally round the Convention. He repeated what he had often said, that the Revolution was greater than any one man. Robespierre might fall, but the Republic would go on. He played on the word "incorruptible" which Robespierre's admirers had bestowed on him.

Marc-Antoine Jullien to His Friends and Brothers in the Popular Society at La Rochelle. 15 Thermidor Year II.

A great political crisis has erupted.

The voice of Liberty cries, "Attach yourselves to no man!"

The voice of Equality cries, "Stop any one individual from standing above others or eclipsing them by his power!"

Yet a man existed who might be called the idol of France. Can there be an idol in a Republic, and isn't idolatry the shameful precursor to slavery?. . .

Individuals are nothing, principles everything. Gratitude in politics is the first step toward idolatry, and idolatry is the first step toward a throne. . . .

A man may be useful, but is never necessary. . . . The pompous title of Defender of the People is sometimes only a synonym for tyrant. Any ambitious man who wished to dominate would call himself their Protector, the better to deceive those that he intended to subjugate. . . . The word "incorruptible" can be applied only to a man whose career is ended, on whose reputation death has set its authentic seal, and who need no longer fear that his laurels will be tarnished by his living one day too long. A man who has always conducted himself well is *uncorrupted*. But if he is still alive, however good a republican he may be, he should no more be seen as *incorruptible* than the ex-bishop of Rome is seen as *infallible*. When you come to celebrate his funeral, if he was the constant upholder of principle and virtue, you can engrave on his tomb: *He deserved the name of incorruptible*.

By this high-minded generalization, mentioning no names, Jullien played for time.

Further along on his journey to Paris he learned that he had been denounced in the Convention as a follower of Robespierre, on 11 Thermidor, only two days after Robespierre's fall. He must have sent this news back to Bordeaux, for the Club National in that city caused to be printed, in his defense, the text of a speech said to have been delivered at the Club in the preceding April. An *avis* or notice prefixed to the speech could not have been published before the death of Robespierre, while the absence of any reference to Jullien's arrest and imprisonment indicates a date before 22 Thermidor. In the speech there is nothing that could not have been said in April. It denounces moderates and hypocrites, threatens traitors, urges good patriots to rally round the Convention, and then goes on:

> The civic crown must never rest on the brow of a living man, but only on the broad forehead of the whole Republic. . . . Let us plant no laurels showing public gratitude except beside the cypresses that shade a mausoleum. So long as a man exists he may change; corruption and error may deflect him from the straight path that he has hitherto followed, and make his life too long by a single day.

These words, spoken at Bordeaux in April, would apply to Ysabeau. Now in print, they were meant to apply to Robespierre. The added "notice" reads:

> **Notice**
> Those who may have suspected, from the denunciation of young Jullien in the Convention, that he was a secret agent or blind instrument of the execrable Robespierre, to foment the idolatry that this monster had begun to inspire by his false virtues, and those who may have conceived of such a suspicion, are invited to read with the utmost attention this short piece by Jullien. They will see that this young republican feared nothing so much for the People as their idolatry for individual persons, and that he ceaselessly called them back to the purest and most severe republicanism.

The use here of one of Jullien's favorite words, "idolatry," and the thought that anyone may be corruptible until he is in his "tomb," as he said at Rochefort, raise the suspicion that Jullien himself inspired this publication of his speech. It was another step in exculpation, and in dissociation from Robespierre.

THREE

DEMOCRAT AMONG THE "ANARCHISTS"

JULLIEN arrived in Paris on about 20 Thermidor, or early August 1794, and the next two years would be the most dangerous and difficult of his life. In prison, in hiding, or as a principal writer for a new journal of the leftist republicans, the *Orateur plébéien*, he would feel himself to be a good democrat, but others would see him as one of the ex-terrorists that they called *anarchistes*. While in prison he met "Gracchus" Babeuf, who, in the same prison, developed ideas that Marxists have seen as foreshadowing communism, while Jullien underwent a change into what Marxism knows as a petty bourgeois or merely bourgeois democrat.

His first move was naturally to rejoin his mother and father. He heard from his father, who as a member of the Convention had been present on 11 Thermidor, a description of the hectic scene in which the younger Jullien had been denounced as a Robespierrist. The attack had been led by Tallien, known as a terrorist at Bordeaux before Jullien's arrival there, and who was also incited by his mistress, a famous adventuress, who thought she had been insulted by Jullien at Bordeaux when she had tried to obtain leniency for some of her acquaintances. Also leading the charge was none other than Carrier, author of the drownings at Nantes, whose excesses had been reported by Jullien to the Committee of Public Safety, which had recalled and discredited him. The elder Jullien had intervened, pleading his son's youth (he was now nineteen), and after a lively commotion the Convention had taken no action. Jullien remained temporarily free, but it was clear that compromised terrorists were trying to unload blame on Robespierre and his supposed acolyte.

With trepidation, Jullien presented himself to the Committee of Public Safety. It was a different committee from the one that he had served. Robespierre and Saint-Just were gone. Tallien himself was now a member. Of those who had been on the Committee for the past year one of the most violent was still present, Collot d'Herbois, notorious as the terrorist of Lyon; and even the relative moderates, Carnot, Barère, and C. A. Prieur, now called the late Robespierre a tyrant. Jullien intended to make a written report on his mission to Bordeaux. But the Committee had already made up its mind. It ordered his arrest the very next day.

23 Thermidor
[10 August]

The Committee of Public Safety orders that Jullien the younger, adjunct of the Commission on Public Instruction and formerly agent of the Committee of Public Safety, is relieved of his functions, put under arrest, and his papers sealed.

He fought back by going public. What would have been a confidential report to the Committee he printed as an open letter. It was a protest as well as a report, in which he joined in the hue and cry against Robespierre while defending his role at Bordeaux as a faithful servant of the Committee. After recounting his constructive activities, as in assuring the food supply of the city, he related his discovery and pursuit of the five fugitive Girondins with evident satisfaction.

To the Representatives of the People
Composing the Committee of Public Safety

. . . I had some suspicions that the outlawed conspirators were hidden in a place near Bordeaux, and I sent two republicans, Laye and Oré, to search for them and pursue them. On 29 Prairial I learned of the capture of Salle and Guadet, who were discovered in the place I had indicated. On 2 Messidor I was informed of the arrest of Barbaroux, and on the 8th of that month I knew that Pétion and Buzot had taken their own lives. I sent you these successive bits of happy news, and your special decree of 7 Messidor approved my conduct.

Meanwhile the just death sentences of Guadet, Salle and Barbaroux were unanimously applauded by the people and advanced the Revolution at Bordeaux. . . .

I was all the more pleased at the discovery of the five conspiring deputies since they had come to the banks of the Gironde only to await a favorable moment for stirring up a new storm, and to avenge their immolated friends, as they themselves told me. . . .

. . . No, I was not the agent of the tyrant. No, I knew nothing of the atrocious plot that your courage has uncovered. I was the first to applaud your energy. . . . As a young man, I scarcely knew the tyrant; I was at a hundred leagues' distance from him. Could I have been able to penetrate and expose his plans?

I have been blamed for having stopped at Rochefort. I left Bordeaux on 13 Thermidor in the evening. . . . At Rochefort, where I had aroused the patriots on a former occasion, I rallied them to the National Convention and I wrote to the popular societies of Bordeaux, La Rochelle, and Lorient to share with them my satisfaction at the fall of the dictator. . . .

If anyone should still think that I was a partisan of this man who deceived so many patriots, I would say that I was deceived myself; but despite the illusion that his false virtues had created in my mind I still feared his great power, his pride, and his insolent and despotic tone; and I had spoken in secret to a few patriots at Bordeaux of the possible need of ending him with a dagger. Did I not then anticipate and even prepare for the revolution that you have accomplished?

I spoke my mind on the very day of the dawn of liberty, 14 July 1789, when I wrote on some little pieces of paper that were imprudently scattered in Paris: *It is not enough to destroy the Bastille, the throne must be destroyed!* At the time of the uprising of 21 June [1792] I demanded the death of the tyrant [Louis XVI] and called for the Republic. Long before 10 August [1792], by letters that still exist, I said that the tyrant's den should be besieged and tyranny overthrown. In December (old style) of that same year I courageously denounced Dumouriez, although I was then employed on the staff of a general who was a friend of Dumouriez. A little before that I spoke out against Brissot. . . .

Citizen Representatives, I await your pronouncement on my fate in order to abide by your decision.

This last sentence suggests that Jullien, dating his report 24 Thermidor, had not yet been served with the order of the Committee, which had decreed his arrest on the preceding day.

The report is so self-serving as to raise doubts about its truth. Yet even such doubts must be modified. Did he really, before the event, call for the attack on the Tuileries and fall of the monarchy on 10 August 1792? He was then in London. Did he really call for dethronement on 14 July 1789? No one else did at that time. His mother, always worried about him, showed no knowledge of such an incident in her long letter of September of that year. But if he scattered such "little pieces of paper" he would have done so anonymously, and it is not impossible that a fourteen-year-old schoolboy, who for years had been hearing stories of Brutus, Cato, daggers, and the Roman Republic in his classroom, might have engaged in such a prank to show his disapproval of kings. Did he really denounce Brissot and Dumouriez in the closing months of 1792? There is no evidence that he did. But his mother and father both warned him at that time against the radicalism of his speeches in southern France. Above all, did he really come to suspect Robespierre before 27 July 1794 and talk with a few Jacobins at Bordeaux about the possible need of his assassination? It seems unlikely, but we have none of his letters after 30 June, and it is possible that during these weeks of July he heard rumors of Robespierre's mysterious absences from the Committee and the mounting dissatisfaction among his own colleagues. There was everywhere a fear that publicized virtue might be false. There had been so many conspiracies, real and alleged, that anyone might be supposed to conspire.

In any case the Committee was unimpressed. It arrested Jullien and sent him first to the relative comfort of a hospice, and then to one of the most famous prisons of the Terror, Plessis Prison, which was in fact the old Plessis College, near where he had lived with his parents in his student days in the rue Saint-Jacques. He was detained for fourteen months, or the whole period of the Thermidorian Convention.

He had reason to fear for his life, for many persons accused of Robespierrism went to the guillotine in these weeks following 9 Thermidor. His worst fears, as well as his highest hopes, were expressed in a short poem written in prison that he published much later. This exercise in rhymed couplets hardly lends itself to effective translation, but the attempt can be made:

My Farewell to My Country

My dear sad country, sole object of my wishes,
Receive at this moment, the last moment of my life,
The last feelings that still live in my heart;
They are only for you, your happiness and glory.

O my country, be happy, and my soul thus contented
Will banish the worries that now torment it.
I have had little taste of life, and have little fear of death,
But I weep for you and your horrible fate.
Crime alone triumphs, and the people are in chains.

I die, but hope follows me to the grave.
Before my eyes I see a new future arising;
I see the factions plunged into nothingness
And the virtues, the laws, and the country avenged.

O sacred liberty, reborn from the tomb,
You will see your enemies hurled into the abyss,
Vice, pride and ambition struck down
And our France standing upright with its tyrants gone.

The prisons, as already noted, were not places of strict incarceration. Inmates could read newspapers, receive visitors, and send out letters. On 21 October Jullien sent a letter to his friends at Bordeaux, to which Ysabeau had returned and where he was denouncing Jullien as a bloodthirsty tool of Robespierre. It was a very long letter, reflecting both Jullien's tendency to repetitious verbosity and the long leisure of his confinement.

> . . . Can you believe, citizens of Bordeaux, that I was a conspirator, an agent of tyranny, as has been said? So I conspired within your walls! Yes, no doubt. But it was with the people and the good citizens against scoundrels, intriguers and swindlers. Yes, I conspired against those . . . who would subject your city to the scourges of famine, discord, terror and enslavement. I conspired against those beings whose atrocious imagination fed on the spectacle of another Lyon devoured by conflagration and war, with your homes destroyed and your blood inundating your ruins. . . .
>
> I conspired against those who would murder virtuous republicans whose only crime was a passing error.
>
> I pursued the chiefs of a liberticide faction that would destroy the country.
>
> To those who were only misled, whose intentions had always been pure, and whose republicanism dated from the fall of the Bastille, I said: No, you will not die. . . . Crime alone will go to the scaffold; mere error will not be proscribed. I said as much to you at the time; I declared myself the defender of patriots of good faith. . . . I wrote to the Committee of Public Safety in their favor. . . .
>
> Did I seem to you unjust, inhuman, avid for power, ambitious, intriguing, or a tyrant? Such are the words used of me today. Was I an accomplice of Robespierre? I, who said to several of you that he must be sacrificed? I, who always warned you not to attach yourselves to one man, not to be dazzled by anyone's reputation, not to raise laurels of popular gratitude except beside the cypresses that shade a mausoleum.
>
> But I corresponded with Robespierre and that is now called my crime. Read my correspondence! I acknowledge it, admit it, glory in it. Its whole object was the welfare of your city and the good of the country. . . . If I was deceived by this man, so was the Convention and the whole of France. Living as I did for a year far from the place where he had made himself a dictator, I might have had no knowledge of his despotism and shared in the general delusion. But I did not share in it, and I proved as much when I returned to Paris in the month of Floréal [April–May], when at a session of the Jacobins I dared to say that the national energy was sleeping. My speech caused them to remove me from the city. Despite my assignment in Paris I was sent back on mission to Bordeaux. They wanted an honorable pretext for getting rid of me.

In this letter, written two months after his report to the Committee, we find the same indignant rejection of Robespierre but also his movement away from an endorsement of severe repression. Jullien would now have it believed that he had been reasonably moderate at Bordeaux. He had indeed said during his mission there that merely misguided patriots had nothing to fear, and he had indeed warned against adulation of one man. But he now makes no mention of the most damaging charge against him, his relentless pursuit and condemnation of the five fugitive Girondins and their relatives, and the destruction of their houses. For his claim to have had doubts about Robespierre as early as the preceding Floréal there is no evidence; on the contrary, he had spoken at the Paris Jacobins and in the Convention in favor of Robespierre's cult of the Supreme Being. And there is no reason to believe that anyone sent him back to Bordeaux to be rid of him. Here again the evidence shows the opposite. He had been a zealous partisan of the Terror at Bordeaux, of a good, honest, discriminating, "surgical" use of the Terror, but of terror nonetheless.

In January 1795 the Convention heard the report of a committee, headed by E. B. Courtois, charged with finding evidence of the crimes of Robespierre. The committee had discovered the letters written by Jullien to Robespierre from the West and from Bordeaux. The Convention published both the report and letters, so that the confident, approving, and admiring tone in which Jullien had addressed Robespierre was now public knowledge. But Courtois was inclined to excuse Jullien and blame Robespierre instead for having employed such a young, excitable, and inexperienced person as his agent. Jullien was left to linger in prison but not to die. He could gradually therefore become more tolerant of his Thermidorian captors.

During his long confinement he occupied his time not only by versification, as seen above, but by composing memoranda and meditations, and a prison journal. These writings reflect his conversations with the various *anarchistes* imprisoned with him, who included the well-known *enragé* Varlet, the Lebatteux whose excesses at Nantes Jullien had denounced, and even for a few weeks Gracchus Babeuf. Jullien in 1795 shared with such men the belief that the Revolution was a class conflict between rich and poor. Unlike them, and a bit inconsistently, he declared that all classes should unite in defense of the Republic. The greatest danger, he thought, and few later historians would deny it, was in a counterrevolution from the right, a victory of the foreign powers, a return of the émigrés, and acceptance of a "Louis XVIII" who at this very time, at Verona, announced his intention to bring back the Old Regime more or less *in toto*.

The trouble with the Revolution, Jullien wrote in one of these memoranda, was that it had paid too little attention to the people.

Before the Revolution could be achieved the people had to be given an interest in it and be identified with it. It was not enough to have popular laws; what was needed was prompt enforcement. The Revolution was a state of war between patricians and plebeians, for whom a distribution of its conquests should not have been postponed. . . . It will be seen everywhere that the Revolution from beginning to end was a continued struggle or war to the death between patricians and plebeians, between the rich and the poor.

Yet he also urged all parties to support the post-Robespierrist Convention. All who were not outright royalists should be included—even the surviving Girondins.

Our only reproach to the Gironde was for opinions different from ours at that time. On the essential point, the indivisible and democratic republic, they seem now to agree with us. Let us then unite. Let such terms as Thermidorians, Girondins and terrorists disappear. Let those who have established the Republic and wish to preserve it, those that can never be pardoned by royalty or by Feuillants or émigrés, now form a holy league to save themselves and save the country. Let us appeal to the true children of the Revolution. Let us stop accusing and persecuting one another. . . . The royalists rejoice in our dissension and are preparing to unite us on the same scaffold. . . . Let us embrace and fight our common enemies. . . . There are more than twenty thousand energetic republicans in houses of detention. . . . The people, the armies and the prisons are with us. With union the country will be saved.

But when a few in the prisons combined with others outside in two great popular insurrections, those of Germinal and Prairial of the Year III, Jullien refused to support them. The winter of 1794–1795 caused great suffering from cold, food shortage, and runaway inflation, and these uprisings of the spring of 1795 were more genuinely of the people, in the sense of the poor, than any earlier revolts since 1789. The demonstrators demanded bread and called for implementation of the democratic constitution of 1793, which had been suspended. Should it be put into effect the Convention would be dissolved. In a mass invasion of the Convention one of its members was killed; his head was cut off, put on a pikestaff, and waved in the face of the presiding officer. Jullien, learning of all this in his cell, made notes of his disapproval. He even thought, as Robespierre might have, that these disturbances were instigated by royalists to discredit the Republic.

The two uprisings and the severe repression that followed had contrary effects. Some, like Babeuf, were made all the more revolutionary. Jullien feared an increased danger of counterrevolution, in which he himself would again face death. He wrote at some time in the summer of 1795:

> I have never been able to get myself heard nor to obtain judgment; I have been given no reasons for my arrest. . . . Every day I hear the sad sighs of a dying liberty. I learn of the deaths of many republicans, and I see a rapid counterrevolutionary torrent swollen with blood and dead bodies. . . . I am on the way to where the Gracchi are. . . . I was born in a volcano, have lived in its eruption, and will be buried by its lava. . . . A virtuous man, a candid and simple soul, lives among men in time of revolution as in a forest peopled by wild beasts.

The reference to the Gracchi may reflect his contacts with "Gracchus" Babeuf. But he was treading the path taken by his mother. She, too, a good Jacobin, had said in 1793 that she was living among wild beasts and wished that quarreling republicans would work together.

Babeuf, in the Plessis Prison, sketched out his ideas on a real equality more clearly. There should be no private property, all would work to put their product into a common store, from which all would receive equally what they needed—just as was done, said Babeuf, "for 1,200,000 men in our armies." Jullien, seeing this paper, recorded his emphatic disagreement:

> All these principles, which have the appearance of justice and truth, are no more susceptible to application in our social condition than it would be for men of today to live on roots and herbs and do without houses and clothing. Only a madman could conceive of an agrarian system [the common term then used for what would be called communism] which would bring the total dissolution of society, and would never prevent the later growth of a great inequality of fortunes. . . . We must improve the lot of the poor by more wise and possible measures.

October 1795 saw another attack on the Convention, remembered as the insurrection of Vendémiaire, but now the assault came from royalists, who if successful would reintroduce a monarchy, constitutional or otherwise. The cooped up prisoners feared for their lives. The horrors of the prison massacres of September 1792 might be repeated. Jullien joined with Babeuf in a delegation to see the warden, asking him to let them out to take part in the defense of the Republic. The warden hesitated. The uprising was suppressed while Jullien and the others remained helpless.

They were saved not by their own efforts but by the army. It was the first time during the Revolution that the army put down an uprising. It did so under the command of General Napoleon Bonaparte, who ordered his "whiff of grapeshot" on this occasion. Royalism was crushed. "I can now breathe a bit freely," wrote Jullien. "I admit that an hour earlier I was ready to kill myself. . . . I thought everything was lost."

Jullien, Babeuf, and the others were set free a few days later. Bewildered at the turn of events, and uneasy at the radicalism of some of his fellow inmates, Jullien decided to use his liberty by removing himself from the scene.

> I am determined to leave Paris. I must find some reason for a sudden departure and make clear my break with revolutionaries who want to enroll me in their phalanxes. . . . I am going away; I would rather look on some milk and cows. . . . I am twenty-one years old, and I hope that the dawn of my life will no longer be clouded by such dark images.

He in fact left the city, but on hearing that the expiring Convention had amnestied the ex-prisoners he was back in a week. With Babeuf and others he founded the Pantheon Club, which became a hotbed of advanced democratic agitation. Jullien found himself again among men who were more revolutionary than he was. He thought again of departing from Paris, and applied to the foreign minister for an assignment out of the country. The reason he gave the minister was that now, as a constitutional regime tried to establish itself, it would be well for controversial figures to be seen no more in Paris.

> Now that a regime of laws and the establishment of a constitution offer the hope of ending a revolution too long prolonged, it is necessary that those who through unfavorable circumstances have been involved in the revolutionary troubles, and so have made many enemies, and whose presence might revive hatreds that it is important to extinguish, it is necessary, I say, that such men should remove themselves for a while and only come back after several years, when peace and union have been achieved.

And further, since the government should be the "conciliator between classes," it would be best to send away

> those patriots whose names might cause alarm, and who must wait for the sponge of time to wipe off the stains of calumny and party spirit that have been imprinted on their reputations.

But he received no foreign assignment, and had to live with his reputation.

The incoming Directory, threatened most recently by the rightist uprising of Vendémiaire, for a few months sought support on the left. It even granted a subsidy to the Pantheon Club. It took a tolerant view of radical journalism, and both Jullien and Babeuf had a brief career as journalists. In his *Tribun du peuple* Babeuf publicized the ideas he had developed in prison, demanding the abolition of private property and a system later seen as an anticipation of communism. Jullien joined with others to found the *Orateur plébéien*. (*Orateur* meant a spokesman, and *plébéien* might mean anyone who was not an aristocrat.)

Babeuf had nothing but scorn for the *Orateur*. "Your taking the title of "plebeian" is a bold imposture; you are only a superficial republican. . . . The people don't listen to you; they listen to me. . . . My pen has always been not only republican but *democratic* and *plebeian*, and always will be. There is a difference. Do you understand?" The difference was between the proto-communist and the incipient bourgeois democrat.

Among those calling themselves democrats there were various tendencies, whose common theme was that they considered the Directory too timid in both domestic and foreign policy. The most intransigent followed Babeuf; they aimed at a "real equality" and preferred to overthrow the Directory rather than cooperate with it. Others, more numerous, favored a democratization of the Directory and the carrying of a democratic revolution beyond the borders of France. Jullien expressed these tendencies in the *Orateur plébéien*.

In almost the first number he reviewed the three parties, as he saw them, in the recently elected and newly forming Legislative Body. By a special law it was required that, for this first election under the constitution, two-thirds of those elected must have been members of the Convention. The law was intended to assure continuation of the Republic, but it aroused strong objection on all sides. Its consequence was that the first legislature was full of the Thermidorians who had removed Robespierre, supplemented by surviving Girondins and others who rejoined the Convention as it became clear that the official Terror had ended.

On his "first party" Jullien had little that was noteworthy to say. It was composed of those in the legislature who thought, or were beginning to think, that the time for a restored monarchy was at hand. These were the faction "favoring the throne." Outside the legislature this faction included perpetrators of the "white terror" in which former terrorists and Jacobins were being sporadically murdered.

It was on his "second party" that Jullien amplified his thoughts. He expressed confidence in the Thermidorians as veterans of the Revolution. He denied that they were "reactionaries" (*réacteurs*, a new word coined at this time); it was only royalists that called them such.

> The second party that is now evident in the Legislative Body, and which can be a powerful force in combating the faction favoring the throne, is composed of men who have been known as *Thermidorians*, men who have figured in all moments of the Revolution, learned the tactics of a large assembly and acquired the habit of guiding popular unrest, and so have the political influence and the degree of audacity necessary for success. . . . These same men have also concurred in the destruction of royalty and in the judgment of the tyrant; they have brought down on their heads the *hatred of kings who know not how to pardon*. . . . Their own interest binds them to the interests of the Republic. They can save themselves only by saving the people.
>
> Royalists may try in vain to divide these men from us by calling them *reactionaries*, by unloading on to them the odium for the evils of true reaction. . . . We will not fall into such a vulgar trap. We will fight against the émigrés, the planners of massacres and the hired thugs of Louis XVIII, and we shall all be united in defense of a cause that is common to us all. . . .
>
> Some of those of whom I speak, alarmed by the hypocritical clamors of royalism, are still afraid of those they call terrorists and "energetics." All such lines of demarcation should be erased. All causes of estrangement and discord should disappear. All prejudices created by party spirit should yield to a sincere union and indestructible friendship among republicans.

These "energetics" are the third party, to which the *Orateur* feels that he himself belongs, though he has little to say about it. He admits that it has fewer representatives in the Legislative body than the second party. It is the party of "austere" republicans, who feel as strongly for equality as for liberty, and who want "the reign of the severe principles that constitute democracy." But the second party, though in a majority, should ally with the smaller party of the democrats against émigrés, *chouans*, royalists, and foreigners. Then the Revolution "will be promptly ended, and turn its attention to the people." Then "the foreign party will no longer govern the Republic, but the fate of the Republic will decide the fate of Europe and the world."

In the following numbers of the *Orateur* Jullien turned his attention to the geographical spread of the Revolution to Europe. By its constitution of 1795 the French Republic incorporated Belgium, formerly a possession of the Austrian empire with which France was still at war. French royalists, crypto-royalists, and cautious republicans took the view that there could be no peace unless France withdrew behind its former frontiers. Jullien devoted a long disquisition to this subject. In this journalists' war he called his adversaries *chouans*, thus identifying them with the antirepublican insurgents in western France.

> Several *chouan* journals would like to persuade us today that these rich countries of Belgium must be ceded back to the Emperor. They would see with a dry eye, or rather a look of satisfaction, the republican Belgians dragged on to their tyrants' scaffolds. They would hand over to the vengeance of the King of Sardinia the Savoyard patriots who have ranged themselves under our standards and shed their blood for the French Republic. . . . These cold-hearted calculators, by their perfidious sophisms, would mislead a generous nation [France] which, if it yielded to their insinuations, would soon see its own liberty perish and be forever buried in slavery and opprobrium. . . . By what pretext do they support this liberticide proposal to return Belgium to its former masters?
>
> It is useless and dangerous, they say, to preserve our conquests . . . . They talk of the prejudices of the Belgians and the political balance of Europe. Such are the dishonest arguments that color this first step toward a French counterrevolution. . . .
>
> Who is this miserable sophist who talks of the prejudices of the Belgians and would have us believe that they are not ready for liberty?. . . In '89 we too had religious and monarchist prejudices; yet we conquered the Bastille and delivered the first mortal blow to the throne. . . . We have taken great strides; the sovereignty of the people has devoured royal tyranny. . . .
>
> Who talks of the political balance of Europe?. . . Is it for our republicans to respect that Machiavellian system of the royal courts and balance of power, which was only invented to perpetuate the slavery of peoples? Wasn't this balance broken at the very moment when the French Republic rose on the ruins of the throne? In *our* political balance we put the rights and liberties of nations on one side, and the scepters and crowns of a few potentates on the other. We shall see whether the invincible arms of free men do not outweigh the gold and baubles of kings. . . .

In February 1796 the Directory closed the Pantheon Club. In March it created a new ministry of police to protect itself against conspiracies by either royalists or "anarchists." Jullien and several other old Jacobins took employment with the new ministry—it was a way of fighting against royalist plots. Babeuf, driven underground, with half a dozen others organized an actual conspiracy against the Directory. Jullien, according to his own later statement, warned the minister that an insurrection was being prepared, while assuring him that most of those called *anarchistes* were not involved. He published a warning also to these latter, the "energetic" republicans, reminding them of the repression that had followed the Prairial uprising of a year before. Babeuf and his "madmen," he said, were luring them to an "abyss."

> Learn from the past. Know your enemies and their designs. You will march to your death and raise your own scaffolds and their triumphal car. . . . Open your eyes, stop this crazy course, abandon leaders who seduce you. I absolve myself. . . from the consequences of this insurrection preached by madmen and scoundrels.

On 30 April he resigned from the police ministry and made more plans to leave Paris. On 10 May the police discovered and broke up the conspiracy. Babeuf and one other were condemned to death a year later. But there were 249 names on a list of suspected accomplices in Babeuf's insurrection, and one of them was the name of Marc-Antoine Jullien.

Jullien again fled from Paris, finding a secret refuge somewhere near Versailles. This time he remained away from the city for five months.

FOUR

BONAPARTE—ITALY—EGYPT—NAPLES

WHILE STILL IN HIDING near Paris, in July 1796, Marc-Antoine Jullien wrote an extraordinary letter to General Napoleon Bonaparte, then in Italy. In it he asked for a job in Bonaparte's army.

At the age of twenty-one, and after seven years of political turmoil, Jullien was isolated and discouraged. He had believed in and been disappointed by each new wave of the Revolution; he had admired in turn Lafayette, then Condorcet and the Girondins, then Robespierre, the Mountain and the Committee of Public Safety, and most lately the advanced democrats gathered about Babeuf, but he had found them all to be less than he had hoped for. Although at times he had warned against extremism, he was now branded as an extremist himself, implicated in the Conspiracy of Equals.

Bonaparte, only six years older than Jullien, was now the sensational Republican hero. He had led his Army of Italy across the snows of the Alps, defeated the Austrians at the battle of Lodi, and occupied Milan, where the Italian patriots welcomed him as a liberator. In the following months he drove the Austrians out of Italy, incidentally inducing the claimant to the Bourbon throne, the future Louis XVIII, to make a hasty escape from Verona. Bonaparte emerged as the international champion of liberty and equality against kings, despots, royal courts, nobles, patrician oligarchies, clerical hierarchies, and miscellaneous privileged classes. While Jullien was an obscure fugitive, Bonaparte had charisma.

There is no evidence that this letter of Jullien's was ever sent, or if sent elicited any reply. But a draft or copy of it is in existence, and it reveals Jullien's state of mind at the time. It is a curious letter, too long for an unsolicited message to a famous man that the writer had never met. It is a bit presumptuous, addressing Bonaparte with the familiar *tu*, as was the habit among zealous republicans, and assuming that the general had suffered as much as the writer from the slanders of faction. It is self-justifying in insisting (rightly enough) that the writer is a firm republican but uninvolved in the later stages of Babeuf's conspiracy. It makes the usual allusions to the ancient Romans, and echoes what his mother had told him about the pleasures of virtue and friendship.

Paris, 18 Messidor IV
[6 July 1796]

General:

All republicans are united by indissoluble ties, and their common interests and sentiments should allow them to identify each other. You also have been oppressed, you have known misfortune, you have won the honor of being hated by enemies of the country.

During the dreadful reaction that weighed upon our heads I spent fifteen months in prison. The day of 13 Vendémiaire, when you had the glory of fighting for liberty, delivered me from my chains so that I saw the light of day. I took up my pen to attack the royalists, whom I had fought against at other times with other weapons. In the Pyrenees, in lands occupied by brigands, I devoted my youth to the defense of the country. . . .

Today I am again proscribed and pursued by a frenzy of slanders in which I am accused of having taken part in the too famous conspiracy of 22 Floréal [the Babouvists]. I cannot stoop to justify myself since I am not guilty. If I were guilty I would admit to my crime, and if I had thought it my duty to conspire I would know how to die. But I had foreseen all the evils that would result for our country from a conspiracy that even its authors could not conceal, and if you will glance at the printed material that I send with this letter, written at the end of Germinal, a month before the discovery of the plot, you will see what my opinion was of the project of the conspirators. You will judge whether I was their accomplice.

Nevertheless, I have been obliged to flee and go into hiding to avoid being thrown again into prison and made the object of party fury. . . . It is blindness for men of the Revolution to destroy themselves instead of fighting their common enemies. They cannot learn from the past, and the example of their predecessors is lost for them. . . . I am often reminded of Cato. . . .

. . . . I have known what the justice of factions is, and seen the servile dependence of law-courts in a revolutionary crisis. The battlefield is the only tribunal where a falsely accused patriot can henceforth justify himself and prove that he has always been a sincere lover of liberty. I write, therefore, citizen, to ask whether you wish to receive me into your army. I would go as a simple soldier if my physical strength and emotional exhaustion made it possible. I will fill any post that you may wish to assign me, and you will not regret calling me to your side. It is a source of happiness, the tenderest joy of a generous soul, to do good and offer asylum to the oppressed. Hearts sensible to glory cannot be indifferent to friendship and virtue.

When you know me better I dare to think that you will congratulate yourself on having found a faithful friend, the most precious treasure to be had on earth. . . .

The camp of the Army of Italy will become for me the school of virtue, the temple of friendship, the sanctuary of glory. O Bonaparte, can the victorious leader of the heroes of the Army of Italy, the liberator of oppressed nations whose laurels are stained only with the blood of enemies of humanity, look with an unfeeling eye on a new palm to be added to his triumphal crown? Ah! if it is well to deliver the earth from kings and their slaves, it is no less glorious to preserve the friends and defenders of the country. In the Roman Republic the man who saved the life of a citizen was no less honored than the one who had killed several of its enemies and won several victories. I salute you with the fraternal embrace and I await your reply.

To this already long letter Jullien added a postscript, giving a summary of his experience and a few references. It is to be noted that he mentions his mission to the Vendée, but not his involvement with the Terror at Bordeaux and the grisly fate of the Girondins there.

P.S. It will be well for you to know something of my past, and I can tell you that I was war commissioner to the Army of the Pyrenees, then commissioner for the levy of 300,000, and finally, under the old Committee of Public Safety, commissioner of the government to the maritime departments and with our troops in the Vendée. Such are the military functions that I have had. . . . I learn on ending this letter, from old journals over two weeks old, that Garrau and Saliceti are commissioners with the Army of Italy. I invite you to show them this letter. Garrau has known me especially well, and is I think disposed to be useful to me. . . . I beg you to let no one else know the secret of my refuge, which I hope will soon be among our brothers in arms. I wish I were already far from this place, where a triumphant royalism threatens to send all patriots and especially the conquerors of the Vendée . . . to the scaffold.

Receiving no answer to this letter, which indeed he may never have sent (and which he never mentioned in his abundant recollections in later years, when such early enthusiasm for Bonaparte was more embarrassing to remember), Jullien lingered on in his hiding place for several months. It seems that when his mother boldly went to the police to inquire about him, she was told that no grounds for his arrest any longer existed. The charges against him were canceled in October 1796.

He was now free from pursuit, but not from his past, and his mother soon again had occasion to intervene. Among the most heated revolutionaries of 1793 was L. M. Prudhomme, who like many others went to an opposite extreme after Thermidor, and in 1797 published six volumes on "the errors, faults, and crimes of the French Revolution." He took note of Jullien's role in the Terror at Bordeaux, where, according to Prudhomme, Jullien had said that liberty must rest on a "bed of corpses" and had conducted an unmerciful program of repression.

Rosalie Jullien wrote a letter of protest to Prudhomme, which he published. She insisted that her son had in fact saved Bordeaux from worse horrors that might have occurred. She quoted at length from Jullien's letters to Robespierre as published by Courtois, from which she noted that he had denounced Carrier and the ultra-revolutionaries at Nantes, and so argued that he had always opposed "revolutionary exaggeration." She ignored what these letters also revealed, that while Jullien had indeed opposed the ultras at Nantes he had feared the "moderates" at Bordeaux. She thought the guilty extremist at Bordeaux had been Ysabeau, whom Jullien had suspected of "moderatism." Prudhomme in any case put more blame on Robespierre than on Jullien, and when he brought out a new edition of his crimes of the Revolution in the 1820s he recounted the same episodes at Bordeaux, with the gruesome fate of the Girondins, but omitted Jullien's name.

Meanwhile, in 1797, it was Italy that provided an escape from such acrimony and recrimination. Among those dissatisfied with the Republic under its constitution of the Year III and the government of the Directory were dissidents of all political stripes and colors, from the most obstinate royalists through constitutional or liberal monarchists, to the unruly democrats that even Robespierre had called ultras and the small extreme fringe of those who were attracted by the alleged proto-communism of Babeuf. Among all these were several Italians, refugees from disturbances in Italy, who believed that a more radically democratic regime in France would promote revolution in Italy, and so were drawn into Babeuf's plan for an uprising against the Directory. One of these was Filippo Buonarroti, whose book thirty years later was to make the Conspiracy of Equals famous. Another was Guglielmo Cerise, who was a revolutionary democrat and hence an early admirer of Bonaparte, and who remained in his service, eventually becoming a baron of the Napoleonic Empire. Cerise had known Jullien when they were both in touch with Babeuf's followers in the winter of 1796. A year later, in the winter of 1797, Cerise was an officer in the Lombard Legion, a formation of Italian patriots attached to Bonaparte's Army of Italy. Cerise wrote to Jullien, inviting him to come to Milan and join the Lombard Legion.

In this way Jullien managed to realize his dream of escaping from the factionalism in Paris and go off on a nobler mission of serving humanity and saving the Revolution beyond the borders of France. There is no record of what his first duties in Italy were. He did soon have, however, one remarkable adventure. He was chosen as a special courier to convey half a million francs to Bonaparte's headquarters about a hundred miles northeast of Venice. Bonaparte had driven the Austrians back within the borders of the Habsburg empire, and was about to arrange a preliminary treaty of peace.

Crossing by ship from Venice to Trieste, Jullien and his half-million francs were captured by an Austrian privateer. Alone and unarmed, he extricated himself and his precious charge by an audacious speech. The best record of this episode is in a certificate signed by one of Napoleon's marshals, Augereau, nine years later, probably at the request of Jullien and possibly even written by him for Augereau's signature, since Jullien was working for the Grand Army in 1806 and Augereau had been in Italy in 1797. The substance of the document consists of one very long and soberly official sentence:

> Frankfurt-am-Main
> 26 August 1806

Marshal Augereau certifies to his knowledge that, toward the end of the first Italian campaign, a few months before signature of the preliminary peace of Leoben, M. Jullien . . . [having suffered various indignities] . . . came to seek an asylum and recover his military status in the Army of Italy; that on passing through Venice, being then an adjunct-commissioner on the staff of the Lombard Legion, he was invited by M. Haller, administrator-general of the army, to charge himself with the conduct by sea to general headquarters in Germany of a half-million in funds needed by the commanding general [Bonaparte] for continuance of his military operations; that he was taken prisoner by an Austrian privateer on the crossing from Venice to Trieste, and that he was able, by great presence of mind, skill and courage, to persuade the privateer that he was engaged on an important mission concerning peace, the success of which would be of more advantage to the Emperor of Austria, menaced as he was in his own states, than to the victorious French army; that he also persuaded his captors that the route of his mission was protected by French vessels cruising in the neighborhood, by which they were in imminent danger of being captured unless they consented immediately to his honorable release; that he prevailed on the sailors by a mixture of seductive incentives, the love of gold, religion, terror, and enthusiasm for General Bonaparte, whose very name exerted a powerful influence, and finally love of their own emperor, whose shaken throne might be restabilized by the success of this mission to accelerate the peace; and that thus, although alone in the hands of armed enemies, he managed to liberate himself and his treasure and land safely at Trieste, from which he arranged for the transmission of the funds entrusted to him to their destination.

This distinguished action would have been better known and better rewarded except that M. Jullien, on leaving Trieste, suffered a broken leg by a fall from a carriage, which deprived him of the advantage of joining the general headquarters himself, taking active part in the close of the campaign, and receiving the reward due for this recent service and previous actions.

In faith of which, the undersigned Imperial Marshal has delivered the present certificate to M. Jullien, now a subinspector of reviews.

Jullien's broken leg (was it really broken?) did not long keep him inactive. We soon find him bearing a letter of recommendation from General Bon at Lodi to General Brune at Padua. These two were among the higher officers in the Army of Italy who sympathized with the democratic wing among the republicans in Paris. (Bon died a year later on the Egyptian campaign; Brune lived to be one of Napoleon's marshals, only to be assassinated by royalists in 1815.) There are two references in Bon's letter that repay close examination. One observes that Bonaparte "appreciated" Jullien, probably because he had heard how the half-million francs were delivered to him. The other, the "proclamation" referred to, means Bonaparte's announcement to his army, only three days before Bon's letter, of a march on Paris in the event of an attempted overthrow of the Republic by royalists, presumably in collusion with England. This "march" materialized a few weeks later in the coup d'état of Fructidor. Jullien was to play a modest part in Bonaparte's preparations.

Bon's letter to Brune was as follows:

Lodi
29 Messidor V
[17 July 1797]

I hasten to take the opportunity through citizen Jullien, my dear General, to renew the assurances of my sincere attachment.

The name of this young republican will recall to you one of the most interesting victims of *reactionary terrorism*. His passion for liberty and his literary talents destined him for an important role in the Revolution, to which he gave himself with all the warmth of his soul. His patriotic virtues are now as well known as the persecutions he has suffered. The general in chief, who has had reason to appreciate him, thinks very highly of him. I feel certain that you will look upon him no differently, and that if he should have need of your services you will take pleasure in obliging a patriot who is so worthy of recommendation. He will not fail to present himself to you in due form on his passage through Padua.

. . . . You must have been pleased with the proclamation by Bonaparte. It is full of vigor and wisdom, and majestically deploys the character of the conqueror of Italy. I think this proclamation will have a good effect, but it will be still better if all the armies make a pronouncement at the same time. . . .

It was at this time also, in July 1797, that Bonaparte, on his own authority without approval from Paris, proclaimed the Cisalpine Republic. This entity, with its capital at Milan, received a constitution modeled on the French constitution of 1795 and a government composed of local Italians under the protection and supervision of the French. The new republic was a product of uprisings that had occurred throughout northern Italy in the year since the arrival of the Army of Italy. The various Italian states, whether monarchies as in Sardinia-Piedmont and Naples-Sicily, or ancient republics as at Genoa and Venice, or duchies as at Mantua and Modena, or cities like Bologna and Ferrara that were subject to the Pope, were alike in being ruled by their own local hereditary patricians and oligarchs. The revolutionaries who opposed them often called themselves democrats, and they considered the French Republic under its post-Thermidorian constitution of the Year III to be "democratic." The Cisalpine Republic, democratic in the same sense, had a territory mainly composed of the old Lombardy, conquered or liberated from Austria, but it also incorporated some adjoining regions where revolts had occurred in Mantua, Venetia, and the Papal States. But Venice and most of mainland Venetia, as well as some other troubled spots, were excluded. Aspiring revolutionaries from these regions congregated in Milan, seeking support for their projects. Among these the Cisalpine Republic represented the constitutional principles of the French Revolution.

Jullien lost no time in putting to work the literary gifts for which Bon had praised him. He hastily composed some "Notes of Advice to the Cisalpine patriots." Young as he was, he presented himself as an experienced revolutionary veteran, offering his assistance to beginners, at the moment when the Cisalpine Republic was organizing itself. Hastily written for an immediate purpose, the Notes consist of sixty numbered but unintegrated items.

The purpose was to portray the Cisalpine Republic as a first step in a revolution of all Italy, and indeed the world. But this revolution was to be carried out gradually, with caution and prudence. Certain members of the Cisalpine legislative body were to form a secret directing committee. Though a small enlightened minority, they must avoid all appearance of faction; they must bring all others into a national unity or consensus, passing laws in favor of the poor without offending the rich, and repressing Catholicism while cultivating the priests. They must introduce a natural and moral civic religion (then briefly expressed in "Theophilanthropy"), but avoid Robespierre's errors in his religion of the Supreme Being. Jullien draws on his experience in the early phases of Babeuf's movement, while warning against its final and unsuccessful attempt at insurrection. Like Babeuf, he illustrates the transition from an eighteenth- to a nineteenth-century kind of revolution, that is, from the improvised revolutions of 1789 and 1792, provoked by immediate circumstances, to a concerted, planned, long-continuing, secretive, and manipulative revolution to be effected by a disciplined minority who know exactly what they are aiming at—all to be done with prudence and moderation.

Notes of Advice to the Cisalpine Patriots

1. The destinies of Italy henceforth rest in the Cisalpine legislative body.

2. Italy, when it shall have proclaimed its complete independence and organized a great republic one and indivisible, will be able in its turn to influence the destinies of the world.

3. The new legislators must have recourse to the lessons of experience and the history of the French Revolution, to guard against errors that might be compromising to liberty.

4. Early mistakes are irreparable. There must be a plan, well conceived and matured, from which should come the developments, step by step, which are necessary for the final achievement.

5. The world must arrive slowly by a progressive course at its point of maturity. To try to hasten the time fixed by nature is to retard it.

6. It is equally dangerous to make exaggerated claims or aspire to an imaginary perfection; you miss your objective if you try to exceed it.

7. All ill-considered or false actions by the republicans are victories for the royalists.

8. In revolutions, prudence is a supplement to force.

9. Tyrants and their underlings depend on Machiavellianism and intrigue, corruption, calumny, and the art of ruling by dividing.

10. Unless republicans are united they will be weak and will perish.

12. Patriotism and enlightenment are almost always in a minority in larger assemblies.

13. Unity and prudence in the minority can assure its preponderance over the majority.

14. There must be a secret directing committee. Different members of the two legislative chambers should meet frequently in private, get to know one another, keep in touch, and prevent unjust suspicions and unfounded distrust, so that they themselves may be in agreement and be animated by the same spirit, and so base their actions on uniform and invariable principles.

18. There are tactics for a legislative body as for an army.

19. The patriot deputies should meet only in small numbers in turn in one another's homes or at dinners or evening gatherings, without openly forming particular clubs or committees, although I myself once used the word, since the thing should exist but should not be seen.

20. By never giving the appearance of an idea of a coalition, even for good purposes, you will prevent the birth of factions, which are the scourge of the state.

22. Republicans, especially in a state newly organizing itself as a republic, must carefully avoid seeming to be a party. They must be for the *nation*, the *people*; they must constantly draw the mass of the citizens to themselves, attach themselves loyally to the constitution and the republic, and combat their enemies solely with such arms.

24. Gradually destroy superstition, which is to religion as anarchy in the true sense is to liberty. But instead of imprudently attacking religion itself use it to republicanize the people. Employ the present influence of the priests. All those of this caste who are inclined to spread your doctrine should be attracted, protected, and brought to share in your principles. Let them associate the words *religion* and *patrie* so as to reconcile the ignorant class of citizens, especially in the countryside, to the revolution. Your blows against Catholicism will be more effective when delivered by its own ministers. . . .

25. Introduce on your soil, in place of papism, a more pure and simple cult that is not founded on fanaticism and intolerance, and which combines religious, moral and political ideas in a wholesome alliance. Look with favor on the meetings of the Theophilanthropists. Keep away so far as possible from public discussions of religion. If you are forced to speak of it, treat such a delicate matter with moderation and an absolute tolerance of all opinions, whatever they may be.

The speech of Robespierre on the Supreme Being did him more harm, and made him more enemies, than all the excesses of the Revolutionary Government.

26. Oppose priestly mummeries with national festivals that appeal to the eyes and the imagination. . . .

27. Give institutions to the people to regenerate them; create a new man. Multiply civic ceremonies having a moral aim, such as marriages, adoptions, schools or gymnasia, prize distributions, military exercises, races, games, and mass meetings.

28. Your republic is small in extent; it must be warlike. From its birth, by its principles and its arms, it must devour the monarchies and duchies that surround it.

29. If you don't destroy the kings they will destroy you.

30. If you don't give a republican and military spirit to your citizens you will be merely a shadow, and the country will perish.

39. It is very important to have assiduous attendance at your sessions, and fidelity in a common vote for those agreed upon to occupy the presidency, the secretariat, and the committees.

46. The French influence must be concealed. Speak of France only with the necessary respect for its government and the constitution it has given you.

47. I have said that this constitution should not be changed by any violent shock, but only ameliorated by the progressive improvement of opinion.

48. There must be popular laws, adapted to local conditions and popular opinion, in favor of the poor, the farm workers, other workers, and defenders of the country, but avoid any direct clash at first with the interests of the rich and the big landowners.

49. *One of the secrets of governing is to use even that which is harmful.* Turn the colossal fortunes, which now exist, to the advantage of agriculture, commerce, industry, the arts, and establishments suited for the development of national activity. In this way you will succeed better in consolidating the republic than if you nourish the germ of internal dissension by irritating and alienating a class of citizens by persecutions and proscriptions.

53. Nourish the martial spirit by small campaigns in neighboring states, in which you never seem to be the aggressor by always leaving to them the apparent initiative in attacking.

55. Isolate your enemies. Take them separately in turn, allying with one by offering him some temporary advantage in order to destroy another. Thus you will successively have Rome, Turin, Parma, Florence, Venice, and even as far as Naples. You will have embraced them all. Your destinies will be accomplished.

56. Yet, I repeat, make haste slowly. To act abruptly is to lose all. . . .

60. If you take to heart the advice I have given, which is the result of meditation and experience, and if you make it the basis of your conduct, you will triumph. . . . Piedmont will be free, and the peoples of Italy will come gladly to be associated with your laws. The Cisalpine Republic will have been the small nucleus. By your efforts, unity and prudence the Italian Republic will exist and flourish, and a people long debased by foreign domination will have been made by you into a new nation, virgin, proud, active, bellicose, free, and powerful. You will amaze the world; you will efface the glory and virtues of your ancestors, the Romans; you will march as noble rivals and faithful friends of the French republicans who have opened to you the way to liberty. That is where the future calls you. It all depends on you and your first steps in this difficult but glorious career.

Events were soon to show that Bonaparte had no such revolutionary intentions for Italy. Nevertheless, he saw that Jullien could be useful, and appointed him to edit a new army newspaper, the *Courrier de l'Armée d'Italie*, in which Bonaparte was to make known his opinions on political questions. He wished to be seen as a peacemaker and upholder of the French Republic and its constitution.

Jullien conferred with Bonaparte on what should be printed in the journal. The first number appeared on 20 July 1797. The message was that the Revolution had degenerated in Paris into factious quarrels and was threatened by counterrevolution and royalism, but that a purer form of the Revolution existed at Milan among Italian patriots and in the French army. Hence the French Republic could be rescued and restored to health by intervention of the Army of Italy. There was a credible danger of a royalist restoration in the summer of 1797, which failed to gather strength because of dissensions between reform-minded monarchists and those hoping for a full restoration of the Old Regime. In any case, on 4 September, the coup d'état of Fructidor dispelled it, and foreshadowed the takeover of the Republic by Bonaparte two years later.

Jullien's prospectus to the *Courrier de l'Armée d'Italie*, somewhat abridged, appears below. It resembles his Notes of Advice to the Cisalpine Patriots in its confusing mixture of revolutionary spirit and moderation. It differs in being addressed not to the Italians but to the French, both those in Italy and those in Paris, and in calling for consolidation of the Revolution in France, while the Notes called for further revolution in Italy. The long periodic sentences, with their complex arrangement of dependent clauses, suggest that the *Courrier de l'Armée d'Italie* was addressed more to the officers than to the rank and file of the French army, and more to the proponents of a "bourgeois" than of a popular revolution. The "sacred flame of moderation" contrasts sharply with Jullien's speech on the "dangers of moderatism" at La Rochelle and Bordeaux three years before. The "telegraph" referred to is the semaphore telegraph invented and built in 1794, one of the proud accomplishments of the enlightened French Republic.

Courier of the Army of Italy
Introduction Serving as a Prospectus

2 Thermidor V
[20 July 1797]

The eyes of Europe and the world are fixed more than ever on the French Republic. They are fixed also on Italy. Paris is the central point from which the political telegraph transmits to all people the various events that can influence their destinies.

But in Paris, a city long racked by the storms of factions, in a closed atmosphere poisoned by party spirit and evil passions that have spread crimes and misfortunes over a land where only Virtue and Liberty should reign, writers are too often the slaves of powerful men, ministering to their fury and their slanders and preaching discord and war. Everything is distorted to profit those who speculate on lies, and the harried truth looks in vain for an asylum.

In Milan, on the contrary, a less populous city, where there are not the same intrigues, the same parties, or the same causes of trouble and corruption, the republican observer can draw back and reflect from afar on the conduct of those who play the principal roles, so that it is easier to offer correct insights, calculate the future with precision, and present to the view of men who are now exasperated, but should be reassured, that sacred flame of moderation that should shine throughout the world, be the basis of peace and public happiness, and the beacon marking the harbor that we all need as a place of repose after our long revolutionary voyage.

It is only this spirit of moderation and fraternity that can obliterate, in France, the memories of past misfortunes, the germs of hatred and division, guilty hopes and liberticide projects. It is this spirit that, in Italy, should prevent the calamities of which France has been the theater, and rally all citizens under the same banners, which are the flags of humanity, reason, and philanthropy.

If, in both countries, the government knows how to replace the spirit of party, the most horrible of scourges, with the spirit of tolerance, union, and love of peace; if, especially in the French Republic, the good citizens, aware of the danger that menaces them, form a sacred battalion around the Constitution and strive in advance to protect themselves from the disastrous necessity of extreme remedies that extreme evils may give rise to; if national pride, based on consciousness of our strength and on our victories, becomes the principle of love of country and brings together all who wish to maintain and consolidate the Revolution that has created the Republic; if, finally, the enthusiasm of the first days of our Liberty is rekindled now that our victorious soldiers will doubtless be returning to the bosom of their families; then we shall see the disappearance of the clouds, portending storms, that seem to obscure the political horizon. Then the handful of factious men who wish to sully the laurels of an invincible army will be unmasked, undone, vanquished, reduced to impotence and contempt. Then the reign of peace and of our laws will come to smile on our long-suffering country. . . .

Such is our hope and our aim. Some of the French, friends of the Republic, eager to take part in the consolidation and to ward off the perils that continue to surround its cradle, believe it their duty, for the reasons given, to undertake a French journal in Italy.

News guaranteed for authenticity; observations on the present political situation in Italy and France; a faithful portrayal of the origin and progress of the revolutions that have occurred in places near the Cisalpine Republic, and are results of the force of things and the inevitable empire of circumstances rather than of any direct or indirect system or influence exercised by the French; an impartial survey of the parties that agitate France and of their efforts, methods and objectives, as well as events that must necessarily follow from a confirmation of the peace [with Austria] or from prolongation of the war; an examination of several interesting questions at the present critical moment; an invitation often renewed to all good citizens to rally to the republican government and the Constitution of the Year III, put aside the resentments that may reawaken old divisions, while appropriating the lessons of experience and avoiding the mistakes in which they were often the parties and the victims; and, finally, a few replies not to particular calumnies but to the perfidious reasonings, envenomed declarations and absurd falsehoods used today to corrupt opinion and make the Republic and the republicans odious: such are the aims which the authors of the Courier of the Army of Italy have decided to pursue. . . . Rally then, O you who cherish the Republic!. . . . Woe to those who like birds of prey feed on cadavers! Woe to those who still want the trumpets of war to alarm women and children in our cities. . . . *Let the royalists show themselves and they will soon be dead!*

Such is the terrible cry throughout the army, heard in the camps and repeated by every soldier.

The royalists are guilty men who would destroy the Republic and the Constitution, who aspire to drown us in a flood of evils, who work to relight the burning torches of fanaticism to raise the steps of the throne, who would open our frontiers to the cohorts of émigrés that the Constitutional Act banishes forever from French soil. The royalists are unnatural beings who want no peace, but an external war to exterminate what they call the revolutionary race. . . .

No doubt it is painful for us to be still obliged to unmask enemies. . . . We rend the veil that hides criminal projects from the eyes of the people. . . .

There are only two parties on earth, the good and the bad. The good are naturally the enemies of despotism, disorder, crime; they are the friends of equality and a free constitution because they love their fellow men and their country. The bad are essentially the enemies of everything good and of all liberty, but they wear a mask of hypocrisy to deceive the credulous. . . .

Let us have equal laws for all. Let the Republic be lovable so as to deserve to be loved—benevolent, generous, destructive of abuses, protective to citizens. . . .

Patriots, meditate on this truth, that the destinies of the Republic depend on your union. Take care to know the traits by which true royalists may be recognized, so that this factious minority can be reduced to nothing. . . . Save your country without the shocks of a new revolution. . . . Prevent the horrors of a civil war which, like the sword over the head of Damocles, seems to hang like a deadly comet about to swoop down on our territory.

Jullien spent only three months as editor of the *Courrier de l'Armée d'Italie*. It soon became evident that he and Bonaparte disagreed. Bonaparte's idea of how reconciliation was to be effected differed widely from his editor's. More willing than the revolutionary democrats to compromise with some elements of the Old Regime, he made peace with the king of Sardinia, thus recognizing the Sardinian monarchy and repudiating the republicans in that country. He reached an agreement with the pope. And to facilitate peace with Austria, formalized in the treaty of Campo Formio, he not only disowned the Venetian republicans, but agreed on the transfer of Venice and Venetia to the Austrian empire. As Jullien later recalled it, Bonaparte dismissed him from the *Courrier* because of their disagreement over Venetia. The Italian patriots, especially those hoping for one great free and united Italy, were enraged by this betrayal of Venice.

Jullien returned to Paris, where he became active in political circles among old Babouvists and more regular political democrats. Bonaparte also returned to Paris as the triumphant hero, victor, and peacemaker. France remained at war only with England, and Bonaparte was appointed commander of a new *Armée d'Angleterre* assembling on the Channel coast for an invasion of England. But the Directory soon changed its mind, deciding instead on the quixotic alternative of an invasion of Egypt. For this wild idea various arguments were advanced—to obtain a new colony now that the French West Indies were lost, to threaten the British in India, and to remove from the scene a triumphant general whose extraordinary popularity was becoming a threat to the civilian authorities. Bonaparte thus received command of an expedition to Egypt. As a minor detail in his plan, he had an interview with Jullien in Paris and offered him a position as a war commissioner in the expedition.

Jullien remained in Egypt only three months, and unfortunately not much can be known of his experiences there. An assiduous writer, he kept a journal and sent it to his family, which, however, never received it, and it remains lost. It appears from other sources that he was stationed at Rosetta (where the famous Rosetta Stone was discovered), and that he crossed the desert, was engaged in fights with the Bedouins, and took part in what he called the "famous and fatal battle of Aboukir," in which the French fleet was destroyed by the British and the French army was thus isolated in Egypt. He received leave to return to France because of ill health, and landed at Livorno in Italy in early September 1798. His health recovered soon enough for him to become involved again in the revolutionary movement in Italy.

During the months of peace on the Continent following the French treaty with Austria the indigenous Italian patriots became very active, while always dependent on French military support. At Rome a republic replaced the old Papal States and the Pope was exiled to France, where he died. The French commander at Rome was J. A. Championnet, one of the generals who befriended Italian patriots and were admired by the democratic republicans in Paris. In December 1798 he made Marc-Antoine Jullien a member of his staff. Jullien now had the opportunity to promote the cause of a great united Italian republic that he had so positively favored in his advice to the Cisalpines.

The king of Naples, spurred on by the British, sent an army to recapture Rome, which the French easily defeated. The French then occupied Naples. Jullien advised Championnet to set up a republic there "based on democratic principles." Against the known wishes of the French Directory, which had little confidence in the Italian republicans either as successful revolutionaries or as allies, Championnet proclaimed the Neapolitan Republic and appointed Jullien as secretary-general to its government.

Jullien's tenure of this position, as of so many others, lasted only a few weeks. He had time only to express opinions, in unpublished memoranda to Championnet and to the Italians in the transient republican government. He showed the same desire as in his advice to the Cisalpines for an eventual sweeping revolution to be accomplished by gradual and cautious measures. The Neapolitan republicans (who were mainly of the upper class) were similarly inclined. They abolished "feudal dues," but only with proper compensation. They aimed at a gradual land reform to reduce large holdings, but they brought rich landowners into the government. They would control the price of bread, and give work to the poor in nationalized workshops, while also lending aid to private commercial ventures.

Jullien's dreams for Italy collapsed in the kaleidoscopic confusion of French politics that came with renewal of the war. First Championnet expelled the civil commissioner sent from Paris. Then the French civil authorities responded by removing Championnet from his command, and they arrested Jullien as an inflammatory subversive. He was imprisoned at Naples. But the resumption of war strengthened the radicals in Paris. They staged another coup d'état; Jullien was released and went to Paris, where he mixed with the "pronounced," "anarchistic," or "terrorist" republicans who tried to reopen the Jacobin club. In Italy the Neapolitan, Roman, and Cisalpine republics all went down before the Austrian armies, which were assisted by the Russians, British, and Turks. In this second coalition against France even the Russian forces operated as far west as Italy, Switzerland, and Holland. The allies expected to invade France; it seemed that the European counter-revolution would at last destroy the French Republic. But Masséna defeated the Russians in Switzerland and Brune repelled an Anglo-Russian expedition that had landed in Holland. Yet the danger had hardly passed.

Jullien feared for the Republic, but he detested the Directory, which had indicted him as a Babouvist in 1796 and as an expansionist ultrademocrat at Naples in 1799. His picture of conditions in France was as hostile and overdrawn as any royalist could have composed:

> ... Who can describe the state of manners today, the luxurious effrontery of the women, the impudent greed of public officials...the debasement of the national representation or rather its absolute annihilation, the enslavement of the press, the oppression of ardent citizens who no longer have any guarantees? The laws are an empty word. Money and women are behind everything ... the 18 Fructidor

only saved the Republic by dealing a mortal blow to the constitution. The vital springs of liberty are dried up. The national representation has disappeared: the executive power has invaded everything.

The "executive power" here meant the five executive Directors who had recently humbled the democrats in the legislature and closed the revived Jacobin club. They were soon to be succeeded by an executive of another kind.

General Bonaparte, having abandoned his army in Egypt and eluded the British fleet, reappeared in Paris on 16 October 1799.

FIVE

FOR AND AGAINST NAPOLEON

JULLIEN was personally acquainted with Bonaparte, having worked with him at Milan in 1797 as editor of the *Courrier de l'Armée d'Italie,* and been one of the numerous civilians that Bonaparte had invited to join him on the expedition to Egypt. Until about 1805 Jullien had occasional conversations with his old commander-in-chief, in which he offered advice. Bonaparte seldom took his advice but undoubtedly found him useful, both as a channel through which to learn what the republicans of the 1790s were doing and thinking, and as a means of transmitting the picture of himself and his plans that he wished them to have. Jullien willingly accepted this role as long as it lasted.

His attitude to Bonaparte was ambivalent throughout, and probably typical of a large body of French opinion. He accepted the coup d'état of Brumaire, the Consulate, and the Empire, while all the while entertaining doubts, on the supposition that any alternative might be worse, whether a relapse into civil bloodshed and confusion, or the restoration of a Bourbon monarchy which until 1814 showed no readiness for conciliation. He served intermittently with the army in quasi-military capacities, reaching a rank equivalent to colonel, and having to do with the inspection and supply of troops. He took part in the Austerlitz campaign and a few others. In private notes to himself he expressed disgust with the Napoleonic system, yet like many other republicans he rallied to Napoleon after the escape from Elba and supported him during the Hundred Days.

His life was changed in 1801 by his marriage to Sophie Nioche. They had four children within five years, one of whom died, and two more in 1811 and 1812. Sophie's father, like Marc-Antoine's, had been a member of the Convention and had voted for the death of Louis XVI. As the babies kept coming there was much visiting with both sets of grandparents, all of whom had been Jacobins at the height of the Revolution and all of whom lived on for several decades, so that the extended family constituted a nucleus of regicide and republican sympathizers, in which the children grew up in an atmosphere of dislike for kings and aristocrats and concern for what a restoration of the Bourbons might mean for them personally. Since Jullien's parents lived until the 1820s, enjoying a modest income from their property, and since he had no training for law or business, he remained dependent for his income on whatever salary he could obtain from the government. Sometimes he was at home with his family, but more often absent on one of his military assignments.

After 1801 and until 1815 he published nothing having any political content. He did, however, submit pieces of advice to Napoleon, and he made private notes on developments as he saw them. Both these kinds of writing appeared in print only after Napoleon's fall. But he published, during the Napoleonic years, works on generally educational subjects that paved the way for his later career as editor of the *Revue Encyclopédique* in the 1820s.

He had several conversations with Bonaparte in the weeks before and after the coup d'état of Brumaire. At the end of 1799 he published anonymously, but apparently with Bonaparte's permission, a pamphlet of seventy-four pages in the form of a dialogue between persons identified only as "A" and "B." Although "B" in the dialogue refers to Bonaparte in the third person, it is evident from the context that "B" is Bonaparte himself, and indeed Jullien said as much when he acknowledged the authorship of the work much later, in 1821. At that time he was accused of having been duped by Bonaparte and having encouraged him in the coup, and Jullien insisted in reply that he had not been deceived, but had tried in vain to give advice which, if taken, would have spared France from many later troubles. A reader of the pamphlet may see truth on both sides, that Jullien did offer good advice, but that he also put Bonaparte's arguments so forcefully and persuasively, and expressed such agreement with them, as to become a "Brumairian" himself. In the following translation, "A" and "B" are presented as Jullien and Bonaparte. The italics were so italicized by Jullien in the printed version of 1799, to signify emphasis.

A Political Colloquy on the Present Situation in France and the Plans of the New Government Frimaire Year VIII [December 1799]

JULLIEN: I have come with your permission to ask for a few moments of conversation. I must express myself with complete freedom. It is not about myself nor for myself that I wish to speak. I have never approached you except to give my frank opinion on matters of public utility, and I think that the truth is the worthiest homage that can be offered to powerful men or those about them.

BONAPARTE: Come into my office. We shall have the conversation that you request. What is the public saying about these latest events?

JULLIEN: Opinion on this point is not yet settled. For a long time people have seen so many changes and so many promises, with so few effects or desirable results, that they dare not yet put their hope in anything, and are weary, uneasy, and apprehensive.

Moreover, it cannot be concealed that some thoughtful men and excellent citizens are alarmed to see the constitution subverted, the national representation dissolved, and the government changed by military force. They would have preferred a stabilization of our affairs by peaceable methods.

BONAPARTE: If that were possible everyone would have preferred it. But one cannot always choose the means he would wish to employ to do good. . . .

First of all, what was the situation of France when Bonaparte arrived from Egypt? Let us not deceive ourselves, let us see things as they really are.

There was no national representation, no government, no constitution. Our conquests lost, our laurels tarnished, peace impossible except on dishonorable terms, our armies destroyed, the French name reviled by both enemies and allies, the republic fallen into the utmost debasement and misery, the aims of the revolution miscarried, the fruits of our labors, sacrifices and victories annihilated, the dregs of faction agitating and disputing with foreigners over the shreds of our country—that is what struck the observer. . . . Organized murders, and the government kept silence, the Vendée rising from its ashes. . . . Armies fighting in the name of a republic that no longer existed, the nation not knowing whether it was at war or at peace. . . . Friendly nations and republics created by us oppressed and despoiled. . . . An open gulf of universal bankruptcy devouring all fortunes, ruining all families, multiplying discontents in all classes of citizens. . . . No stable laws, no constitution, no liberty, no institutions, no guarantees. . . . Invisible legions of spies and secret informants. . . . Suspicion and fear everywhere. . . . No one knowing where he was or where he was going. . . . The state like a reeling drunkard unable to stand.

Such is the horrible situation from which we have barely escaped.

JULLIEN: I admit it. This picture of our misfortunes is only too true; the republic was falling to pieces. A change was necessary; something better was possible, but it was hardly possible for things to get worse.

BONAPARTE: Only a kind of national instinct survived, a profound sense of evils past and present, the fatigue of long suffering and an imperative need to recover.

For ten years we have had no government except the Committee of Public Safety before 9 Thermidor. It did great things, which were dishonored by great mistakes. It pushed force to the point of atrocity; but it governed, and it saved France from the greatest perils.

JULLIEN: Royalists, foreign writers and even the émigrés grant as much, and posterity will also. All other administrations before and after the Committee, from 1789 until this moment, have devastated our country instead of governing it.

BONAPARTE: What was needed then was a strong and robust government. . . .

JULLIEN: That is all true. . . . *But if in well-constituted states it is institutions that should form the leaders of the republic, at the birth of societies, or at the moment of their regeneration, it is the leaders of republics that must form the institutions* . . . and hence this first choice may determine the fate of a great people for several centuries.

BONAPARTE: There is another principle, equally recognized by publicists and sanctioned by the example of the freest peoples of antiquity and by republics that most scrupulously respect the political rights of their citizens. It is that a nation cannot be well constituted, or entirely reformed, except by one man or a very few. . . . A kind of dictatorship, or supreme magistracy with a concentration of power, was imperiously demanded by the circumstances. . . .

The constitution of the Year III had been so often violated that it was only a phantom. Salvation had to be found outside its limits.

JULLIEN: There was general agreement on these truths. . . . A crisis was inevitable. People foresaw it but dreaded it, not knowing how or by whom it could be ended.

All eyes were fixed on Bonaparte. He has cut the Gordian knot.

The two men discuss for several pages whether Bonaparte aims at personal power, which "B" denies:

BONAPARTE: He has not made war on kings and surrounded the cradle of the republic with trophies, only to debase himself by raising a throne. He too is a *Jacobin* in the sense meant by the émigrés and partisans of the Bourbons.

There are some, seeing him from afar, who have supposed he had narrow personal views and wished to take power for himself alone.

They failed to observe that he had already tasted supreme power and knows what it is worth. In Italy and in Egypt his power had no limit or borders; it was a despotism of fact. He knows that *whatever is excessive cannot be preserved; that an authority unlimited in its exercise and duration has no safeguard for itself since it offers none to anyone else.* . . .

Hence he aspires to justify the confidence of his fellow citizens, to persuade them that they are right to put their hopes in him, that he has no object except their welfare and liberty. He will be known and judged by his actions.

JULLIEN: May he persist in these magnanimous resolves! He will be a great man and bring happiness to his country. Nor will he be mistaken in his true interests. His power will not be ephemeral, and the most distant ages will bless his memory. . . .

BONAPARTE: Bonaparte has declared publicly that he bears no grudges and feels no resentments. He knows no parties but only Frenchmen. He means to use all men of ability who love their country. But it must be said frankly that if the government is to save the republic the friends of the republic must unite behind it. . . .If there are madmen, royalists or others, who want to struggle they will be put down, to their great loss. If prudence and calm prevail there will be no passions and no vengeance; we will work harmoniously to do what is good.

JULLIEN: Above all it must not be forgotten that, *instead of creating opposing parties in order to combat them, it is better to let them exist up to a certain point, since they are in the nature of things*; but also to neutralize them, or even guide them by indirect influence and skillful dissimulation; *and never to push irritability too far.* . . .

To *resist the abuses of government is a way of supporting it.* Powerful men should convince themselves that they are never better served than by stern and forceful citizens who speak to them honestly and sometimes combat their opinions. But machine-men, low automata, passive agents are always ready, for the slightest self-interest, to betray the authority that commands them. A stupidly blind and servile obedience is a sign of cowardice and contemptible character. . . .

BONAPARTE: The men now in our government come after the Revolution. They know that he who overthrows on one day is overthrown on the next . . . that one must respects one's equal and even one's rival, to be safe oneself. The common maxim applies in politics: *Do nothing to another that you would not wish done to yourself.*

Above all, the barbarous habit of proscription and deportation for factious quarrels must be forever abolished. . . .

Bonaparte has no desire to be alone at the helm of state. Whoever, by vanity or ambition, may wish to concentrate all in himself, as Robespierre did, and gather all the weight of a vast empire on his head, has no security for his glory and offers none to a people for their well-being. . . .

JULLIEN: Everything collapses and dissolves after him. The smell of his carcass spreads; chaos reigns about his grave; posterity blames him for working only for his own lifetime and not foreseeing the future.

BONAPARTE: It is in Bonaparte's own interest, as in the interest of France, that the public destinies should not be so dependent on him that, were he unfortunately to die, the country would fall back into uncertainty and faction.

He has and will keep about him auxiliaries who share his sentiments, men who have made commitments to the Revolution, and have liberal ideas.

Such men mean to save France from the fluctuation and anarchy in which it was perishing, give it settled institutions and government, make it independent of men and parties and especially of foreign parties.

JULLIEN: Yes, no doubt there still are such generous souls. . . . They are inspired by the glory of rescuing the French from their long sufferings; giving us peace, the chief benefit that all Europe begs for; restoring to its bed the raging torrent that has changed its course; bringing back the Revolution to its natural original direction. . . .

How many fond hopes have been deceived! How the illusions of our well-meant imaginings have vanished! What an ocean of blood we have traversed! What bastilles! What scaffolds! What sinister influences of calumny! What barbarous intolerance of factions! What murders! What frenzies! . . .

It is inevitable either that the hideous counterrevolution should show itself in its entirety, and royalty reappear over our dead bodies, or that the republic, sustained by powerful hands, should rise again and strengthen itself on imperishable foundations.

These foundations can only be national independence; civil and political liberty; equality; the sovereignty of the people; a wisely and strongly organized representative system; a precise and guaranteed division of powers; an independent judiciary; a graded and effective responsibility for agents of the executive; a restoration of moral values through education; a good system of finance and taxes; property guaranteed, industry encouraged, abundance and prosperity spread among the citizens; in a word, the public happiness, a new idea on earth, and the one goal in the formation of societies and progress of civilization.

BONAPARTE: The constitutional edifice that we are to construct will rest on no other foundations. . . .

Jullien proceeds at some length to offer some ideas of his own, which include law codes to replace the confusing laws left by the Revolution, and a constitution which, "since theory is insufficient unless accompanied by practice, will be, so to speak, experimental." Once every five or ten years numerous assemblies should meet throughout the country, isolated from one another and hence from the pernicious influence of party, faction, clubs, and intriguing personalities, to express public opinion and pass judgment on the wisdom and legality of the government's actions. "B" does not like this idea.

BONAPARTE: What we need is a government. You can't govern by the chatter of large assemblies. Let us organize the liberty of the press, I agree; it is the boulevard of liberty. . . .

Let the laws and acts of authority be wisely and moderately discussed. The truth will be heard with pleasure. But we must banish the mania of denunciations, personal attacks, insults, and incitements to insurrection and the dissolution of government.

In good writings and reasoned works on government you will hear the voice of the people and find an alternative to clubs and popular assemblies. To assure the triumph and dissemination of public enlightenment is to give an unshakable basis to liberty. It would be well for the government to know how many copies of a good book have been bought by readers. It would be a sound way to know the national will and have valid instructions for legislators and magistrates.

JULLIEN: Don't you think that that would too much limit the number of citizens, and restrict intervention in public affairs by the mass of the people, and by the middle class, which reads little because it is working in the fields, manufactories, shops, and armies, but is nevertheless an integral part of the state?

BONAPARTE: I know that after falling into one extreme one should not fall into the other. . . . But enlightened men, through the benefit of national education, will emerge from the different classes of society and be better *representatives of the people* than those who usurp this imposing title to oppress and betray the *sovereign* so much vaunted by hypocrites.

Bonaparte goes on to sketch the constitution devised mainly by himself, promulgated at the time of this conversation, and known as the Constitution of the Year VIII, with its three Consuls, its various levels of voters, its Preservative Senate, whose members sit for life and select members of a Tribunate which discusses proposed legislation, and of a Legislative Body which enacts it without discussion. Jullien agrees in part, but would prefer a touch of democracy.

JULLIEN: It may be observed that, although the desperate position we have been in, the misfortunes we have undergone, the resentments of diverse factions, and the extreme corruption of our time may have obliged us to *oligarchize* the government a bit (so that with less variability there is less chance for ambitious men and agitators), it would be no less easy to *democratize* our institutions up to a certain point, to prepare a race of men better than those now existing.

BONAPARTE: Yes, no doubt. National education will be cast in a truly popular mold. . . .

Bonaparte next describes schools resembling the *lycées* that he was to introduce in 1802, renews his assurances of liberty to all men of good will, and promises amnesty and a welcome return to France to all "except royalist émigrés who have divorced themselves forever from the Revolution and from their country." He concludes with a stern warning:

BONAPARTE: As for factious men, forever dissatisfied, they should receive this salutary advice: *When some men are displeased by the results of a great political operation they should ask themselves, before decrying it publicly, whether publicity for their opinions would be useful; and if the matter is irreparable they should suppress imprudent murmurs, impose on themselves a necessary silence, and at least accept the advantages that remain for them. Everything on earth has its good and its bad side. What is necessary, even with events thought to be harmful, is to get the good out of them and take advantage of fortune.*

JULLIEN: I have gathered this information and these precious details very eagerly. With your permission I shall publish them in part. . . .

Meanwhile France remained at war with Austria and Great Britain. In the following summer Bonaparte again led an army across the Alps and defeated the Austrians at Marengo, a village between Genoa and Milan. The Austrians withdrew from Italy, the Second Coalition was broken up, and it seemed that the Cisalpine and other republics introduced by the French and their Italian sympathizers in 1797–1798 would be revived. Jullien submitted more advice to Napoleon, this time unpublished, in July 1800. He still wants revolution in Italy, but a mild and peaceable one.

Memoir on an Independent and Federalist Organization of Italy

Citizen Consul:

As I am about to leave Italy to rejoin the reserve army at Dijon I think myself authorized, as you indicated in our last conversation, to write to you frankly and confidentially on the present condition of Italy, and on the great political interests that have now been entrusted to you. . . .

Austria must be detached from Italy, but France also must know how to detach itself from Italy and allow it its independence.

The idea of making Italy into one indivisible republic has long been the favorite plan and hope of Italian friends of liberty. But prejudices and fears militate against this idea, so long as Europe will not consent to a peace based on this provision, and so long as one great Italian republic might become someday dangerous to the very France that created it. . . .

It might be admissible to have a division of Italy into four or five separate states: the Venetian Republic, bordering on the [Holy Roman] Empire; a state of Naples that would strengthen us in the Mediterranean; a third state formed from Genoa, Piedmont, and Lombardy; and one or two states in the middle, under whatever names might be thought suitable, and which might be assigned to princes of the royal family of Spain, to bind the ties that join that power with the French Republic. . . .

The only way to end the dependency and oppression from which that country has long suffered might be to *establish a federal pact and a defensive league among the Italian states.* . . .

[In this arrangement] political necessity might bring the transfer of the seat of the church to Lucca, where the pope, reduced to his spiritual powers, would possess a small territory sufficient to his needs, with a revenue of about five millions. . . .

To conclude these general reflections on the administration of the parts of Italy now occupied by our troops, I believe that you will agree, Citizen Consul, for your own interest and glory, on the need of preventing and ending the abusive system of arbitrary requisitions and levies that crush and paralyze the government and authorities of the country, reducing them to hollow and absurd pretensions, as, for example, in demanding enough food in certain cities to furnish ten or twenty tables for thirty men each every day—organized robberies committed brazenly and with impunity.

You will get control of brigandage. You will not tolerate the venality that infects all parts of the administration and puts liberty up for sale.

You will encourage that spirit of moderation, good order and wisdom that will make your influence lovable and the regime established under your auspices dear to all citizens.

Religion will be respected, but seditious fanaticism will be repressed, and the influence of the clergy turned gradually to the advantage of the government. Finances will be administered with economy and probity. A mild and conciliatory political system will heal the deep wounds left by revolution and war. . . .

Revolutions are electric and contagious when they make peoples happy, since the first need of all men is happiness. . . .

But only a few months later Jullien had reason to swing to the other side in his estimation of the new regime. As Bonaparte's victory at Marengo made his position all the stronger in France, little groups both of royalists and republicans formed their separate conspiracies to overthrow him. The most spectacular and nearly successful was the attempt to assassinate him by an "infernal machine," or bomb, while he made his way from the Tuileries to the Opéra in December 1800. Bonaparte escaped unhurt, but twenty-six others were killed. Although the police produced evidence to show that the conspirators were royalists, Bonaparte used the occasion to intimidate the republicans. Calling them Jacobins and followers of Babeuf, he ordered the deportation of 130 known republicans without trial or further inquiry. He thus made good on the warnings he had issued, as reported by Jullien in the "political colloquy" a year before, while reverting to "the barbarous habit of proscription and deportation" which, according to Jullien, he had said must be ended. Jullien submitted another private memo to Bonaparte, protesting at this arbitrary action. It had no effect.

A few weeks later Bonaparte signed the treaty of Lunéville with Austria (February 1801). France was now at peace except for sporadic maritime hostilities with Great Britain. Jullien took the occasion to publish, anonymously, a two-hundred-page pamphlet, half of it composed of the peace treaty and other documents, to review the achievements of the year and a half since the coup d'état of Brumaire. Called *An Appeal to True Friends of the Country*, it asked the reader to compare France before and after the Revolution. The worst features of the Old Regime, he said, had been abolished, such as nobility and "the appalling inequality in the distribution of wealth." Now there was peace on the Continent, the Vendée had been pacified, the finances reorganized, buyers of the nationalized properties reassured in their new possessions, and trade and manufactures, arts and letters, all encouraged.

As for the Revolution itself, Jullien now used the language of a moderate but shocked conservatism, with a denunciation of abstract ideas worthy of Edmund Burke.

> First of all, if we recall the systems of homicide, proscription, spoliation, massacres, deportations and contradictions that devastated our country under the various revolutionary dynasties, we shall recognize in the administration of the Consuls in the Year VIII a mild, conciliatory and peace-loving government, which has not tried to put itself between two opposing parties simply to balance them, combat them and destroy them by strengthening and neutralizing them in turn; a government that has sought to put an end to the flux and reflux of passion and violence. . . .

But I think I speak as a faithful interpreter of opinion in recognizing that the Consuls have governed a country that most preceding administrations have devastated; that they have realized in one year a vast plan of improvement whose execution would have seemed chimerical when they took up the reins of State; that they have overcome almost insurmountable difficulties, and have had the rare merit of profiting from experience and avoiding the mistakes of their predecessors; that, in a word, they have done all the good possible in the circumstances. . . .

Put no trust in those intolerant sectaries who, once they have adopted a doctrine, become fixed irrevocably in a few abstract principles, never departing from the geometric line they have traced, never considering that everything about them has changed and that other circumstances require other measures and another system; who still dream either of an *absolute monarchy* or of a *democracy without bounds or limits*, and who in an imaginary world never subject themselves to the sight of reality.

But disillusionment soon set in. Much happened to displease one who favored a touch of democracy within bounds and limits. In notes addressed only to himself Jullien deplored Bonaparte's actions, which were roughly as follows in 1802 and 1803. Ignoring Jullien's advice for Italy, Bonaparte failed to restore the Venetian Republic and combined it instead with the Cisalpine in what he called the Italian Republic. He simply annexed the kingdom of Piedmont to France. He set up what looked like a royal court for himself in the Tuileries palace. He purged the Tribunate, dissolved the class of Political and Moral Sciences at the Institute, and created a Legion of Honor. For a few chosen members of the Senate he created a few ostentatious dignities and emoluments called "senatoriates." He reached an agreement with the pope. He brought in young men for training as "auditors" attached to his council of state. He obtained the enactment of a law on education, a major step in the history of education in France, affecting several hundred secondary schools; a few of these were called *lycées*, and in these lycées a few thousand students were to receive scholarships by appointment of the First Consul. He also proclaimed a new Constitution of the Year X, by which large property owners should dominate the elections, and Bonaparte became Consul for Life.

To all such developments, while remaining in the government service, Jullien responded with suppressed cries of solitary anguish. He wrote in a note of July 1803:

O France! You were to be an example to the world! O England! You were to rival France only in wisdom and prosperity! O Italy! You were no longer to be a bloody arena but a federal state independent of your neighbors! O Holland ... Helvetia ... Spain ... Egypt ... Poland ... Germanic Body ... Europe ....

All has been lost. A unique moment in history has been missed. . . .

Republicans, royalists, peoples, kings, religious persons, the French nation, philosophers and men of learning all hailed this star that offered to preside over the destinies of European states; all listened to promises that flattered all hopes and passions; but all these hopes and passions have been deceived and betrayed. . . .

And in another such private memo, in January 1804, he vented his outrage at what the First Consul had done, going into further particulars addressed only to himself. The old revolutionary democrat was indignant. It is doubtful whether public opinion was as hostile to Bonaparte as he says.

We have no constitution but only an absolute master who absorbs everything into himself. We have a few institutions which are now being organized under his orders and auspices, though slowly and cautiously, and all of which have for their object to bring back the prejudices, customs, and abuses of the old regime. This wrongheaded idea of government, by misunderstanding, scorning, and crippling public opinion, must sooner or later inevitably bring its fall.

At the head of these institutions is the *conscription*, which as established in the Year VI under a free regime was to produce a generous and martial nation, composed of citizens ready to defend their country, but which is now cunningly altered for the benefit of the despot, while it delivers the children of French families to his arbitrary will and caprices, and assures him a more absolute possession of the persons of his subjects than our kings ever enjoyed.

After the conscription comes the *institution of the lycées*, which abandons equally to the Supreme Chief that portion of the youth not yet old enough to bear arms. No one is admitted to the lycées except by nomination by the First Consul. The power of opening the public schools and hence education only to those who have received his favors attaches all parents to him through their affection for their children and concern to give them a good education.

This complaint was grossly overstated. It was only holders of the national scholarships that had to be nominated by the First Consul.

A third institution is in the creation of *auditors*, attached to the council of state and the various ministries, law courts, and administrations, exclusively destined for the sons of public functionaries, and having the same purpose of attaching parents to the chief of state. . . . Bonaparte has another aim in this institution; it is to establish gradually a hereditary aristocracy of public office, a kind of substitute for nobility. The sons of rich families, large proprietors, men to whom the government is obliged to allow a certain influence and authority, will be the only ones initiated at an early age into the management of public affairs. They will be a kind of privileged body, composed of patrician families created by Bonaparte, who alone occupy all the lucrative and important places.

The *legion of honor* . . . is a *fourth institution* designed to make the chief of state absolute master of the army and distributor of the favors, honors, titles, and marks of distinction that he will award exclusively to his creatures. This legion is a praetorian cohort of new nobles that will bind the whole military class and many civilians to the dictator's chariot.

A *fifth institution* is the establishment of *senatoriates*, introduced with the same intention, and making dependent on the master the only authority created by the so-called constitution of the Year VIII [i.e., the Senate] that seemed designed to protect the rights of the nation. . . .

The *electoral colleges*, presided over by nominees of the First Consul, composed of the wealthiest proprietors and of citizens designated by the Consul, form a *sixth* link in the immense chain by which an astute master gradually fetters a whole nation. . . .

Such are the *six institutions* which, by their nature and object, demonstrate that all the master's ideas are uniquely and exclusively devised for the aggrandizement, indefinite extension, preservation, and transmission of his usurped domination. . . .

He was thinking of war even on signing the last treaty of peace. He used this peace to arouse the enthusiasm and gratitude of the French and assure his becoming *consul for life*; and he would soon use war to turn the attention of the French from their internal situation. . . .

But only a few months later we find Jullien veering in the other and more favorable direction, this time in a long paper that he said he submitted to Bonaparte. We have only his word that he did so; there is no evidence that he actually sent it or that Bonaparte ever received it. It is so flattering in its approach, and so contrary to his private notes, as to raise the question of his sincerity. It may be (he was still not yet thirty years old) that he was ambitious to remain in public life, that he hoped for promotion in Bonaparte's service, that he still thought his advice might be useful, that he felt a need for strong government as a protection against counterrevolution (as in the days of the Committee of Public Safety), or that actual events had recently made him change his mind. More conspiracies and assassination plots had just been discovered in western France, a resumption of war seemed imminent, and the idea that France needed a hereditary chief of state was being openly discussed in the Tribunate and elsewhere. Jullien's paper seems to have been written just before the proclamation of the Constitution of the Year XII on 18 May 1804.

"The government of the Republic is entrusted to an Emperor." These words, with which the new constitution of 1804 began, seem today to be a pure oxymoron, a contradiction so transparent and ludicrous as to defy belief. Jullien attempted to reconcile them in his advice to Bonaparte. It should be remembered that the words "republic," "empire," and "dictatorship" did not then have the connotations that they took on later. "Dictatorship" suggested the ancient Roman device of a brief temporary authority invoked in emergency; there had been all kinds of "republics" in ancient, medieval, and more recent times; and "empire" connoted an overarching majesty rather than actual power, as in the Holy Roman Empire or the hazily remembered empire of Charlemagne. It is to be noted, too, that Jullien calls for a *charte constitutionnelle*, an expression not used until the restoration of the Bourbon monarchy ten years later. For this "charter" he lays down much the same conditions, or gives the same advice, as in his Political Colloquy of 1799. He was not merely a weather vane turning in every wind; the preferred wind, for him, always blew in the same direction.

General and First Consul:

I. Character of the Present Epoch
A new era is about to begin for France. Common minds will see only a change of title and new name for the government, but political observers will see the basis for the institutions that you have promised to the French. . . .

III. A Power Regulated By Law, More Durable
Than an Unlimited Authority
Today you can do anything; the gratitude of the nation will give anything to you. But unless you yourself set bounds to the new authority you are invested with, your authority will be less real and less durable. . . .

V. Public Opinion
Though often invisible, opinion exerts a great influence.

In 1791 it declared against the court and the court was overthrown.

In 1794 it pronounced against murderers, and the reign of blood and terror gave way to a milder government.

In the Year VIII it called for the dictatorship of a man of genius, so as to escape from a lethargic anarchy, and your supreme authority was confirmed by general consent.

Today this same public opinion, alarmed by frequent conspiracies and uncertain of the future, demands that a vague, indeterminate, personal and absolute dictatorship should be replaced by stable institutions, which should not depend even on your own life. . . .

IX. The Words "France" and "Republic," Which Some Would Suppress

The nation and the army cherish these words "France" and "Republic," consecrated by your glorious victories and by five years of your administration. Words have a great influence on opinion. The French empire should not renounce the word that Europe has learned to respect; the Nation would be sorry to lose it.

The word Republic, synonymous with "public thing" or "public interest," was always applied in former times to different forms of government, and even to royalty. This word alone, as a principle of public spirit and national pride, seems to remind the people of their part in the general interests of the state. The government finds in it a powerful force, a means of arousing the patriotism that produces great actions. . . .

XI. The Act Proclaiming Bonaparte EMPEROR Should at the Same Time Consecrate the Principal Rights of the Nation and the Basis for a New Organization of the Government

The day when you are proclaimed *Emperor* should be the day on which you voluntarily and unselfishly put aside the dictatorship, to take the reins of a free government in which all parts are coordinated, balanced, and lend each other support.

The act newly installing you will be more agreeable to France and honorable to yourself if it includes the elements of a CONSTITUTIONAL CHARTER and a guarantee of the public destiny.

This charter should consecrate both your rights to power and the rights and liberties of the people; heredity in your family; independent organization of the national authorities; personal inviolability of the chief of state with real and strict responsibility for his ministers and the agents of government; grandeur and dignity as befits the highest rank in a great empire; a direct and necessary but not absolute or exclusive participation of the executive power in the formation of law; force, energy, and speed of executive action but with the right of voting taxes and levying troops reserved to the nation through its representatives; civil liberty protected and guaranteed; private properties made safe from dispossession; liberty of the press modified by law but sufficient to allow a certain power to opinion.

After a few words on how the "immortal Charlemagne" had levied no taxes except by consent, Jullien goes on to praise some of the very "institutions" that he had privately condemned a few weeks before.

XIV. Nine National Institutions Now Existing and Created or Confirmed By Bonaparte

The *senate*, with its organization and powers already settled.

The *legion of honor*, whose members are chosen from all parts of France and in all classes of society in which their services and talents have distinguished them.

The *camps for veterans* established on our frontiers, both as ramparts of the state and as a reward and place of asylum for its defenders.

The *conscription*, which calls up all Frenchmen in succession to the colors *for five years* to serve the country.

The *concordat*, which has brought freedom of worship and peace for consciences.

The *electoral colleges*, sitting for life, and composed of citizens having the greatest interest in the preservation of order and of society.

An *annual report on the condition of France*, which is the homage rendered by the government to the nation, a means of maintaining public spirit, and of incorporating, so to speak, private wishes into the interests of the state.

The *lycées* and *special schools*, fertile nurseries of educated men and useful citizens of all kinds.

The *National Institute*, the home of enlightenment, standing next to the government, under its august protection at the center of the Empire, to watch over the precious deposit of the arts and sciences.

These are the *nine institutions* founded, consolidated or brought to perfection by you, which do honor to France and which must be part of the new order of things that is to fix our destinies.

It is curious and inexplicable that he does not mention the Civil Code, which had been proclaimed about two months before. He had recommended law codes in 1799.

A year later, in May 1805, shifting to the other side, he gave vent to his private thoughts in a long lamentation. Was he leading the double life necessary under a despotism? Or was he only the honest and candid soul that he said he was, who also now had a family to support? In any case, he continued to serve the state. He was present with the army assembling on the Channel coast for an invasion of England, and when that plan was given up he accompanied the army to central Europe, where Napoleon won his great victory over the Austrians and Russians at Austerlitz in December 1805 and over the Prussians at Jena in October 1806. Jullien's diagnosis of the ills of France, written only a few months before these earth-shaking events, mark him as a poor prophet for the immediate future. His description of the army in 1805 can hardly be accurate, and it is understandable that Napoleon found him less useful as an informant. But his account of the internal weakness of the Empire, with its extravagant and compulsory ostentation, was more true to the reality. In the long run his predictions were borne out.

Here are his thoughts as of May 1805, not made public until ten years later:

The excesses of flattery and display, of which the new court sets the example, mean that no one can be rich enough to reach the level of others to whom he thinks he should be equal. Such excesses undermine all principles of morality by producing an inordinate thirst for wealth no matter how acquired. They cause a perpetual and progressive augmentation of taxes, and hence a growing public discontent. In the organization of his own household the Emperor gives the example of a disordered luxury that becomes a goal for those who surround him. It is part of his political system, which resembles the one adopted by Richelieu to humble the great magnates of the kingdom. Bonaparte's aim is to make dependent on himself men who must forever feel new needs and so cannot do without the treasures he heaps upon them. If these new rich were to use their fortunes with a sensible economy they would easily become contented and too independent. They are ruined on purpose by the luxury demanded of them. . . .The use of wealth for useful objects would have produced greater prosperity for the state without rendering the owners of large properties dependent on the prodigality and largess of the prince. . . .

The army is disorganized in several ways. The colonels have an exclusive and dominant preponderance. All appointments as officers go to young men of the leading families of the present regime. The colonels, with their powerful connections, are independent of generals who lack such advantages. The heads of regiments are as imperious and insolent within their commands as they are subservient in the antechambers where they pay their respects. They are honored to be titled servants. They fill and inflate their mouths with the words "sire," "majesty," *mon empereur, mon prince, monseigneur,* "excellency," and "highness." They enjoy using such words of which they have been so long deprived. The soldiers, under an arbitrary authority, lose a part of their modest pay, which is withheld on various pretexts and goes for the benefit of some who should be responsible for its proper use. Every officer takes a soldier as his personal servant. Chiefs are flunkies to the master and princes of his family; soldiers are flunkies to their officers and chiefs. This comfortable arrangement is hardly consistent with the martial spirit that wins victories. *An honor founded on baseness rests on a false principle and can produce no great result.* Can soldiers who are more or less servitors and lackeys, soft and submissive, be a match for those who are citizens, free, poor, sober, proud, inured to fatigue, in the habit of scorning danger, loving their country, and avid for glory? . . .

The military form a class apart and look down on mere citizens. They call them *bourgeois, manans, pékins.* They oppress them when they can, as if they were in a conquered foreign and enemy country. . . .

Jullien is especially scandalized that Bonaparte has even taken the title of "king." (He had done so by converting the Italian Republic, of which he was president, into a Kingdom of Italy of which he became king, sending Eugène de Beauharnais, son of the Empress Josephine by her first marriage, to represent him as Viceroy of Italy at Milan.)

He had the empire conferred upon him, knowing that the word *king* would shock the ears of those who had rejected it as odious for ten years. He obtained the longed-for title in a republic of which he was president by erecting it into a kingdom, always justifying such changes, in the eyes of a gaping and imbecile populace, by the pretext of public interest and the well-being of peoples. Members of the Legion of Honor, who had gladly taken an oath against return of the feudal system . . . now saw new grants of fiefs, principalities and baronies; they heard the master cite Charlemagne, not with the intention of imitating him by being ahead of his time, as Charlemagne was in many ways, but in order to throw back the present age to the state of barbarism in which the contemporaries of Charlemagne were plunged. Liveries, lackeys, chamberlains, equerries, almoners, pages, ribbons and decorations reappeared, more than in the old court before the Revolution, and with more importance attached to them. Corrupting, degrading, debasing, and shrinking the minds of men are the means by which the new order is to be consolidated. To exhaust the people, to make them miserable, are the means of preparing them to accept the yoke. These symptoms of decadence presage the approaching fall of an order of things that rests neither on ancient prestige nor on new ideas.

He then reviews the threat posed by Napoleon to all countries, naming every European state in turn, then Turkey and the Barbary coast, and finally the United States and Great Britain.

America, guided by the wise counsels of the virtuous Jefferson, views the recent events in Europe from afar, and deceived by pleasant illusions thinks the evil may not be as great and dangerous as it really is, and that America will not soon be menaced. . . . If England succumbs (as is possible, for it is divided, corrupt, and fearful), the balance of Europe and the world will be destroyed. Nations and kings will fall one after the other before the young conqueror, who aims at a universal monarchy with a European scepter, and sees no glory except in a world subjected by his arms and bowing before him.

But the Emperor of the French and King of Italy (his official title) only went on to more majestic heights. He had the pope come to Paris to officiate at his imperial coronation. He made three of his brothers and a brother-in-law into kings, and elevated three German princes to that royal station. He created a new Napoleonic nobility, complete with dukes, counts, and barons. He gave some of his generals the title of marshal, with lavish emoluments, and revived Poland as the Grand Duchy of Warsaw. This array of crowned heads and imperial dignitaries, together with France, constituted his "greater empire," *le Grand Empire*. Throughout this empire he undertook to reorganize the civil, legal, fiscal, and educational systems of western Europe, along lines anticipated in the Enlightenment and laid down in the first years of the French Revolution.

Overcoming his republican sentiments, Jullien continued to perform official assignments and errands for the imperial government. He even became a chevalier of the Legion of Honor. In 1806 he attended the wedding of Eugène de Beauharnais and the daughter of the king of Bavaria, one of the seven kings who owed their royal titles to the Emperor of the French. This connection with Prince Eugène proved useful to him later. But in the leisure available from less than full-time service he developed other interests, especially in education. In 1808 he published two books, a *General Essay on Education* and an *Essay on the Employment of Time*. Both these books went through later editions and translations into the 1830s. More will be said of them in a later chapter.

Certain features of the *General Essay* are nevertheless relevant at this point. It appeared semianonymously, with only the initials M.A.J. on its title page and an address at which he might be reached in a footnote; the author thought it best neither to assert, nor quite conceal, the connection between his official status and his personal reflections. The book appeared at the very moment when Napoleon was organizing his Imperial University. This "university," despite its name, was mainly a system of schools for adolescent males, of which there were hundreds called "secondary," "communal," etc., and a few called "lycées" that offered a somewhat more advanced instruction. Almost all these schools had existed since long before the Revolution, the lycées, in their new form, since the law of 1802. The new university created very little; it merely reorganized.

The point at present is that Jullien said openly the opposite of what he had said privately to himself in 1803 and in his jeremiad in 1805. He is now wholly on the side of the government. He still hopes to be useful, or, in his own words at the end of a very long subtitle, "to accelerate the march of the Nation toward civilization and prosperity." He is frankly elitist, recognizing that his purpose is to help create what amounts to a hereditary class of public servants.

A General Essay on Education
Preface

A father of a family, still young, occupied for fifteen years by public functions far removed from the sciences and unfavorable to reflection and study, has thought it well to devote his occasional leisure to observations and researches on *Education*. . . .

The present moment seems favorable to bring out this Essay, which is only a simple theory of education but contains, in a more complete and methodical form, a number of general principles. . . .

All institutions are being reorganized in France and most of Europe, and all should be coordinated and aim at the same end. The education of the children of families surrounding the government is especially important for the government itself and also for the mass of the nation, over which these children, when adult, will necessarily exert a great influence. For their own interest and the public interest they will have to justify, by their talents and virtues, the kind of hereditary prerogative, due to their birth, which will have placed them in an elevated situation near the throne and its favors. They will have to provide the government with the incalculable advantage of being served, and the nation with the advantage of being administered, only by capable and distinguished men whose personal qualities have been the chief means of their fortune and high position.

He then quotes the Englishman Francis Bacon, who two centuries before had observed that no schools existed to train men to assist kings in the public service.

Our government, whose views extend to everything concerning the prosperity of the Empire, has wished to meet this need by three equally useful kinds of institutions: *for the armies* a special military school and schools of artillery and engineering; *for diplomatic functions* the establishment of student diplomats and a graded scale of progressive advancement; and for *administrative, civil, and political* employments the salutary institution of auditors attached to various branches of the administration and admitted to meetings of the Council of State, where, by hearing informed and widely ranging discussions of political and legislative matters, they are enabled to develop the knowledge that they will someday apply. But these measures would be insufficient unless young men destined for various careers are prepared by a well-directed earlier schooling. Such seems the purpose of the new creation now added to the three preceding ones: THE IMPERIAL UNIVERSITY, which is to embrace and favor all branches of teaching and give the whole system a more complete and rapid movement; and in which, as in the INSTITUTE, in a magnificent organization of all the sciences, each moves freely within its own sphere while they communicate with one another and tend toward a common center.

The imperial decree organizing the teaching body seems to call on all persons who have ideas in education. A practical educational treatise, mainly concerning the children of upper classes in the State, should both have a present and immediate usefulness, and be no less useful for the future.

During the following years, the apogee of the Empire, Jullien spent much of his time in Italy on tours of inspection of French troops in that country, where he was on good terms with the Viceroy, Eugène de Beauharnais, having been at his wedding in Munich in 1806. Meanwhile Napoleon, in 1810, in need of a male heir to perpetuate his empire, divorced Josephine and married Marie-Louise, a daughter of the Austrian emperor. The marriage gave Napoleon a certain legitimacy in the eyes of conservative Europe, and it sealed the uneasy alliance between France and the Habsburgs. It also produced a male infant and successor, for whom Napoleon invented another royal title, the King of Rome. Outwardly, at least, Jullien accepted all these developments. In his book on Pestalozzi's educational ideas, published at Milan early in 1812, he praised Napoleon as the "immortal regenerator" of Italy.

But in June 1812 Napoleon launched his invasion of Russia with an army drawn from all over central and western Europe (only a third was French), in which Eugène de Beauharnais as Viceroy commanded a sizeable Italian contingent. Eugène played an important part in the disastrous retreat from Moscow and in the subsequent battles in Germany as Napoleon's forces were driven westward. He returned to his capital at Milan in the spring of 1813. The Grand Empire was falling to pieces. As a Russian army moved through Germany various German states switched to its side, the king of Bavaria urged his son-in-law Eugène to abandon Napoleon, the emperor of Austria declared war on *his* new son-in-law, and an Austrian army of 60,000 men invaded Italy in August 1813. Eugène remained loyal to Napoleon, and resisted the Austrians in pitched battles until early in 1814.

Jullien, in October 1813, somewhere in north Italy, as a passive spectator to these events, wrote the most violent diatribe against Napoleon that he ever penned. It was called *The Preserver of Europe*. He said later that it was "addressed to the sovereigns of Europe several months before their entry into Paris," but he also said later that, when Napoleon's police heard about his intentions, it was buried in the ground in a garden near Mantua and then returned to him, with his other papers, through the good graces of Eugène. Whether or not anyone ever read it, it was not calculated to please Eugène, who in October 1813 was still fighting on Napoleon's side.

The Preserver of Europe was full of unsolicited advice to the rulers of Russia, Austria, and Prussia. It denounced Napoleon as a shameless tyrant, demanded his deposition by the Allies (with a regency in the name of his infant son), and urged that while dismantling the Grand Empire they recognize France within its "natural frontiers" of the Rhine and the Alps. By this plan France would retain its annexations in Belgium and the German left bank of the Rhine.

Such was the setting for Jullien's plan for a new Europe, which filled eighty pages when published after Waterloo. It resembles the actual Peace of Vienna of two years later in calling for a balance of power.

The Preserver of Europe
or
Considerations on the Present Situation in Europe and the Means of Restoring a Political Balance of Its Different States, and a Solidly Established General Peace

All Europe is in flames. No one can foresee where, when, how, or by whom the fire can be put out. The crisis is universal and decisive; it affects both states and individuals, both public and private destinies. The result must be either the consummation of domination and tyranny, bringing the complete ruin of a Europe devastated for twenty years by the scourge of a war of extermination, *or the rebirth of European civilization through the reestablishment of a political balance and a solidly guaranteed general peace*. . . .

The French Revolution, soon deflected from its original course and precipitated into all kinds of excesses, appeared like an ominous comet threatening to burn and consume all governments. Issuing from this revolution and becoming one of its most active and redoubtable instruments, the present chief of state in France, on taking up the reins of government at the end of the last century, promised to abjure the destructive principles of the Revolution and make its true principles prevail, principles that were favorable to the free development of human faculties and the prosperity of nations. By his false promises he inspired a blind and imprudent trust, a deceptive sense of security, of which France gave the example of Europe, and was the first victim. *A useful lesson is to be gained by a comparison and contrast of what he said and what he has done.* . . . In his happy reign not only would peace flourish, but also agriculture, industry, trade, the arts and sciences and all elements of prosperity.

Yet what are the results of these pretentious protestations?

All thrones have been shaken and several subverted. . . .

The fugitive Bourbons and the small number of their still faithful supporters find no asylum on the continent. . . .

Religion is profaned and destroyed; the venerable pontiff, who had been weak enough to sanctify the usurpation, believing it to be in the interest of the Church and of Europe, has been taken from prison to prison, subjected to humiliation and outrage, with no voice daring to demand his liberty.

The sciences, arts, enlightenment, true philosophy, all elements of civilization have been sacrificed to unheard of violence, plans of conquest, devastation, brigandage. . . .

The friends of a wise liberty, of a moderate monarchical government . . . have seen the rise of an appalling system of despotism, terror, servitude, demoralization, corruption, and universal ruin, not only in France but in the conquered countries, annexed or allied, over which the dominant power extended.

Even the anarchists and the wildest Jacobins, who had based atrocious hopes on the overthrow of legitimate authorities, the dissolution of all social bonds and disorganization and license made into a system, have had to shudder at the chaos wrought everywhere by a destructive conqueror who had become, so to speak, the very revolution personified, clothed in turn by the insignia of a general, the purple of a consul, and the robe of an emperor, to roam, ravage and desolate the earth. . . .

The same fate awaited his companions in arms. . . . Of all classes of society the military has been most cruelly sacrificed.

Property owners and agriculturists, friends of order and peace . . . have seen all public and private resources exhausted, swallowed up in the gulf of eternal war without legitimate cause or reasonable and acknowledged motive. . . .

If we listen to the class of merchants, whose interests have been the pretext to justify the bizarre, gigantic and absurd conception of the so-called *continental system*, we hear unanimous but suppressed and muffled groans from one end of the continent to the other. . . . An avaricious, inquisitorial, murderous system of taxation. . . .

Education and instruction directed solely to the profession of arms; booksellers and printers subjected to a vexatious and oppressive police. . . .

At last the war and disaster in Russia, so ruinous to the Grand Army in its campaign of 1812, have aroused Europe from its long lethargy. Opinion has suddenly changed; courage is restored by a hope of salvation. France itself, while mourning its losses in an expedition that was extravagant, unjust, impolitic, impious and *disavowed in principle by the unanimous opinion of the nation and even the army*, has shaken off its chains and begun to think it can at last breathe again.

An amazed Europe has blessed the memory of Peter the Great, who in the last century created a nation destined to become in our century the liberator of the continent. . . .

All our misfortunes, all our false steps that have produced them and aggravated them, come above all from a feeling of *fear*, which causes us to arm against one another. It is *fear* that creates obedience and acceptance of warfare in places subject to the usurper; it is *fear* that makes other states sign treaties with him and shut their eyes to his successive conquests. The power of *fear*, proportionate to his audacity, so different from the true courage that he has never known, is what gives him all his strength in his empire and elsewhere.

In France, the remnants of factions are mutually *afraid* of each other; by *fear* they serve the master who immolates them to his ambition. Those who passed judgment on the unfortunate Louis XVI, all Frenchmen who took part in the Revolution, whether by criminal intent or by weakness, cowardice or necessity, or in good faith with pure, noble and generous goals, in the hope of reforming abuses and obtaining a better order of things, *fear* a vengeful reaction of which they might be victims. The whole nation *fears* a dismemberment of its territory; for this reason alone it sees in the odious author of its calamities a necessary protector of its independence.

In Europe some statesmen *fear* the great bulk of France and seem to entertain plans for dissolving it, an impolitic and barbarous project that would rearouse all the French national energy, inspire a resolution to perish to the last man in defense of the integrity of their country, and furnish by the very excesses of despair the incalculable forces and means of resistance to a common enemy.

The cabinets of Europe *fear* each other, and so are sometimes ready to yield to the secret intrigues used to divide them.

There must be an end to this *fear* that makes governments, peoples and individuals suspicious, distrustful and hostile, when their

interest alone and their common salvation should unite them. There
must be a frank proclamation of principles of conservation to rally all
opinions, dissipate all fears, and stabilize all hopes. . . .

He notes that because of revolution, counterrevolution, and war,
not only the French but other Europeans were responsible for Napoleon's success.

The French faced a frightful alternative, on the one hand menaced by
the ambition of the Allied powers, on the other, sacrificed to the unbridled ambition of their own leader; and not knowing where to find
a protector or the means of salvation they abandoned themselves in
despair to the same dominating influence that had caused their dangers, but seemed their only hope for escaping from them.

For this reason, many reasonable, estimable and enlightened men,
friends to their country and to humanity, employed in various civilian and military capacities, and sometimes clothed with the highest
dignities, followed regretfully and by necessity the laws and stan-
dards of the chief of the French. They were condemned to serve him
while awaiting the favorable moment when they might help to extri-
cate their country from the abyss into which it had been pushed by
the mistaken policies of the powers, the imprudence and blindness
of nations and individuals, the force of events, and a kind of fatality
in it all.

But the cabinets of Europe have no ground for reproaching the
French for cooperation in the destructive plans of the usurper, since
they themselves made treaties with him as a sovereign, consecrated
his dignity and dynasty by family alliances, and deprived the peoples
dependent upon him of any means of escape.

The weakness and disunity of the continental powers have paralyzed all efforts at resistance and conservation. They have more effectively contributed to the success of the common enemy than the
forces available to him in his own states. . . .

The powers must therefore unite, and act with restraint.

To remain united the kings must avoid ambitious views and ideas of
partition, which would become the germs of disunion and the seed of
further wars.

To show themselves *generous, moderate and disinterested*, the kings
should abstain from new personal acquisitions and dismemberment
of ancient states. They should guarantee independence and integrity
to *France*, bounded by the Rhine, the Ocean, the Pyrenees, the Mediterranean and the Alps, and governed by the Empress-Regent, assisted by a council. Otherwise, I repeat, the fear and despair of the

French would make them rally, in defense and preservation of their country, to the very man who has begun to destroy it.

In the remainder of the *Preserver of Europe*, Jullien proceeds to indicate, one by one, how each of the states of Europe should be treated by the victorious Allies. Napoleon should be exiled to his native Corsica, if it will take him. England and the continental monarchies should reorganize Europe in a spirit of moderation and good will.

> Today, it is by a deep and unanimous feeling for their *common interest*, and for a *system of political balance and general pacification, firmly established in Europe*, that kings will be able to preserve and strengthen their thrones, and provide happiness and tranquillity for their peoples.

A few weeks later, as the Allies pushed the French army back into France, they in fact offered Napoleon about what Jullien recommended. The Austrians, always fearful of Russian expansion, and now with a Habsburg daughter as Empress of the French, had reason to favor France as a balance against Russia, and so for it to remain an important power. While insisting on Napoleon's abdication, they proposed that France retain Belgium and the west bank of the Rhine, with Napoleon's infant son as emperor and his Austrian mother as regent. But Napoleon spurned any such ideas. The Allies invaded France, Napoleon abdicated, and the Bourbon monarchy was restored in the person of Louis XVIII.

The dethroned Napoleon was sent off in exile to the island of Elba on the Italian coast.

SIX

THE HUNDRED DAYS

THE "first" Bourbon restoration lasted scarcely a year. The new king (who was sixty years old) proved to be more conciliatory than he had been in the past. He issued a constitutional charter with assurances of parliamentary government and civil rights, and he retained most of the legal and administrative reorganization that had taken form since 1789. But in calling the constitution a charter he signified that it depended on the royal will, not on the will of the people or nation. He called himself King of France, not King of the French, the title assigned to Louis XVI in the constitution of 1791. He styled himself Louis XVIII, implying that his nephew, the ten-year-old son of Louis XVI who had died in 1795, had really been a hereditary king. He dated his own accession as the nineteenth year of his reign. He rejected the tricolor and adopted the white flag of the Bourbons. It was thus made to appear that a continuous monarchy had existed throughout, only temporarily subverted by revolutionaries and usurpers. And with the new king all sorts of more extreme enemies of the Revolution made themselves heard. It was reasonable to expect further efforts to reinstate other features of the Old Regime. All sympathizers with the Revolution and the Empire were alarmed.

Napoleon escaped from Elba, landed on the coast of Provence, proceeded north through cheering crowds, and reached Paris on 20 March 1815. For about three months, remembered as the Hundred Days, it seemed that the Empire might exist again, though on what terms remained an open question. It depended also on what the Allies would do; they had made peace with France and recognized Louis XVIII, but they had not disarmed, and were at this very moment meeting at Vienna to redesign the map of Europe.

Marc-Antoine Jullien welcomed the sudden return of Napoleon as another revolution. He published (anonymously) two hastily written tracts. One was a short *Profession of Faith of a French Military Man*, the other a longer work called *The Conciliator: or The Seventh Epoch*. By the seventh epoch he meant the seventh phase of the Revolution, the first six being the well-recognized series of the Constituent Assembly, the Terror, the Directory, Consulate, Empire, and Restoration. For Jullien this seventh epoch should be the last. It should consolidate and perpetuate the goals and principles of the true Revolution.

The *Profession of Faith*, the earlier of the two tracts, was also the only occasion during his long writing career when he presented himself as a soldier. He was annoyed to learn that certain German publicists were accusing the French army of betraying its rightful king. But, said Jullien, this abandonment of Louis XVIII and enthusiasm for Napoleon

were only the necessary result of the violations of solemn promises and the grave wrongs by which the king and the princes have alienated the people and the army.

These publicists should have considered that the French army is an essentially national army, composed of citizen soldiers and officers who regard themselves, not as the property, patrimony or servile flock of a prince, but as the defenders and preservers of the independence, glory and prosperity of France. . . .

The Bourbons, on returning to France, had no idea of their own position or of the spirit and character of the nation, nor of the ground on which they wished to establish themselves. They supposed that they were returning to a property acquired by inheritance, which they could administer without the aid of those who had taken part in its administration for twenty years, who knew its resources and needs, and who could advise on the best means to improve its exploitation.

The Bourbons were lured into a mistaken course by the corrupt remnants of a privileged caste whose self-interest and exclusive pretensions are repugnant to the nation. This caste badly advised them, badly defended them, and has brought on their ruin.

Napoleon has been welcomed by the people as the defender of its rights, and by the army as the avenger of its glory. He is guided, supported and sustained by a national movement. . . . The sudden return of Napoleon was not the *cause*, but the *occasion*, of the revolution that has occurred. This revolution has prevented civil war. It has saved the nobles themselves, whom the outraged peasants in their fury might have exterminated.

When the unanimity of the national will in the towns, the countryside and the army has demonstrated to Europe France's positive refusal to accept the Bourbon yoke, why should foreigners wish to impose it on us again? Have they not solemnly promised to allow us a free choice of our government? By what right do they meddle in our internal affairs? Have they not themselves recognized the Emperor Napoleon by contracting treaties and alliances with him? When he entered as a victor into their capitals, at Vienna and Berlin, did he abuse his victory to the point of depriving their rulers of their thrones and forcing their peoples to accept other dynasties? What would the

English say if we wished to impose some descendant of the Stuarts upon them? What would the Russians say if we found some obscure offspring of their dynasty to claim ancient rights to their empire, and if we were to relegate their sovereign to some distant island?

Let us apply in politics the great principle of morality: do nothing to others that you would not wish done to yourself.

The kings and nations of Europe have an equal interest in the independence of France. They had best not rekindle the wrath and courage of a nation that henceforth aspires only to enjoy on its own soil a reasonable liberty, a flourishing industry, and a contented tranquillity. . . .

It is not now a dynastic quarrel between Bonaparte and the Bourbons, but a final struggle between the remnants of feudal nobility and the nation, between privileges and equality, between the Inquisition and the freedom of religion, between the Old Regime and the new institutions.

After these observations, which were only prefatory, the "French military man" goes on to enlarge on the faults of the Bourbon restoration in eleven numbered paragraphs. He incorporates a kind of restatement of the Revolutionary declarations of rights.

I.

In a sudden and unexpected revolution, in which the army is honored to have played a large part. . .[it must be asked]. . .what are the real and durable gains that the army and nation have a right to expect from the return of the Emperor? . . .

II.

The first and imperious needs of France, both for the military and for civilians, are glory and liberty. No one better than Napoleon can procure for the people and the army these two benefits of the social order.

IV.

The Bourbons have proved themselves to be the enemies of our glory, having been imposed on France by foreign armies, and bringing with them the criminal Frenchmen who have been in arms against their own country for twenty-five years. . . .

V.

The Bourbons, instead of honestly rallying to the French nation and army, espousing the national glory, adopting as a noble heritage the results of the immense labors of the present generation, began by surrendering all the forts occupied by French garrisons and putting themselves at the mercy of our enemies, whom they called their *allies* and our *liberators*. They renounced the natural boundaries of France because these had been conquered by other Frenchmen than the former kings. They adopted the white cockade that revives the hateful memory of civil wars, and proscribed the three national colors that consecrated the heroic efforts, sacrifices, labors and victories of twenty-five years. They have not blushed to sign their royal acts with the absurd formula of their nineteenth or twentieth regnal year, which is both an insult to the other powers and an admission of their own profound and absolute nullity, and which tends to criminalize the Revolution and anathematize everything done, in the army and in our internal affairs, since their expulsion. With conceited affectation, they have talked of their so-called legitimacy, which puts the nation and army in a state of rebellion by recognizing no other government than theirs. They have been afraid to support the throne with a true representative body arising from election by the people. In the upper chamber they placed former noble émigrés who had lost all French feelings. In the lower chamber they kept the remains of a legislative body whose powers had almost expired, and which had betrayed the nation by its cowardice. They degraded the Legion of Honor, that sanctuary of the brave, by depriving it of its most noble prerogatives and awarding its decorations to the very men who had constantly borne arms against their country. After promising to forget the past and to treat all Frenchmen alike, they have exclusively called to their side, admitted to their intimacy, employed, and favored all the returned émigrés, former nobles and known enemies of the Revolution, while they rejected, removed and abused all those in France who had faithfully served and defended their country. Obliged to give France the semblance of a guarantee, they promulgated their pretended constitutional charter simply as a royal ordinance, a concession necessarily revocable and always precarious, without even the formalities required by all laws, and to which they were afraid to add the sanction of the national will through the consent of bodies appearing to represent the nation. . . .

So, all the solemn promises of the Bourbons having been violated and undone, the nation and army are released from unjust oaths imposed by violence and necessity. The social pact, resting on no consent, is nullified. A universal and irrepressible discontent has exploded against the Bourbons. Their ephemeral reign has vanished.

VII.

The Emperor Napoleon recognizes the need of reigning over a free people, by and for the people, with the concurrence of its representatives. . . .

VIII.

The French people and army, in serving the Emperor and his dynasty faithfully, demand a free constitution. . . .

IX.

The fundamental principles consecrated in the different constitutions drawn up by our national assemblies in 1791, in the Year III, the Year VIII, and the constitutions of the Empire, together with their strict observation, are the faithful expression of the national will.

These principles, supported by the opinion of the thinking class, the middle classes, and the vast majority of the nation, can be reduced to the following:

1. Equality of rights for all citizens and their admissibility to all civil and military employments.

2. Free consent to levies of men and taxes.

3. Public and individual liberty assured.

4. Freedom of the press, the primary guarantee of individual and public liberties and the necessary safeguard of peoples and governments.

5. Inviolable secrecy of private letters, so necessary to the peace of families and to free communication of heartfelt thoughts and feelings.

6. Inviolability of properties, the essential basis of social order, and abolition of the penalty of confiscation.

7. Freedom of religion guaranteed.

8. Irremovability of judges, necessary to secure the independence of their judgments.

9. The institution of the jury preserved, and applied also to what are called *political* offenses.

10. Inviolability of the head of state, and strict and positive accountability of ministers.

11. Guarantee of the public debt; freedom and inviolability of the Bank of France.

12. Assurance that no military man, having attained the rank of officer, can be deprived of his grade except by a legal judgment. . . .

X.

A national representation, divided into two chambers and deliberating in public, is demanded by the immense majority of the French, to exercise legislative authority with the concurrence of the supreme head of the executive power.

XI.

The power of the Emperor Napoleon and his dynasty will be the more solidly and unshakably affirmed by taking root in a freely manifested public opinion, and by preserving and guaranteeing the rights of the people, reflecting the national power and the national will.

By the time the *Profession of Faith* was in print, Napoleon's constitutional arrangements were already known, and Jullien hastened to expound and criticize them in his *Conciliator*, which he published, again anonymously, in a hundred pages.

The "constitution" of the Hundred Days reflected a compromise between Napoleon and his supporters. These included many old republicans such as Lazare Carnot, who had served on the Committee of Public Safety in 1793–1794, and many of those who were beginning to be known as "liberals," notably Benjamin Constant, who had been ousted from the Tribunate by Napoleon in the purge of 1802. Both Carnot and Constant, like Jullien, had turned against Napoleon during the Empire. Both, nevertheless, were among those invited by Napoleon to prepare a new frame of government. They did so by drafting a document that in fact closely resembled Louis XVIII's constitutional charter. They preferred to call it a "constitution," but Napoleon, to defend his own record, insisted on calling it an Act in Addition to the Constitutions of the Empire. He offered this *Acte Additionnel* as a liberalizing continuation of the constitutions of the Years X and XII, in 1802 and 1804. It was submitted to a popular plebiscite, which yielded 1,300,000 affirmative votes out of some six million potential voters.

Jullien's *Conciliator* for the most part only repeated at greater length what he had said in the *Profession of Faith*. Its main interest lies in what he said of the Additional Act. Written just before the plebiscite, it recommended adoption.

As for the Act in Addition to the Constitutions of the Empire, it has been generally criticized for the veil of mystery that enveloped the moment of its formation. The absence of publicity for the names of its authors gives us no assurance. Unless the urgency of our circumstances made it impossible, it should have emanated from a constituent body, chosen by the nation, which could easily have been convoked in the last days of April. This constituent body would have needed only to collect from our previous constitutions, as accepted by the people, the fundamental principles consecrated by the national will. . . .

1. The principle of all sovereignty resides essentially in the Nation.
2. The national sovereignty being the legitimate and necessary source of all power, it follows that the legislative, executive and judi-

cial power can only be exercised by virtue of special and defined mandates as set forth in a constitutional code.

3. The *constitution* of a state is not exactly a pact, or an agreement, as has too often been repeated, but an actual delegation of power by the nation to its mandatories. . . .

4. The condition of heredity in a ruling dynasty, to which the free will of the nation conveys supreme power of government, is only an agreed upon method of continuous peaceful election to prevent troubles.

5. Civil and political equality, recognized as flowing from a natural and imprescriptible human right, requires the admissibility of citizens of all classes to all civil and military employments on the basis of their virtues, talents and services. In consequence of the same principle, honorific distinctions and recompenses are purely personal, never hereditary. (We do not prejudge here the question whether, as a safeguard to public liberty, it may not be useful to adopt a hereditary Upper Chamber; anything clearly necessary and convenient for the good of the state becomes just and good.)

6. A National Representation, divided into two Chambers, deliberating publicly, and permanent in the sense that they cannot be adjourned except by their own formal and public consent, should exercise legislative authority in concurrence with the supreme chief of the executive power. . . .

7. The Law, whose essential character is to be the faithful expression of the general will, should result from the agreement and fusion of three wills: those of each representative body and of the chief of state.

8. The *division* and *harmony of the constituted powers*, independent of one another in their respective spheres, but equally subject to the force of law, are one of the necessary guarantees of public liberty.

9. A simple, clear and precise provision, whose infraction must never go unpunished, should guarantee *individual liberty* and *security of persons*.

10. *Freedom of the press*, the palladium of public and individual liberty and the necessary safeguard to government itself, should be guaranteed by a special law.

11. *The inviolability of properties, the essential basis of social order, requires as a necessary consequence the abolition of the penalty of confiscation.*

After touching more briefly on a number of other principles, such as the right of petition, Jullien goes on to express his doubts and reservations. It was unnecessary and unfortunate, he thinks, to pretend that a new constitution for the Empire should be only an "additional act," because Napoleon after 1804 had governed too much by *senatus-con-*

sultes that were arbitrary, secretive, illegal, and incoherent. And the provision for a hereditary upper house of the legislature, or House of Peers, with the right of the Emperor to increase their number at will, was contrary to all principles issuing from the Revolution. But Napoleon now said that future improvements in the Additional Act were to be expected, and Jullien, hopeful as ever, or indeed credulous, was willing to believe him. Therefore:

> All good citizens should hasten to cast their votes for the Additional Act, which will receive later the modifications and improvements to which it is susceptible. The first need of the nation and of the government is to reconstruct the social pact, to reestablish and strengthen the regular and legitimate rule of the laws as freely deliberated upon by representatives of the people. It is to organize a national body, capable of resisting foreign powers that may wish to attack, divide, and destroy us. A coalition is always helpless against a strongly united nation. To cement this union of all Frenchmen there must be assurance of public liberty, a good Constitution. This constitution, urgently and immediately needed, will be the real and legal expression of the will of the people only so far as the people can clothe it with their positive and solemn sanction, after public discussion in an assembly of their representatives. . . .
>
> The *definitive outcome of the French Revolution* must be neither the absolute abandonment and destruction, nor yet the disorderly abuse and exaggeration, of its principles.
>
> He only will finish the revolution with success and glory who knows how to conciliate and combine in durable institutions . . . the opinions of two classes, both truly estimable and respectable, of which the mass of the French nation is composed. . . .
>
> These two classes, which formed only one class in 1789 in the first days of the Revolution, really constitute the nation, because beyond them are only penniless beggars [*mendiants prolétaires*, but "proletarian" did not yet have its later sense], robbers, gamblers, intriguers, and political speculators eager for trouble and revolution, who put themselves beyond the limits of the social order. . . .
>
> One of these classes is made up of those citizens who took a direct and active part in the revolution and the war for liberty. . . .
>
> The other class is of those who still have a profound memory of the evils that the nation suffered during the revolutionary storms. . . . The supposed establishment of a free government, which for this class meant the devastation and fury of a blood-stained anarchy, led them to confuse the abuse of an institution with the institution itself. . . .
>
> The first hold essentially to the ideas of *political liberty and equality,*

consecrated in our successive constitutions, and to the fundamental principles of *national sovereignty* as the source of legitimate power, of the *representative system, constitutional government*, judgment by *juries, liberty of the press*, and *accountability of ministers* and agents of authority.

The second adhere more strongly to the ideas, no less necessary and fundamental, of *real property* as the principal basis of citizenship, of *security, social peace, impartial administration of justice, public order*, and a *strong, energetic and centralized government*.

To conciliate and combine these two great elements, ORDER and LIBERTY, should be the task of deputies of the nation, to satisfy the unanimous will of the French. . . .

France is tired of revolutions and political commotions. It wants a strong but national government suited to the present state of civilization and enlightenment, which will guarantee its independence and security against the outside world and, internally, its liberty and tranquillity under protection of the laws. It recognizes as laws only those that come from free and public discussion by a truly national representation.

A legislative body was set up under the Additional Act, consisting of a Chamber of Peers whose members were first appointed by Napoleon and were in future to be hereditary, and a Chamber of Representatives chosen under the system of electoral colleges dating from 1802, in which the electors were the owners of substantial real property, but with an automatic right for all members of the Legion of Honor to belong to an electoral college. Jullien qualified for the electoral college of the department of the Seine, probably as a member of the Legion of Honor rather than by the possession of property. He offered himself as a candidate for the Chamber of Representatives, and indeed the name Jullien exists on a list of its members, but if we may believe his later statement he was deprived of election by the manipulation of his enemies, who contrived the election of another person of the same name instead.

The two chambers sat for only about a month. No one can say how a reformed Empire might have turned out, since the powers meeting at Vienna immediately prepared for a second invasion of France to be rid of Napoleon a second time. Napoleon hurriedly reassembled his army, but was defeated at Waterloo, on 18 June. He left the army to attend to his political future. On 21 June the Chamber of Representatives called for his abdication. He abdicated for the second time on 22 June. On 23 June Jullien wrote another tract, *On the National Representation on the Days of 21 and 22 June 1815*.

The title page bore no author's name; no one at the time could accuse its author of contradicting what he had said in the two anonymous tracts written a few weeks before. No one, indeed, could or ought to have been consistent in such a moment of confusion and crisis, with the Allied armies about to occupy Paris.

Some in the Chamber of Representatives, which was composed largely of old republicans and of those now called liberals, favored the proclamation of the four-year-old Napoleon II as Emperor. Jullien demurred; he now reached the strange conclusion that France, in a great upsurge of patriotic national unity (which did not exist) should negotiate with the Allies and receive, by agreement with them, a king from another country. The idea was not wholly absurd; the Frenchman, J. B. Bernadotte, who had been a general in the French Revolution, was now the crown prince of Sweden and would soon be its king; and in the following years the Powers would provide a German prince to be king of Greece. But to propose such an arrangement for France was a counsel of desperation.

The Chamber of Representatives, said Jullien, instead of listening to pleas for Napoleon or his family,

> should have shown that some of the nation repudiated Napoleon and would henceforth make no sacrifice for him or for his family; that some others of the citizens rejected the Bourbons and their dynasty; that the unanimous cry of the French, and their necessary rallying point, was *neither Napoleon nor the Bourbons.* . . .
>
> An appeal could have been made to our armies and to patriots within the country: "You have believed Napoleon to be the defender of your rights, of public liberty and independence. You accepted him on his return only on the condition that he would save France. This condition is violated, the pact is broken. But France, restored to itself and the noble energy of its citizens, France whose sacred treasure has too long been entrusted to criminal hands, has within itself the resources needed to save it. It wants neither the Bourbons who have humiliated and betrayed it, nor Napoleon who has worked only to exhaust it for his own ambition, and to enslave it."
>
> Then the long suppressed truth would have been heard with its noble accents.
>
> An appeal could have been made to Europe, to the kings and foreign nations: "Kings, you declared war on Napoleon; he is no longer our chief. We, like you, have groaned as his victims. His yoke is now destroyed. He now belongs only to history and posterity. Allied kings, be faithful to your promises. Hold back your armies, respect our independence; the war has no further purpose; take care not to

reduce a great nation to despair; it will rise unanimously to throw you back if you advance further.

"Foreign nations! Would you be instruments of your masters to carry on a war that is henceforth unjust and wicked, and could not be continued except to destroy a people that wishes to be free and independent, and which defends the sacred rights of man, the cause of all peoples. . . ."

All talk in the Chambers of a regency under Napoleon II, said Jullien, was a mere evasion. The Chambers were meanwhile doing nothing to stop the advance of the Allied armies.

Yet let no one think that I despair of the public safety. I have tried to explain honestly the reasons for what the Chambers have done. There was a fear of agitation among the people and in the army unless Napoleon II was proclaimed as successor to his father. But the simple truth expressed by only one deputy was ignored: If the abdication of Napoleon was judged necessary, because he had demonstrated his inability to save the country after leaving his army, how could the proclamation of his son, a child, far away, and a captive in the hands of our enemies, rally the parties within France or impose on the foreign powers?

It would have been the part of moderation and wisdom . . . to send a deputation from the two chambers to the powers of the Coalition. The real question should have been faced, and a formal negative basis laid down for negotiations: *Neither Napoleon nor the Bourbons*. The wishes of France would have been satisfied. Europe would have had no further pretext for pursuing the war. It would have recognized our right to choose our own government. Then later, perhaps in concert with Austria, we could either have proclaimed Napoleon II with a council of regency, or a continuation of the present government commission, or, by agreement with another power, call on a foreign prince to be received among us on condition of accepting and observing our constitutional pact, as made by representatives of the nation. We would have arrived at a solution of the problem: to guarantee our internal liberty, our independence from outside powers, our national institutions, and the peace of Europe. We would have avoided simultaneously the double danger presented by the faction that wants a prince of the house of Orleans and by men still blind enough to desire a return of the Bourbons.

But on 23 June, as Jullien was writing these words, the chambers did in fact proclaim the four-year-old Napoleon II as Emperor of the French. Jullien added an afterword to his pamphlet, dating it 24 June.

The printed work appeared the next day, carrying the date 25 June on its title page.

In this afterword, he announced that as a good citizen he accepted the decision of the two chambers, and that he understood their reasons, namely that unless Napoleon II were proclaimed there might be revolt in the army and revolutionary disturbances throughout the country. Nevertheless, for the long run, he remained of his opinion:

> *Neither Napoleon nor the Bourbons.* Such is the rallying cry of all Frenchmen who are above party and want only to see their country happy and pacified.
>
> The national representation and the government are placed between the debris of two dynasties that still cause agitation and can only bring new troubles upon us. The nation firmly rejects them both. It wants a new head of whom no party need be afraid, who has no vengeance to exercise, and who accepts a constitution freely discussed and consented to by representatives of the nation. Whoever this head may be, if he offers the desirable guarantees against every kind of reaction, he will be favorably received by the immense majority of the French, and there will be peace in France, which is the necessary condition for Europe itself to enjoy a durable peace.

So Jullien, the former revolutionary zealot, the bold young agent of the intrepid Committee of Public Safety, firm in his resistance to counterrevolution for more than twenty years, was reduced in 1815 to imagining the coming of a foreign prince to protect France against "reaction." It is to be noted that with his slogan, "Neither Napoleon nor the Bourbons," he never mentions the possibility of a republic, to which he had devoted the best years of his youth. Dreading fanaticism and violence, he had become a liberal. The Revolution was not the war of the poor against the rich, as he had said in the 1790s. It was the struggle of enlightened and progressive persons against obstinate, backward, and selfish upholders of outworn ideas.

As the Allied armies marched inexorably toward Paris under Wellington and Blücher, the victors of Waterloo, members of the two chambers were thrown into a state of helpless consternation. They continued a futile discussion of a new constitution for the Empire, to which they intended to attach a declaration of rights. The Chamber of Representatives adopted such a declaration and sent it to the House of Peers in the afternoon of 5 July. Several members, however, while voting for it, thought it hardly adequate or relevant to the actual menace of their impending doom. They favored a second declaration, to be issued by the Chamber of Representatives without reference to the

Peers. Their proposal was sent to a committee of five, one of whom was none other than Barère of the old Committee of Public Safety. After adjournment for dinner this committee reported that evening, submitting a text which the Chamber immediately adopted, so that in fact, on its deathbed, it adopted two declarations on the same day.

This second declaration was written by Marc-Antoine Jullien. Though not a member of the Chamber, he was in touch with several who were, and met with fifty of them to whom he submitted a draft. It was necessary, he said, to fling a final verbal defiance in the face of the victors, and leave a political testament for the future. He had the satisfaction, denied to him when he had tried to advise the Directory, the First Consul, the Emperor, and the Coalition in 1813, of at last finding men who agreed with him and acted on his proposal.

The Chamber, in this declaration, announced its determination to remain in Paris whatever happened, affirmed its adherence to the principles of the Revolution, and added a few provisions more suitable to the moment. Its action may be contrasted with what happened in France during another German advance on Paris in 1940.

Declaration of the Chamber of Representatives
Session of 5 July 1815

The troops of the Allied powers are about to enter the capital.

The Chamber of Representatives will nevertheless remain in session among the inhabitants of Paris, to which it has been called as mandatories by the express will of the people.

But in these grave circumstances the Chamber of Representatives owes it to itself, and owes it to France and Europe, to make a declaration of its sentiments and principles.

It declares its solemn appeal to the fidelity and patriotism of the national guard of Paris, which is charged with protection of the national representation.

It declares its highest confidence in the principles of morality, honor and magnanimity of the allied powers, and their respect for the independence of the nation, so positively expressed in their manifestos.

It declares that the government of France, whoever may be at its head, should both rest upon the will of the nation legally ascertained, and reach agreement with other governments to become a common bond and guarantee of peace between France and Europe.

It declares that a monarch can offer no real guarantees unless he swears to observe faithfully a constitution deliberated upon by the national representation and accepted by the people.

Hence, any government having no other credentials than the acclamations and wishes of a party, or which would be imposed by force, or any government that would not adopt the national colors, and would not guarantee:

The liberty of citizens

Equality of civil and political rights

Freedom of the press

Freedom of religion

The representative system

Free consent to levies of men and taxes

Accountability of ministers

Irrevocability of sale of nationalized lands

Inviolability of properties

Abolition of the tithe, of feudalism, and of old and new hereditary nobility

Abolition of all confiscation of wealth

Amnesty for political opinions and votes up to the present

The institution of the Legion of Honor

Distinctions and rewards due to officers and soldiers, assistance due to their widows and children

The institution of the jury

Irremovability of judges

Payment of the public debt

would have only an ephemeral existence, and would not assure the tranquillity of France or of Europe.

If the principles announced in this declaration should be ignored or violated, the Representatives of the French people, performing this day a sacred duty, *protest in advance before the entire world against violence and usurpation.* They entrust the upholding of these principles to all good Frenchmen, to all generous hearts, to all enlightened minds, to all who are jealous of their liberty, and, finally, to future generations.

Two days later, on 7 July, the Allies entered Paris and a small force of soldiers dispersed the Chamber of Representatives without more ado. Louis XVIII was again restored. The two declarations received no publicity. There could be no public discussion of their contents, and they were forgotten except for those who had been present in the Chamber on 5 July 1815.

SEVEN

CONSTITUTIONAL MONARCHIST

FORTY YEARS OLD in 1815, Marc-Antoine Jullien had half his adult life still before him. It would bring him some modest satisfactions, for he was already known as a writer on education, and would soon enjoy a limited repute as editor of the *Revue Encyclopédique*. He would have liked, however, to take a more active part in public life, as he had done with the Committee of Public Safety in 1793–1794, and again on his missions under Bonaparte after 1799. He was never again to have any such official duties.

Louis XVIII, restored to his throne for the second time in July 1815, immediately reinstituted his constitutional charter of the year before. It provided for a parliament in two houses, a Chamber of Peers appointed by the king from among persons of noble rank, and a Chamber of Deputies elected at meetings of electoral colleges, which were distributed throughout the country. Jullien qualified as a member of the electoral college of the department of the Seine. There were only about 100,000 such electors in all France, who qualified by paying a direct tax of at least 300 francs, and so were a small affluent minority, but the law also set a lower tax requirement for certain military persons and members of the Legion of Honor, and in this way Jullien became an elector. On several occasions he described himself as an *électeur éligible*, that is, qualified also to sit in the Chamber of Deputies. There were only about 20,000 *éligibles* in the whole country, who paid a direct tax of 1,000 francs. Since Jullien was not so rich he may have qualified as a member of the Legion of Honor.

He attempted repeatedly to play a part in the elections. He did so by publishing pieces of advice to the electoral colleges, and even hoped to be elected himself. He worked in conjunction with more eminent liberals, for example the Marquis de Lafayette, who in 1817 supplied him with information on the British parliamentary system. Yet the result was always frustration. An unpleasant note of self-pity became evident in his writings. He complained that he had always been misunderstood, unappreciated, and calumniated. The "calumnies" concerning his past, as he called them, must have circulated by word of mouth, very likely at meetings of the electoral colleges themselves. What he had written about Bonaparte, the Empire, and the Hundred Days had been published anonymously, if at all. He had put his name to tracts and speeches printed during the Terror, but these were all ephemeral productions, later destroyed or hidden by their frightened recipients. His letters to Robespierre had been published by the Convention in 1795, but only as a pamphlet which few would possess twenty years later. But there were many still alive in 1815 who could remember Jullien as the young terrorist at Bordeaux.

Or some might think him merely a trimmer, willing to work for any regime in his own interest, and then abandon it. He had served Robespierre, and turned against him. He had welcomed the Directory as a constitutional republic, and then denounced it. He had accepted the coup d'état of Brumaire, and rejected its consequences. He had worked for the Empire, but scorned it. He had hailed Napoleon's return from Elba, and repudiated him after Waterloo. All this was true, but he would argue that each of these regimes had deviated from its own principles as announced at its outset; and this was true also. He could say with some justice that except in 1793 and 1794, at a time of foreign and civil war, he had favored the same principles and given the same (unheeded) advice to every regime in turn.

This is evident in his speedy acceptance of the second coming of Louis XVIII. Barely a month after coining the slogan, "Neither Napoleon nor the Bourbons," he published two tracts calling for support of the Bourbon king. He made known his authorship of both. The earlier one, and the longer, took the form of advice on the coming elections to the Chamber of Deputies. It attributes the troubles of the first Restoration not to the king but to the most obstinate partisans of Napoleon and to those who longed for the Old Regime—and who wanted to recover their lost property. The electors, he said, should avoid both these kinds of men. The country needed unity, and a firm center.

> A common center is necessary for us to preserve and guarantee this precious unity. The king alone, and the unity of a responsible ministry, will henceforth offer this central point around which all the strength of the nation should be combined. . . .
>
> But if the whole nation feels the need of joining with the king or his ministers . . . the king and his ministers must see that it is equally important to win over the opinion and sentiment of the nation, and to adopt honestly, with this in view, the principles and institutions that the national will has sanctioned. . . .
>
> The authority of the king would have been easily strengthened, a year ago, if only some persons who returned with him, misled by their own preconceptions and concerned more for their own interests than for the great interest of the monarch and the country, had not used their influence in public affairs to make it seem that a project

was afoot for gradual establishment of the older order of things, or I might say the old abuses.

Thus a part of the French people were attacked in what they held most dear. The nine or ten million citizens who had acquired nationalized properties, purchased under guarantee of the laws, feared to lose them. All citizens of the old bourgeoisie feared the reestablishment of the privileged caste and the abuses, humiliations and vexations that would follow. The peasants, whether owners or tenants of their land, feared the return of the tithe and the *corvées*, as publicly announced by some writers and by some priests in their sermons. Military men and their families were mortified to see that the services they had rendered to the country for twenty-five years would no longer count, if indeed they were not branded as crimes, and that the career of promotion would be open only to noble families, whose sons would have a special right to admission to the royal military academies, which would be almost totally closed to other classes of the nation. All Frenchmen who had taken any part in the Revolution, either by publishing writings favorable to its principles or by exercising public functions, were disturbed by semi-official pamphlets which, by recalling the past, now suggested as grounds for proscription the political votes and opinions which the king had guaranteed should be forgotten.

The constitutional charter, said Jullien, repeating himself, was only a "royal ordinance, revocable and precarious by its nature," and should be turned into a true constitution

> by the free and solemn consent of representatives of the nation, so that the charter, modified and improved as needed by the agreement of the two chambers and the king, would be converted into a fundamental law of the state.

Jullien concludes this advice to the electors (which was of course meant also as advice to the king and the public) with half a dozen pages restating what he had tried to say to Napoleon a few weeks before. There is virtually the same numbered list of principles and political and civil rights. There is the same description, verbatim, of the two classes now composing the French people: those who had been active in the Revolution and stressed the need for liberty and equality, and those who had suffered from the Revolution and now yearned for security and order.

The second of the two pamphlets of August 1815 restates more briefly the ideas expressed in the first, but is notable for two newer points: a more explicit repudiation of "revolutionary spirit" and the entrance of the word "Bonapartism" into French political language. It is now the extreme royalists and the Bonapartists who are the real revolutionaries.

The citizens called upon to exercise the electoral right . . . should fear above all the *revolutionary spirit* that has caused us so many evils, and prevent men in whom this spirit predominates from arriving in the Chamber of Deputies, where they would inevitably stifle true patriotism, justice and reason. . . .

But may it not be believed that this *revolutionary spirit*, the fertile germ of our troubles, would be no less pernicious, antisocial and destructive to morality and virtue in 1815 than it was in 1793, and that it is more active and dangerous today in the camp of the old royalists than among the partisans of a liberal and constitutional system? The former, in effect, want to reclaim the properties of which the Revolution despoiled them; they want to wreak vengeance for the evils they have suffered; they cannot yield to their passions without troubling the social order again. The latter wish to keep the properties acquired under guarantee by the laws and maintain the present institutions that the Charter has consecrated. (The principal bases of these institutions are set forth in my previous tract on the coming elections.)

Of these two classes, I ask any honest man which is the more likely to expose us to new chances of revolutions? . . .

Bonapartism, which some bitter and impassioned men would make into a party label and ground for proscription, applying it in a vague, arbitrary, senseless and dishonest way to the very persons that Bonaparte constantly persecuted [read: M.-A. Jullien], is by its most exact definition a system of terrorism, absolute despotism, suppression of all liberty, destruction of all social guarantees, whose results we have learned to appreciate, by long and cruel experience, from the imperial regime of odious memory. . . .

Let us refuse our vote to those true and dangerous *Bonapartists*, those over-excited *revolutionaries* who would wish, under whatever banners, to substitute arbitrary power, or a reign of anarchy and license, for the regular and peaceable rule of law. . . .

We have a wise and enlightened *King*, who wishes to found a constitutional and temperate monarchy. We have a strong and united *Ministry*, which will be the more inclined to enforce an impartial justice the more it is shielded from agitation. It is no less essential to have a calm but energetic *Representative Body*, entirely free from all spirit of faction, whose sole and dominant passion is for the public good, in love of country and of the king. The dearest interests and most sacred duties of the Electoral Colleges depend on the wisdom of their choice; they are *responsible to the whole of France*.

Several observations can be made on these pamphlets of August 1815. "Revolution" now means breakdown and disorder, not a high-minded struggle to bring on a better world. And although Jullien devoted many pages to describing the qualities to be looked for in candidates for the Chamber of Deputies, these qualities are singularly bland. He offers no program, no suggestions on how members of the Chamber should vote on disputed issues. It is simply a choice between good men and bad. Private interest is likely to be corrupt. The Chamber should be composed of patriotic, unselfish, disinterested, and right-thinking men who belonged to no faction. Legitimacy of party is not recognized. Contention and a clash of interests are to be avoided. What is wanted is unity, that is agreement, on measures to promote the welfare of the nation, which is regarded as obvious. Such advice was a surviving shadow of the idea of virtue, which since Machiavelli and Montesquieu had been said to be necessary in republics, and which Robespierre had associated with the Terror.

At this time also, late in 1815, to prove that he had never been a Bonapartist, he made public the papers that he had written privately during the Napoleonic years. He did so, as already explained, by showing them to Friedrich Schoell to put into Schoell's final volume of documents "to disabuse the French" from their attachment to Napoleon. It is hard to see why he used a pseudonym in this volume of Schoell's collection; perhaps it was from embarrassment at his own tergiversations, but he undoubtedly let some persons know of his authorship, which he publicly claimed a few years later. In any case, one could now see in print what Jullien had privately written to Bonaparte in 1800 and 1804 containing advice that Bonaparte ignored; the notes written only for himself deploring the course taken by the Empire; and the *Preserver of Europe* of October 1813 urging the Allies to press on until Napoleon was driven from power. Naturally he did not give Schoell what he had written in Napoleon's favor, and in fact published, during the Hundred Days.

The elections produced the opposite of what Jullien desired, a Chamber with a majority of ardent enemies of the Revolution and Empire. A "white terror" broke out in which various persons designated as Jacobins or Bonapartists were assassinated. For Jullien the atmosphere became inhospitable if not dangerous, and in 1816 he went off to Switzerland, where he visited his friend Pestalozzi and wrote another book on education. He remained outside of France for eighteen months.

Louis XVIII and his ministry, as Jullien would wish, managed with some success to hold the counterrevolutionary fervors in check, so that when Jullien returned to France in 1817 the country enjoyed a more uninhibited parliamentary life and more freedom of the press than at any time since the early years of the Revolution. Jullien therefore published another *Manuel électoral* in 1817, reprinted in 1818, and still another in 1824. It would be too repetitious to set forth their contents, which were always the same: that France should loyally accept a mild and beneficent constitutional monarchy; that deputies should be men of conscience and reason, free from faction, intrigue, obstinacy, and vindictiveness; and that extremists should not be elected, neither partisans of the Old Regime on the one hand nor vaguely described revolutionary troublemakers on the other. No fear of the popular or working classes is expressed. The only class consciousness is feeling against the old aristocracy. The word "democracy" has disappeared from Jullien's lexicon. There is no demand for a widening of the narrow suffrage. The very watchwords of French liberalism at this time fall from his pen. His advice in 1815 calls for the *juste milieu*, and in 1824 he concludes his fifty-page *Directions for the Conscience of an Elector* with a plea for "order and liberty."

> The final result of our revolutions should be neither the destruction and abandonment, nor yet the abuse and exaggeration, of principles which the general spirit of the age has made triumphant. . . . We must combine and mold together in our political organization the two distinct and pronounced opinions of the two great and truly estimable classes that constitute the nation. Some want LIBERTY above all else; they prefer even a stormy liberty to a tranquillity that would lead to servitude. Others want ORDER above all else; to obtain it they would if necessary sacrifice even the guarantees of liberty, which they too readily confuse with the excesses committed in its name. To reconcile these two elements, ORDER and LIBERTY, is the problem to be solved.
>
> *The organization of a well-regulated liberty*, which is simply the spirit and letter of the Charter, or the full application of its principles, is both the base and crown of our social edifice, the common goal of apparently contradictory opinions, and the end of the Revolution.

But while Jullien hoped to end revolutionary agitation in France, he looked with favor on it everywhere else. During the wars of the 1790s he had argued for the liberation of Belgium, offered advice to revolutionaries in Italy, and seen signs of republicanism even in England. In the 1820s movements of liberation asserted themselves, or continued, in many places—in Spain, Italy, and Greece; in Russia with the Decembrist revolt; in the struggling new republic of Haiti; in Spanish America from Mexico to Buenos Aires; and in demands everywhere for the abolition of slavery. On these matters Jullien touched frequently in a book of his collected poems, *My Regrets and My Hopes*, published in 1825, and in the *Revue Encyclopédique* which he edited at this time. He himself wrote pieces on these subjects for the *Revue,* and he published book reviews and specialized articles by his contributors. He glorified Kosciuszko as the fighter for freedom in America and Poland, and Lord Byron as the poet whose inspiring work was translated into French, Italian, Polish, and Russian and who died fighting for the independence of Greece. Lafayette's triumphal visit to the United States in 1824 prompted further reflections on the transatlantic spread of struggles for liberty.

The new freedom of the press in France after 1815, such as it was, did not favor the liberals only. It had been one of Napoleon's purposes with press controls to impose silence on both revolutionary and counterrevolutionary polemics. With the new freedom the advantage lay for a while with outright counterrevolutionaries and with former revolutionaries who accused others of excesses.

Jullien was vulnerable to two kinds of these writings. One of these was in new multivolumed biographical dictionaries in which he was included. Against these he published a "Provisional Response" first written in 1819, reprinted in 1821, and again in 1831. He presents himself as the honest man always surrounded by villains, the lonely believer in true liberty. It was at this time also that he began to sign his name as "Jullien de Paris," probably to avoid confusion with his more heavily compromised regicide father, Marc-Antoine Jullien "de la Drôme."

Provisional Response to Some Articles in the Collection of Lies, Defamations and Calumnies Entitled *Biographie Universelle, Biographie des Hommes Vivants, Biographie Moderne,* etc. . . .
By M.-A. Jullien, de Paris

It is characteristic of the philosophical spirit and of a truly generous mind to rise above particular facts to a general consideration of public utility. This thought makes me cite the striking example of the *misunderstandings* that have had such disastrous effects for an isolated individual that I have long observed [i.e., himself]. His whole life has been a long series of cruel vicissitudes, persecutions and misfortunes. . . .

This victim, both proud and timid, wraps himself in the innocence of his conscience as behind an impenetrable shield. He disdains to fight against unjust prejudices and judgments made in anonymous libels, or in perfidious private conversations in which poisons are circulated in the dark. . . .

The numerous agents of this active conspiracy of bad men against good, of mediocre against superior minds, of good men who are deceived against good men who are calumniated and who disdain replying to personal attacks; these gross *misunderstandings*, all too frequent in times of troubles and revolutions, fed by a blind, unjust and intolerant party spirit, have perhaps deprived our country of the citizens most able to support public morality, liberty, virtue and national glory. . . .

It would require the gifts of a great writer . . . with the victorious power of reasoning and the warmth of a keen sensibility, to present the fate of a man distinguished by superior talent and honorable character, but independent and solitary in the world, supported by no party, sect or coterie, abandoned as a dedicated victim to the influence of all kinds of defamations and calumnies, and to be compensated only after his death for the ingratitude and injustice of his contemporaries.

Such was the destiny of the wise Socrates among the Athenians, of the divine founder of Christianity among the Jews, and of the virtuous Malesherbes among the French. . . .

After this astounding piece of self-righteousness, in which nothing whatever is said about the French Revolution, Jullien proceeds to envisage a better time ahead:

All our efforts should go toward that desired era when intrigue and villainy, political prostitution and apostasy, crime and infamy will no longer be the means of enrichment and self-advancement. One of the benefits of representative government, when firmly organized, will be to weaken the empire of prejudices, false ideas and injustice produced by ignorance and by the *misunderstandings* that divide men and corrupt opinion. . . . To favor this progression by legitimate and peaceful methods of education, legislation, public morality properly understood and applied, a widely diffused instruction, persuasion and enlightenment, is the most certain means of extirpating the germ of violent commotions and revolutions by which Europe is threatened.

And as if realizing that such moralizing was not enough, and that the "misunderstandings" should be more clearly specified, Jullien added a postscript when he reprinted this Provisional Response in 1821. He announced an intention to write and publish his memoirs, which in fact he never did.

P.S. I have long felt the need of replying with more positive facts to the mendacious, vague and odious allegations with which the anonymous authors of several biographical sketches have vainly attempted to vilify me. . . . But a complete and faithful record of my conduct for the past thirty years, of the difficult circumstances I have lived through, the honorable persecutions I have suffered under all regimes from 1793 and 1794 to 1815 and 1816, and the cruel vicissitudes that have filled my career, would require much freedom for meditation and recollection, and a long period of time which I am far from having. I must therefore postpone the writing and publication of memoirs which I hope some day to produce at length.

The other writings to which Jullien was vulnerable were the memoirs of men who had taken part in the Revolution. In actuality, Jullien had been too insignificant in the 1790s to be much remembered, or even mentioned, in the recollections that could be published in the freer atmosphere of the Restoration. There were two, however, those of J. B. Louvet and L. J. Gohier, in which enough was said about him to draw his rejoinder.

Louvet, who had died in 1797, had been a member of the Convention and one of the most outspoken and influential of the Girondins. From papers left at his death his editors put together what they called his memoirs and published them in 1824. Louvet in these memoirs called Jullien the murderer of Guadet and the other Girondins and their relatives at Bordeaux in 1794. Jullien sent the editors a letter of protest in over three thousand words. He insisted that the blame for this "atrocious act" had lain with Tallien and Ysabeau and a military commission that they had created. It was this commission, he said, that initiated the search in which the fugitive Girondins were discovered.

> In consequence of this search, during the time I was at Bordeaux, several unfortunate victims were discovered whom the fury of factions sent to their death. I had neither the power nor the will to concur in acts of this nature.

This may be how Jullien remembered it, but it was flatly contrary to what he had said in his report to the Committee of Public Safety of 24 Thermidor of the Year II (11 August 1794), in which, while denouncing Robespierre, he had claimed the credit for the discovery and death of the fugitives at Saint-Emilion. Louvet's memoirs also revived for the 1820s the old charges against Jullien, that as a terrorist he had said that liberty must lie on mattresses for corpses. Jullien insisted that he had been misunderstood, that this libel had been generated while he was in prison (almost dying, he claimed) by the real terrorists, Carrier and Tallien, to save themselves by unloading the blame for excesses on an innocent young man.

> I was detained in prison, and could not know until long afterward the infamous machinations and atrocious and profoundly Machiavellian system, combined with infernal malevolence, that were used to make

an obscure young man, dying in prison of lung disease, into the sacrificial lamb for representatives of the people at Bordeaux who wanted to rehabilitate themselves at his expense. I was accused of speeches at the Club National at Bordeaux in which I used the expression, among others, that "liberty has no bed except mattresses for corpses." But here is the language that I really used: "One of the leading orators of the Constituent Assembly, Mirabeau, let fall these terrible words, 'Liberty has no bed except mattresses for corpses.' Far from us such a bloodstained liberty! Only a virgin liberty free of blood and crimes, the inseparable companion of humanity and justice, is suitable for the French. To make the Revolution loved let us make it lovable."

Men who wished to sacrifice me without knowing me had no scruple in attributing to me maxims that I had rejected. I have learned that the same lying supposition has appeared in several current biographies, in which anonymous libelers have tried to put an imposing historical form on lies and slanders collected from many pamphlets, often anonymous, published at different periods of the revolution.

It was true that Carrier and Tallien in 1794 intended to discredit Jullien to save themselves from the guillotine. But at La Rochelle and Bordeaux, in his speech on the "dangers of moderatism," put into print in 1794, Jullien had called the phrase about mattresses for corpses "a true saying."

L.-J. Gohier, still living in 1824, published his memoirs in that year. He had been locally active during the Revolution, but his only moment of prominence came for a few weeks in 1799, when he had been a member of the Executive Directory overthrown by the coup d'état of Brumaire. In his memoirs he argued that the constitutional republic, whatever its faults, had been a viable regime that might have survived except for the violent intrusion of a military adventurer. While writing his memoirs he met and talked with Jullien, who told him that he had been the author of the anonymous *Political Colloquy* published shortly after the coup d'état. Gohier then said, in the memoirs, that Jullien had been deceived by Bonaparte and had contributed to Bonaparte's success by writing the *Political Colloquy*. Jullien, replying in a review of Gohier's book, put the blame for Bonaparte's success on the weakness of Gohier and his colleagues. He also justified his own purposes in 1799.

Gohier has persuaded himself in good faith that this author [of the *Political Colloquy*], still a young man when the constitution of the Year III was overthrown, must have been the dupe or even the accomplice of Bonaparte, because he so forcefully pointed out the faults of the Directory, and because he sketched the views and plans of the new government in such a way as to inspire confidence in the future. But M. Gohier has failed to note that the author of this pamphlet, which was mainly historical, presents two interlocutors, A and B, who used words exactly as attributed to them. One of them, Bonaparte himself, developed in his own way the reasons for his conduct and the measures by which, he said, he would reassure the nation and consolidate the republic. The other, all alone in the presence of an absolute and irritable master, was bold enough to speak up as a sincere patriot and warn the new head of state that he would enjoy no security, glory or well-established power except by organizing a free government. This young and courageous spokesman for the truth, who betrayed himself and destroyed his own future to save his country, at a time when so many public men betrayed their country in order to save themselves, paid for this generous imprudence by remaining out of favor during the whole reign of Bonaparte as consul and emperor. In the last months of the empire his liberty and even his life were endangered because of the constant opposition he had manifested against the supreme master's system of ambition and conquest. M. Gohier could not foresee, at the first news of Bonaparte's landing in France from Egypt, that the very existence of the Directory was threatened. He rejected the prophetic advice offered *by the very man he accuses today*. He cannot, in these memoirs, recognize and admit the faults of the government that was entrusted to him, which was overturned without being defended, and whose abrupt fall produced the deplorable results of a prodigious usurpation. No doubt if a man of action, a true statesman, a foresighted, honest and energetic citizen, such as Bernadotte or Marbot, had been M. Gohier's colleague, the conspiratorial general would not have succeeded in his enterprise, the national representation would not have been outraged, violated and annihilated by parricide bayonets, and liberty might have been established in France in a peaceable, regular and durable manner after the vicissitudes of the Revolution.

Here again the note of self-pity mixes with the recollection of fact. Jullien in 1799 had in fact advised Bonaparte to establish a free government, but he had also heartily agreed with Bonaparte's sweeping condemnation of the Directory. In the light of his subsequent services under Bonaparte, and award of the Legion of Honor, it is hardly true, except in his own estimation, that he had thereby "destroyed his own future" or remained "out of favor" under the First Consul and Emperor. It is clear in any case that in the 1820s, as in 1799 and indeed since 1795, he wanted no more revolution in France.

But in 1830 an uprising occurred that was celebrated at the time and has been remembered as the Revolution of 1830. It was a revolution that Jullien could approve of, for it was hardly a real revolution. It was only the overthrow of a king together with his followers and his principles. The violence lasted for only three days, 27–29 July, after which Charles X abruptly fled from France, as he had fled forty-one years earlier within a few days after the fall of the Bastille.

Jullien immediately published, under date of 6 August 1830, another piece of advice for whoever would listen, *Le bon sens national*, or the *Common Sense of the Nation*. In it he declared that Charles X had violated the charter of 1814, which was indisputably true. He offered much the same counsel as he had given to Bonaparte in 1799 and to both Napoleon and Louis XVIII in 1815: that the new chief of state would be the stronger by having an explicit mandate from the people. He firmly warned against any attempt at a republic. But he went beyond what the leading liberals had already accomplished in proclaiming the duke of Orleans as provisional Lieutenant-General of the Kingdom. He favored their idea of the duke as king, but only after, not before, a new constitution with a declaration of rights should have defined the royal office and formally conferred it.

Events, as usual, followed Jullien's wishes only in part. There was no wholly new constitution or declaration of rights, nor any express delegation of authority by the people. But the duke took the name Louis-Philippe, a curious neologism, as if to show that he meant to be no Louis XIX or Philippe VII. He adopted the tricolor flag of the Revolution and Empire, called himself King of the French (not "of France"), and consented to some liberalizing changes in the charter of 1814. He became, for his supporters, the "citizen king."

Jullien wrote before these arrangements were quite completed:

The Common Sense of the Nation
6 August 1830

All the newspapers have given the details and results of the heroic week rightly called the *Week of the People*. We have lived more than a century in these last eight days, during which France has resumed its rank as the Great Nation. The mere appearance of counterrevolution, throwing off its hypocritical mask to show its bold and menacing face, was enough to raise up the whole population of Paris in a unanimous and electric upheaval, and almost at the same time the whole population of France. The admirable conduct of the people of Paris, wholly aroused, free, and left to itself without leaders or direction, produced surprise and respect even among those who have so misrepresented the people as to conceive of no popular revolution without a hideous parade of pillage and massacre. No excess, no act of cruelty or vengeance has soiled this great and memorable moment.

The national colors have again provided a rallying point, and the old flag, the cherished symbol of liberty, has produced the most pleasant and lively emotions. . . .

The two names of General Lafayette and the Duke of Orleans today serve to rally all minds, affections and opinions. They express and represent the two great ideas of LIBERTY and public ORDER, the two necessary elements of any durable society. LIBERTY has been conquered by a heroic patriotism. Only ORDER can and should consolidate liberty, prevent internal dissensions and a new shedding of French blood, and ward off any plan of foreign coalition and intervention in our affairs. . . .

We have been carried on by events; let us now know how to remain calm, cool and reasonable, so that events can be better observed, guided and controlled, or used to advantage as they may occur. . . .

The explosion of a long-suppressed discontent, the irritation and wrath of the people, were brought on by the recent excesses of a mad and reckless ministry that broke the social pact and tried to establish absolutism by bayonets, gambling on the blood of citizens when confronted by soldiers. . . .

On *Monday 26 July* the counterrevolutionary ordinances were published. They were met with surprise, affliction, stupefaction and indignation.

On *Tuesday* the first shots were fired by the royal guards and the Swiss. Lancers, cuirassiers and gendarmes treated citizens as enemies, and a veritable Cossack invasion frightened the inhabitants of our peaceable capital, which thought itself protected by the laws. The armed resistance of the people began. On the same day a strong protest against the violation of fundamental law was published by young and courageous writers in the periodical press.

Wednesday was the first day of the barricades and civil war. There was fighting in almost every quarter of Paris. The improvised general insurrection had an admirable character of order and moderation in the midst of disorder and sanguinary fighting in many places. Several cases of courage and heroism, shown by young men and even boys of fifteen or sixteen years, recalled the prodigies of valor of our old soldiers. The students of the Polytechnic took command of hastily formed troops, composed of men badly clothed and hardly armed, whom they led in assaults on barracks, public establishments, guard-houses, the Louvre and the Tuileries, and who captured all the places that they attacked. These brave young leaders inspired respect and confidence, obtained obedience and established discipline in the insurrection, and maintained order and moderation in the victory. . . .

On *Thursday*, while small skirmishes continued in Paris, members of the Chamber of Deputies met at the house of M. Lafitte and named M. Lafayette as commander in chief of the National Guard. . . .

On *Friday* the popular movement received a central direction; local officials and provisional leaders reinforced the spirit and organization of the multitude that had taken the initiative. But already on *Friday* and *Saturday*, while some energetic Deputies were active and braved proscription and death by joining the people, their colleagues, meeting in their usual chamber, seemed more frightened by the insurrection and anxious to stop it than able to understand its significance or profit from the great progress made. Real statesmen would have taken firm action to found liberty and constitutional monarchy on a broad and durable basis, instead of being content with a bad patching up of the charter, which would leave much to be done and bring on new troubles. . . .

They forgot that the same mistake in 1815 had been the ruin of Napoleon, who was more afraid of a free France than of a Europe armed against him. . . .

After detailing what the Chamber of Deputies had failed to do, day by day of the past week, Jullien went on:

Now we must summarize the situation and see what it requires. . . .

1. General Lafayette and the Duke of Orleans, both worthy of the popular cause, are enough to bring together all shades of feeling and opinion. They represent the two great ideas of liberty and order, the necessary elements of a society shaken in its roots. . . .

3. A republican utopia may have seduced ardent imaginations, generous hearts, and admirers of George Washington. But the very word *republic* would frighten pusillanimous or prejudiced minds, and even very enlightened persons, in both France and Europe. A representative monarchy, if it is well constructed, cast in bronze and not molded in plaster, can give us as much liberty as the sternest patriots desire. We become thereby the model of peoples without being the terror of kings. No foreign bayonets will come to serve our fallen throne if by a strong and wise monarchical organization we reassure kings and prove to them that we know how to reconcile monarchy and liberty.

4. But the immediate naming of a king before the constitution to which he should swear has been presented to the nation and confirmed by it would have no less serious consequences. The throne should rest upon and be supported by the law. If you set up a throne before the fundamental law is established you will renew the same

great error that threw France, in 1814, into the trap of a royal charter that was improvised and proclaimed only by royal authority. . . .

5. It is better to remain with our present Chambers, and a Lieutenant General of the Kingdom who offers sufficient guarantees of order and liberty, than to preempt the solemnly and legally expressed will of France as a whole by prematurely adopting incomplete, hazardous or vicious decisions that sooner or later would be overturned by the nation. . . .

6. Men who think only of their own position and personal interests . . . would like to surround the prince with a court that would become a barrier between him and public opinion. They are already hurrying into salons and antechambers to form such a court and obstruct the truth. Can we so soon forget that courtiers were the undoing of Louis XVI, of Napoleon himself, and only yesterday of Charles X? The good sense of the Prince Lieutenant-General of the Kingdom, his character as an honest man and excellent citizen, will be a guarantee against this inrush of courtiers, intriguers and low flatterers that are the plague and scourge of monarchies.

7. If we hasten too quickly to name a king before arranging for the throne to take root in the law and the nation, the throne will be less solid and more easily shaken. What is done too fast is not durable.

A man of common sense and foresight, truthful and energetic [i.e., M.-A. Jullien] addressed such language to heads of government during the Revolution, to Napoleon when he was intoxicated by his own pride, genius and success, and to Louis XVIII and Charles X himself under grave and critical circumstances. This man was said to be factious, a complainer and malcontent; he was dismissed, persecuted, proscribed, and treated as a veritable pariah. The future justified his predictions, and the errors that he pointed out found their due punishment. May his voice not be again ignored! May disinterested advice, inspired only by love of country, not be rejected by a prince worthy of the truth, called to one of the finest roles in history, to march gloriously at the head of a great people and of the civilized world!

9. Today any hasty action would be fatal. The wishes of our departments and of thirty-two million Frenchmen must count for something. . . .

10. We must now give a rallying-point and guarantee for opinion by a *Declaration* or *Bill* of *Rights*, to be accepted and sworn to by the prince lieutenant-general, as the basis for a great national Charter, of which the definitive text cannot be the work of a day, nor of a Chamber that has no special mandate for so important a task.

11. What has triumphed in these recent days in Paris is the cause of order and of the laws, European peace, the freedom of the world and of civilization. Let us not compromise it. This triumph, if wisely and moderately conducted, far from frightening the monarchs, can protect their states from popular commotions and bloody revolutions, if only they can learn this great lesson.

In 1831 Jullien again offered himself as a candidate for the Chamber of Deputies. To support his cause he published a pamphlet, or rather a booklet, of ninety pages addressed to the electors. It consisted of three parts: a survey of the political situation in France, a biography of himself, and an appendix containing sixty-three documents or *pièces justificatives*.

In the survey, besides repeating what he had often said before, he made a specific proposal reflecting his democratic past. He declared that the Chamber of Peers should not be hereditary. It was still hereditary, by the charter of 1814, in that the king appointed the Peers from among men enjoying hereditary nobility, in which nobles of both the Old Regime and the Napoleonic empire were included.

> ... The time has come to bring France out of its present provisional condition, to give an explicit and solemn national sanction to a government born on the barricades, to end an uncertain and embarrassed situation, to constitute definitively one of the great powers of the state [the Peers], which for ten months has been an obstacle rather than a source of strength. By showing open hostility to the new order of things and proclaiming its regrets for the fallen dynasty, it has helped to obstruct the course of government and prolong the general feeling of unease, discontent and irritation that has been evident in several parts of the country.
>
> This Chamber, hereditary until now, should be reconstructed in harmony with a regenerated monarchy, which has recognized that its powers come from the people. ... If the vital principle of popular election, or at least presentation of candidates by the electoral colleges or by the Chamber of Deputies, is accepted, ...and if appointment for life with irremovability should replace the principle of heredity, our constitutional royalty will be strengthened by having deep roots in the nation, instead of depending on an aristocratic body that is removed from public opinion and our way of life. ...
>
> But as the public conscience rejects a hereditary peerage, with which we have had fifteen years of experience, so also the reason of the nation firmly rejects the republic as antipathetic to our opinions, habits and customs. ...

He then briefly lists various other evils to be corrected, and turns to the qualities desirable in candidates for the Chamber of Deputies. They should be the decent, honest and unselfish men such as he had often recommended before. He offers himself as one of them.

> . . . I have consulted my conscience and the memories of a lifetime and of our long revolution. I think myself the faithful interpreter of the sentiments of all good Frenchmen. I have outlined the conduct that I would engage myself to follow if I had the honor to be elected a deputy. . . .
>
> Since we recognize the need to scrutinize the opinions and actions of men called upon to guide the destinies of France, and so influence those of Europe and the civilized world, it should be permitted to a candidate seeking choice by the electors to make known the services he has rendered, the public functions he has discharged, the circumstances he has lived through and the writings he has published, which reflect an honest and open mind. The electors should be all the more attentive to the following materials since the man who now submits to them his conduct, actions and writings has been the object of odious calumnies and honorable persecutions. . . .

And in a footnote he adds that some day he will write his memoirs, claims authorship of the Declaration of Rights of the Chamber of Representatives of 1815, whose demands have been realized in 1830, and goes on plaintively to say that

> perhaps my fellow citizens will think they owe me compensation for what I have suffered by honoring me with their confidence, if they agree with me, by giving me a new opportunity for serving France. . . .

The following biography was only a reprint of a long article in a "Universal Portable Biography of Contemporaries" published in 1829. This article was entirely different from those in the biographical dictionaries against which Jullien had written his "provisional response" in 1819. It was highly laudatory and full of exculpations, and in style and content suggests that Jullien may have written it himself, or at least furnished much detail for use by the editors. It is a main source for our knowledge of his career, but not without misstatements and evasions. On the sensitive point of the death of the Girondins at Bordeaux it denies that Jullien had the powers to order any such executions, and it puts the blame on Tallien, though Tallien had been in Paris in May and June of 1794. On Jullien's activities in Italy in 1797 and 1799 it obscures the fact that he had been a radical democrat at that time. Bonaparte had in fact thought him too radical in favoring a revolutionary republic at Venice, and the Directory had regarded him as too radical in the revolutionary republic at Naples.

The sixty-three documents, which fill over half the pages of this publication of 1831, are a miscellany ranging from a letter of commendation for his "brilliant success" at school, written by the head of his college in 1792, to a letter from Lafayette of September 1830 expressing support for Jullien's candidacy for the Chamber of Deputies. They contain, in between, numerous other complimentary letters and a few more informative sources already used or quoted in the present book.

But all this analysis, apologetics and documentation set forth in 1831 was unavailing. Jullien was not elected to the Chamber. He had to content himself with the activities in which he had been mainly engaged since 1815, as a theorist of education and as a publicist of what he liked to call "civilization."

EIGHT

THEORIST OF EDUCATION

A S A WRITER on education Jullien enjoyed a flurry of post-humous fame about a hundred years after his death. In 1942 he was rediscovered and publicized by an American professor at Teachers College, Columbia University. At about the same time a Swiss professor at the University of Geneva, who was also an official at the International Bureau of Education, singled him out as the father of comparative educational history. In 1948, in Paris, at a centennial observance of Jullien's death, an associate director of UNESCO hailed Jullien as a precursor to that vast (and then new) international enterprise. All these eulogists had in mind those of Jullien's writings that were specifically devoted to education. They showed little interest in his activities during the French Revolution and Napoleonic Empire.

He nevertheless had ideas on education throughout these changing regimes, because for him education was always closely related to politics, or was a branch of political science. During the Revolution "public instruction" meant both schooling for young people and a reorientation of adults to make them citizens of a new kind of society. Jullien, during his missions in western France, had accordingly established political clubs, organized local festivals and patriotic pageants, and even written a political ballet, his *engagements des citoyennes*. He spent a month in Paris in Floréal of the Year II as a member of the Executive Committee on Public Instruction. After the Revolution education became more exclusively concerned with the young, as an activity to be conducted in schools, still with the thought of producing useful members of society, but of a society undergoing progressive improvement rather than revolutionary regeneration. Jullien reflected this transition. In education, as in other respects, he turned from the Jacobin into the liberal. Where he had once seen education as part of the revolutionary process, he came to see it as a substitute for revolution, or as a means by which revolution could be prevented.

But the transition was gradual. It may be remembered that in 1797, as he became more doubtful about the revolution in France, he went off to Italy to serve in the Lombard Legion in Bonaparte's army. Here he hoped that the Cisalpine Republic, newly proclaimed by Bonaparte, might become the vehicle for a better and more successful revolution in Italy than had occurred in France. In his *Notes of Advice to the Cisalpine Patriots* he recommended both a re-education of adults and a better schooling for children. With France and Austria still at war, and the Italian patriots on the side of France, there is a military undertone in both cases.

> . . . **27**. Give institutions to the people to regenerate them. Multiply civic ceremonies having a moral purpose, such as marriage, adoptions, schools or gymnasiums, prize distributions, military exercises, races, games, and numerous assemblies. . . .
>
> **57**. Youth is the age of passions. With youth you will set souls afire, make them volcanic, and so have legions, victories and an Italian Republic. It is because the French neglected national education at the beginning of their political regeneration that young people corrupted by idleness became the instrument of counterrevolution in the hands of royalist reactionaries. Consecrate the principle that children from the age of five belong to their country and should be set apart from society; do not leave them at home unless their fathers have a useful occupation to pass on to them; and even for these children combine the benefits of an education in common with the pleasures and advantages of education at home.

"Education in common," or *éducation commune*, echoes a phrase often heard in Paris in 1793, when one plan, to remove the inequalities arising from family influence, had proposed putting all children into mandatory state boarding schools; this plan, sometimes cited by historians as "Jacobin," had never in fact been approved by Jacobins or sansculottes, or enacted by the Convention.

Two years later Jullien touched on education in the advice he gave to Bonaparte shortly after the coup d'état of 18 Brumaire. In his *Political Colloquy* of 1799, in a list of desirable attributes of the new regime, "a restoration of moral values through education" came between a few words on purely governmental bodies and the reform of taxation. He also advised Bonaparte "to democratize our institutions up to a certain point, to prepare a race of men better than those now existing." Bonaparte had answered: "Yes, no doubt. National education will be cast in a truly popular mold," and had then sketched a plan for highly regimented and militarized schools, to which Jullien made no objection, perhaps because he could not, since Bonaparte went on talking at great length.

In 1801, in his *Appeal to True Friends of the Country*, urging support for the First Consul, he invited his readers to compare the condition of France before the Revolution with what was emerging in the year-and-a-half since Bonaparte had taken over the government. He now developed his thoughts on education more fully. Education was to include all levels, from the highest to the lowest, and to be judged by its usefulness to society.

> The old France made no better use of the talents and minds of its citizens than it did of their arms and hands.
>
> It was covered with schools, colleges and academies. The French language had its own special academy in the capital [the Académie française]. Literature, science, painting, sculpture and music each had its own academy. All the provinces had their academies in rivalry with one another. However numerous, they were never lacking in members. Their very number, their competitions and prizes, the ambition to be admitted and to be crowned, gave birth to an infinity of writers who were removed from agriculture, trade, and the useful arts. The profession of author, in France, was an exclusive, privileged and sterile profession which excused a person from having any other. How many bad writers of worse books might have been good agricultural workers, industrious artisans, active merchants, and useful citizens!
>
> If we examine the different questions that occupied these academies and were treated in books, we find the sciences and arts of pure enjoyment always preferred to those offering real advantages. Wit and manner of writing were valued. Substance was sacrificed to form, ideas to style, things to words, thought processes and choice of material to harmony and grace. Everything was sacrificed to the mania for frivolity.

He then recalls the old *collèges* , such as he had attended himself. He gives them a mixed verdict: their concentration on Latin and Greek had taught liberty and equality, but had also been too much a matter of words. He pronounces this verdict in one of his very long sentences:

> Public education, so admirably organized in some ways, and which planted republican ideas in the bosom of the monarchy; which offered in our colleges so many little states where rank and fortune gave no superiority and merit had to be recognized; where independence and equality were the highest good; where the students, by learning the eloquence of Demosthenes and Cicero and the love of liberty from Trasybulus and Brutus, were constantly transported into an imaginary country and no longer lived in their own; where, as among the Greeks in their Olympic games, the only awards were crowns of laurel and the only passion was the desire for glory, the necessary enemy of despotism; where finally the very games bore the imprint of the ideas in everyone's soul: this public education was

nevertheless not exempt from the general vice of the academies; and the study of languages, which almost exclusively occupied these precious years of childhood, often only prepared those who left school to be literary people, pedants, authors and half-learned persons, and very few to be useful citizens suited for social occupations.

If national education since the Revolution has not yet been coordinated with the political constitution of the state. . . it must nevertheless be admitted that in many respects it has lost much of that frivolity by which it used to be dominated. Our long political discussions, our debates, clubs and assemblies, our parties, and even our misfortunes and proscriptions have turned our minds towards important objects and serious reflections. The various branches of political economy have gained our attention. Agricultural societies have been formed throughout France. Questions of real usefulness have been set as subjects for prizes, and have produced valuable observations. Many discoveries and salutary inventions have shown a creative genius to rival the genius of battles, to make the Republic strong and illustrious.

Talents, liberated from many obstacles, are better employed; they have taken a new flight, and been directed at a greater and nobler goal, the glory and prosperity of the nation.

The most useful occupations have been raised from the scorn and low regard which prevented citizens from entering them.

The parasitic classes that devoured all the others have been diminished or destroyed.

There is now a respect for utility rather than show, for real merit rather than the titles of vanity and a haughty donothingism.

Farm workers have seen the end of tithes, *corvées*, hunting rights, and seigneurial justice. Abundance has come to smile on their labors. The remains of feudalism have vanished. The cottages are less oppressed, and land formerly uncultivated has become productive.

Artisans are less blocked. Competition and rivalry have stimulated industry. Freedom has become a protection for commerce.

It is evident why Jullien thought of education as an aspect of political or social science. The ideas expressed were not his alone. They may be found, more piecemeal, in the educational plans formulated before and during the Revolution, including those of Talleyrand in 1791, Condorcet in 1792, and a plan endorsed by the Paris Jacobins in 1793. They resemble the ideas of Jeremy Bentham and the emerging "Philosophical Radicals" in England. And they reflect a belief that the French Revolution was of economic importance.

The comprehensive educational law of 1802 imposed an organized system on several hundred existing schools, of which in the next ten years only thirty-six became lycées and the rest were designated as "secondary." It left elementary schooling to the vagaries of local government, religion, and private initiative. It could hardly meet with Jullien's approval, especially since Bonaparte became consul for life at about the same time, and emperor two years later. We have seen how in a private note for himself he denounced the lycées as a means of enhancing Bonaparte's personal power, but later accepted them as an accomplished fact and even praised them as an achievement of the imperial government. Indeed, since three of his sons, born in these years, were later admitted to the École Polytechnique, they must have had at least some of their earlier schooling within the system introduced under Napoleon.

It was in the years beginning in 1805, while serving with the French army in Germany, that he began work on his books on education. At Frankfurt in 1806 he printed a short fifteen-page "succinct analysis" of a plan for "using time" which was published in full in Paris in 1808, and grew by its third and fourth editions in the 1820s into a thick volume of 568 pages.

He also in 1806, in Frankfurt, made the acquaintance of Franz-Joseph Gall, a German physician who launched the supposed science of phrenology. According to phrenologists, differences in the exterior surface of the skull, popularly called "bumps on the head," gave evidence of inborn differences in faculties or aptitudes among human beings. Phrenology had a short scientific life, but Gall is favorably remembered as one of the first to attempt a scientific study of localization of functions within the brain. Such a scientific endeavor would appeal to Jullien as an admirer of science, and might offer a scientific explanation of the differences in human abilities. No educational plan during the Revolution had supposed that all persons were mentally equal at birth; the most democratic or Jacobin plan of all, in 1793, had made generous provision "for subjects whose difficult study is not within the capacity of all men." For Jullien the problem was to coordinate different abilities with different social needs. He assisted Gall in a move to Paris, where Gall gave a lecture to a scientific society for which Jullien wrote a commentary when it was published. But he made no reference to Gall or phrenology in his own later writings on education.

His *Essay on the Employment of Time,* first appearing in 1808, proved to be the longest lasting and most widely diffused of Jullien's works. Its title page for the third edition of 1824 made clear both its practical purpose and the imposing credentials of its author: *Essay on the Employment of Time, or Method for a proper regulation of life, the basic means to happiness, designed especially for use of the young, by Marc-Antoine Jullien, of Paris, Chevalier of the Legion of Honor, Member of the Royal Soci-*

ety of Turin [ten more are named] *and several other learned, literary and philanthropic French and foreign societies; Founder-Director of the Revue Encyclopédique.* Jullien was very proud of this work. The copy of the 1824 edition in the Library of Congress is inscribed in his hand "to the Columbian Institution at Washington" (a short-lived learned society in that city) "under the auspices of Mr. Adams, President of the United States."

As a book of 568 pages, *The Employment of Time* hardly lends itself to selection, but a few passages illustrate its relationship to a more widely conceived social science. After much other discourse, Jullien reaches chapter XV, where he develops the conception of intellectual capital.

Chapter XV
On the Two Portions of Time, Distinct In Their Use, of Which Life Is Composed

The public fortune in a state and the fund available to any private person, as has been demonstrated by the famous Adam Smith, who was both a moralist and an economist, are naturally divided into two classes. One is the *fund for consumption*, whose distinctive character is to bring in no income. The second is the fund or *capital* employed to produce an income. . . .

Time used to procure the means of existence . . . is like the fund destined for immediate consumption. The use one makes of it is for necessities; it is driven by need.

The portion of disposable time that can be employed at will, well or badly, is lost for many, who consume it in useless, frivolous or harmful actions. It is employed by some others to develop their physical powers, education or self-improvement. It becomes for them a kind of capital, which is destined to bring in a profit in the future, and also procures the most true and pure enjoyments at the very moment of its use.

And later, in chapter XXXI:

The effective employment of time, men and capital, and generally of wealth of all kinds, material and intellectual, is an essential part of the *art of governing*. The *bad employment* of these three elements of prosperity, characteristic of bad governments, is a vast subject of meditation and affliction for anyone seriously interested in the progress of the social art and the general good of humanity.

To speak only of the *employment of men*, it comes about by a deplorable absurdity that they *are almost never in the right place*; and being always in false positions, they cannot fulfill their true potential, either for society or for themselves. Every man, in effect, may be suited for one definite thing, and quite unsuited for another.

A footnote here suggests a quantitative and somewhat mechanistic measurement of human abilities:

> An individual may have in himself a force or power equal to 100 if in function A, but is obliged to consume or lose this force if employed in what I call function B, where his faculties, badly applied, are hardly equal to 10. Hence a real value of 90 percent is lost for him and for society. He might have been a great *poet*, but is only an inferior *jurisconsult*. He had the talents of a good *administrator*, but is only a mediocre *man of letters*. He could have distinguished and enriched himself as an able *businessman*, but vegetates as a *soldier* in an obscure subaltern rank. The loss is even greater for the state and for government when a position requiring a force or capacity equal to 100 is occupied by a man whose capacity is only 10.

And returning to the main text:

> Certain inborn primitive abilities can be distinguished, which it is the concern of religion, education, legislation and morality to develop, direct or modify, but which always retain a great influence. Every person may succeed in what is analogous or relative to his own organization. The essential is to be employed precisely in the sphere for which we are suited. . . .The lowliest occupations are raised and ennobled by the same principle. The *worker*, *artisan*, or simple *shoemaker* who would excel in his trade should take pride in it and even exaggerate its utility. It is by the work of the shoemaker that communication among men becomes easier, a greater activity is imparted to commerce, and armies march rapidly over great distances. Every occupation should seem honorable to those who pursue it. Everyone should pursue, so far as possible, the occupation for which he is most qualified and which is attuned to his tastes and talents.
>
> Happy is he whose *destinée* allows him to fulfill his *destination*!

The play upon words here in French cannot be reproduced in English, where the word "destination" lacks the scope of its French twin. The idea is clear enough. Happiest is the person whose destiny, or fate in life, allows him to work at a task for which his powers seem to be "destined" or suited. Jullien was well aware that few people were so fortunate. But he believed that with the progress of civilization, and of education, more would become so.

The voluminous contents of the *Essay on the Employment of Time* were digested at the end in an elaborate table, composed of blank spaces which the user was to fill in every day. Vertical blank columns were crossed by horizontal lines, one for each day of the month. The column to the left was for noting the weather. The next three columns, under the category of *Physical*, were for noting the hours spent in sleep, eating and exercise; the next three, under *Moral*, were for recording the hours given to meditation, family life, and domestic management; the next three, under *Intellectual*, were for hours spent on professional concerns and various kinds of reading; and the next four, under *Social*, were for the hours in conversation, visits, letter writing, and travel. A wider and final right-hand column was reserved for comments on one's use of the day. Hours added up horizontally would total twenty-four, and addition of hours in a column would show the time spent in that category for a week, a month, or any period of time.

This table, with adaptations, and with or without other passages from the *Employment of Time*, was printed and reprinted under various titles, most often as a *Biomètre*, once as a *Thermomètre*, or again as a *Mémorial Horaire*, and alternatively as a *Montre morale*, or moral timepiece. It was translated and published in English, German, Italian, and Russian over some twenty years. A *Biometer, or Moral Watch*, appeared in English at London as late as 1833.

A reviewer of the *Employment of Time* claimed that Jullien's table was derived from Benjamin Franklin, whose autobiography had been translated and published in Paris in 1798. Franklin there told how, as a young man, he had defined thirteen virtues in which he had tried to train himself, and had devised a boxlike table in which he recorded his progress (or regression) in each virtue for each day of the week. Jullien was in fact well aware of Franklin's autobiography. In his other book of 1808, the *General Essay on Education*, published soon after the *Employment of Time*, he referred to Franklin several times (as to John Locke and others), and reproduced in a long note about a dozen pages of the French translation of Franklin's autobiography, complete with the boxlike table of virtues. It is not possible to say whether Jullien got the idea for his own table from Franklin, or only brought in Franklin to add prestige to his own invention. He later declared, rightly enough, that his table was more detailed, systematic, and far larger than Franklin's.

Jullien hoped, as already observed in chapter 5 above, that his *General Essay on Education* would be useful to the organizers of the Imperial University. Its purpose was to improve society by improving the education of an upper class of decisionmakers and power-holders, or, in the words of the title page, "the first families of the State."

Never hesitant to repeat himself, he incorporated much of his earlier book into this new one. He also spent many pages in debating matters that had long been debated in France, such as the relative merits of private and public education ("private" meaning education at home with a tutor, and "public" meaning at a *collège* or the like), which had been discussed at least since Charles Rollin's *Traité des études* of 1732; and the question of whether civilization was a good or bad thing for human beings, which had been discussed at least since Rousseau's *Discourse on the Arts and Sciences* of 1750. Jullien came out firmly on the side of public education and civilization, with which, in fact, few at the time would disagree. He admitted, however, that one of the bad effects of civilization was to divide people into two social classes. His classes, somewhat as in the "socialism" of his contemporary, the Marquis de Saint-Simon, were the idle and useless persons on the one hand, and on the other the workers or useful persons, including not only workers in a later sense but all those who labored productively in professional, governmental, and managerial positions.

On the March of Civilization and Its Consequences

Civilization is in the nature of man, one of whose distinctive characteristics is sociability. It is a mixture of good and bad, like all human things. But its advantages greatly outweigh its drawbacks. We must try to improve it, to diminish the evils produced by it and impacted in it, and augment the benefits that it can diffuse over society and the human race.

The *division* and *employment of men* are both the principal consequences and in turn the most important causes of civilization and its progress.

Our civilized societies are divided into two great classes. One includes the idlers (*les oisifs*), or those who do nothing, and who live by the work and sweat of the others. "In politics as in morality, says Rousseau (whose opinion seems indeed overstated), it is a great evil not to do good; and every useless citizen can be regarded as a pernicious being." In the second class are the workers (*les travailleurs*), or those who are active and industrious. But this class itself is subdivided into two sections: first, those whose work and activity produce useful results; and second, those whose activity is not only sterile and unfruitful but harmful. The number of these latter is unfortunately only too great. Even among those occupied in useful work there are many who are not engaged in work for which they are suited [here he has a note citing his *Employment of Time*], and whose activity is therefore a pure loss or less productive than it would be if they were better employed. Many others are obliged to use their powers in work I call *negative*, although necessitated by the nature of things in society. Such are the judges, administrators, priests, physicians, etc., who render important services and whose functions are necessary, but whose number should not be disproportionate to the real needs of society, since they consume the product of the work of others while producing nothing of immediate value themselves. This class must be kept within proper bounds, so as not to encourage the growth of this part of the social body, or give it an artificial girth which is harmful to other parts of the body.

In our present societies hardly a twentieth of the population is employed in really productive work. This twentieth must support and nourish by its labor all the others, namely, the useless idlers, the misplaced workers, and the unproductive.

Let us restore the proportion for the benefit of society. Let us bring more art and wisdom to the arrangement of individual and general activity, which is now often badly conducted and applied. Let us make a great combined effort, multiply our powers a hundredfold, and employ them better. We have so far raised only a very small part of the veil in which nature hides herself.

Instead of condemning civilization we must seize what it provides that is good and useful, the means and resources that it offers, and above all strive to improve it by a better understood application of these three great moral and political forces: *the division of labor, the employment of time*, and *the employment of men*.

Like the *Employment of Time*, the *General Essay on Education* was summarized in an enormous tabulation, in this case running for many pages, with one table for each year of age up to 24. Where in the *Employment of Time* the table is left blank for the user to fill in, in the *General Essay* the columns are crammed with small print telling what the young person should learn. For each year there are columns for Physical, Moral, and Intellectual Education. The advice is given in the second person singular, as if addressed to a parent, tutor, or teacher. Here, for example, is the program for Intellectual Education, beginning with the 17th year, or at age 16:

> You arrive this year at *modern history*, and you continue to follow with your pupils a theoretical and practical course in social economy, having them observe in the annals of nations the causes of their rise and decline, their progressive, retrogressive or stationary condition, the principles of public administration and the true foundations of the wealth, power and well-being of empires. . . .

Over five hundred words follow in this column on what the young person should learn from modern history. Then at age 17 (he is now thinking only of the boys) the pupils

> should spend a year in a regiment or camp, or on a naval vessel, to extend and apply their knowledge of mathematics and algebra, to make a serious study of tactics and military science and of attack, defense and fortification. . . .

and of the discipline, supply, accounting, etc. necessary in a military unit, with readings from Julius Caesar, Frederick the Great and others.

> After the year of novitiate in a regiment each of your pupils passes the first six months of his 19th year (or 20th if he remains two years in military service) in the office of a notary, trial lawyer or other legal practitioner to acquire at least a general knowledge of legislation, the affairs of civil life, the operation of the law-courts . . . the laws relating to fidelity in engagements, guarantee of property rights, sanctity of contracts . . . to be able to avoid the pitfalls that lie in wait for ignorance, candor and good faith. . . .
>
> The other six months of the 19th (or 20th) year are used for employment with an experienced and reputable banker, who often has widespread connections. Your pupils will there obtain ideas on commerce and its procedures, on the relationships that it establishes among peoples, and on the object and influence of commerce and the kind of protection it has a right to expect from the government. They will thus complete their course in political economy, which develops their reason and judgment, lets them see things both in the mass and in all details, and understand the mechanism and workings of the political administration of society.
>
> The pupil also continues during this year to speak German and English, or if he became at ease in one of these languages the year before, to turn to the study of the other.

The young man, now nineteen years old, is next to spend a year in gaining some knowledge of medicine, anatomy, surgery, and pharmacy, and then spend three or four years in foreign travel, under an experienced *gouverneur*, and to come to understand other peoples and sharpen his powers of observation. He has also, since childhood, following the columns for Physical and Moral, become healthy and vigorous and acquired humane values and feelings. Finally, this paragon will choose some fixed occupation suited to his taste and abilities, in which he will avoid the superficiality of pretending to know everything, will be useful to humankind, and promote social advancement.

Jullien says nothing on the question, vital to any such a planned society, of how his pupil's individual choice and particular qualifications are to be exactly coordinated with the multifarious needs of society. Nor is it likely that any real person was ever educated according to the abundantly detailed program that he set up.

It will be asked what he said about the education of women. In fact, the *General Essay* actually begins with this subject, in the form of twenty lines of verse "On the Influence of Women." These verses introduce the book, says the author, "because of the empire that nature and society accord to them as women, wives and mothers." That he thought the power of women very great is evident in many of his writings. No doubt he had not forgotten his own mother. Much of the *General Essay*, especially in his categories of Physical and Moral, could apply to both sexes, and in the Intellectual category with some modification. Since women were so influential, both in bringing up their children and in their impact on husbands, grown sons, and other male associates, it was important that they too should be strong and healthy, have keen moral sensibilities, and be literate, intelligent, and reasonably well informed. All this was well within the usual wisdom of the day, and possibly more generally accepted in France than in some other countries, though hardly in line with the thinking of more positive feminists of that time or later.

In 1810, falling out of favor with Napoleon, Jullien was sent off to the Napoleonic kingdom of Italy, the region of Lombardy and Venetia where Prince Eugène was Napoleon's viceroy. Still occupied with administrative affairs of the army, Jullien considered this move a demotion, one of his "cruel vicissitudes," but Prince Eugène gave him a warm welcome, and soon granted him a three-month leave of absence. As author of two recent books on education, Jullien used this free time for a visit to Switzerland to observe the famous school conducted by J. H. Pestalozzi at Yverdon. The school had pupils from various countries, and was often visited by important persons from all over Europe. Jullien spent over two months there, talking with Pestalozzi, interviewing the teachers, and sitting in classrooms. He did so with difficulty, which he acknowledged, since the language of the school was German, which Jullien could not understand, and Pestalozzi and his assistants spoke only an imperfect French. He nevertheless was so favorably impressed that in 1811 he put his two older sons at the ages of seven and nine into Pestalozzi's school, where they remained for five years. He also produced a book in two volumes, *The Spirit and Educational Method of Pestalozzi*, which was published in French at Milan in 1812.

In 1812 the Grand Empire still stood, since the invasion and disaster in Russia came only later in that year. Jullien begins his book by paying his respects to Napoleon, perhaps to advance his own prospects, and perhaps with a lingering belief that the Empire provided a means for the advancement of civilization in Italy and all Europe.

> The time and place of publication of this work seem favorable. The place is in the heart of Italy, . . . while this fair country is seeing in the various parts of its territory the organization of a great many educational establishments for both sexes, whose creation is due to its immortal regenerator [Napoleon] and to the young and august Prince [Eugène], the adopted son of this great Monarch, and in the midst of newly born institutions designed to form a generation of new men to revive the national glory and virtues. It is in this Italy that a Frenchman who followed the victorious banners of the first Army of Italy [Jullien in 1797] comes to pay his feeble tribute to the great work of an improved education. The *Imperial University* of France, which embraces all human culture in its vast domain, together with its illustrious chief whose mission is to work tirelessly to perfect teaching of all kinds, will perhaps not disdain to welcome and examine the Method [Pestalozzi's] that I explain.

The book expounds the Method at length, that is, Pestalozzi's objectives and procedures, which Jullien believed to resemble the programs he had outlined in his two books of 1808. In fact, Pestalozzi's school, and hence Jullien's description of it, departed in significant ways from the main ideas in Jullien's earlier books. Jullien had previously stressed social needs and social utility, and thought of education as part of the political or social sciences. Pestalozzi, more in the Rousseauist tradition, stressed the self-development of the individual. With much discussion of definitions, classifications, and interrelationships, and his usual verbosity, Jullien finds twelve "principles" in the Method, of which the following are examples:

Fourth Principle
Complete Liberty in Development of the Natural Faculties or Inclinations and the Individuality of Each Pupil

> The *fourth general* principle, whose germ is contained in the preceding, and especially in the *first* and *third*, consists in allowing a full development of the original faculties and inclinations of each pupil as they reveal and express his true nature. Each inclination shown by the child furnishes the signs needed for directing it well; and since it then is one of the results of training it becomes also the means. The child grows and in a way instructs himself; the teacher is only the external means of development and instruction.

Education should make each child capable of rising to all the perfection that his physical, moral and intellectual nature allows. Each teacher, required by the principles and laws of the Method to study, recognize and respect the particular character of each of his pupils and the freely manifested expression of each one's nature, observes with a kind of reverence this nature revealed in them. The teacher regards himself not as the master to influence or direct this nature, but as a minister to serve it; he notes its impulses, satisfies its needs, obeys its laws; he lets the germs existing in each of his pupils develop by themselves; he restricts himself to following and supporting their march, progress, and action. . . .

It is important here for the teacher to use scrupulous care and great insight in studying and discerning the *basic inclinations* that pertain to free development of the child, as distinct from *secondary propensities* or caprices. All too often, by a strange aberration that has deplorable consequences, an ordinary educator stifles a child's real inclinations by yielding to his fantasies or bad and harmful wishes; he enchains the true freedom of nature by accepting deceptive appearances. Delicate tact, sure judgment and careful habits in the observation of children are necessary in the application of these distinctions.

Fifth Principle
Harmony between the Development of Faculties and Acquisition of Knowledge, or Instruction

This principle has as its object to combine the development of faculties, or *what one is capable of*, with the acquisition of knowledge, or *what one learns*, and so to give children an intimate consciousness of the auxiliary resources that instruction adds to their natural powers. . . .

At the same time as one studies in each child the first appearance of each inclination or natural faculty . . . one sets beside each faculty, according to its progressive growth, the body of knowledge that is analogous to its nature and aim. Each level of instruction, in each branch of knowledge, is always proportioned to the strength and capacity of the corresponding faculty. The horizon of knowledge and intelligence is enlarged in proportion as the faculties of mind develop and intellectual power becomes stronger. . . .

In ordinary modern education the effort is too often limited to *instruction* in the strict sense, without effective attention to *education* in the broad sense, so that the instruction becomes superficial, insufficient and empty. And even in instruction itself the *acquisition of knowledge* is seen as the principal aim, and the *development of faculties* is seen as a purely secondary byproduct, necessarily neglected. The result is often to give *knowledge* to pupils whose *faculties* are quite undeveloped.

By the Method, on the other hand, the *development of faculties* receives special treatment, as an essential and fundamental objective achieved by well-directed gradual and continuous action. The intellectual faculties are exercised and augmented at the same time as knowledge is acquired. . . . Some pupils who have spent only a few years at the Institute leave it with a small fund of acquired knowledge but with a real development of their natural faculties which is quite advanced and complete for their age.

It may be said in general that the *development of faculties*, neglected in ordinary education, receives a religious attention at M. Pestalozzi's Institute, while the *acquisition of knowledge, or instruction*, the special and even exclusive aim of all other educational establishments, may be somewhat neglected at the Institute. This fine but accurate distinction . . . is one of the principal differences between our Method and other methods of education and instruction.

Jullien notes the difference between this theory of education and a theory arising from the sensationalist psychology, in which the mind at birth was seen as a *tabula rasa* or blank tablet to be written on by sensory perception of the environment.

Sixth Principle
A Method of Education Essentially Positive

Education, as viewed by the Method, should not attempt at an early age to instil opinions suited to this or that form of society, which most often tends to generalize its errors and vices and produce false thinking and corrupted hearts. . . .

The Method is essentially positive in all its operations. It looks for the first germs of *development*. . . . It is based on a truth furnished by experience and confirmed by multiple observations, that human nature is itself essentially *positive*, that is, creative and endowed with a productive power . . . and not *negative* or limited to the ability to receive impressions by the act of *perception*, as seems to have been established by Locke, Condillac, Helvétius, and almost all modern philosophers who have written on education. These philosophers, for not having penetrated deeply enough into the inner nature of man, have seen in it only a receptacle to be filled rather than recognizing a fertile germ able to develop by itself.

He recognizes Rousseau as an exception, as one who penetrated to the inwardness of human beings, but who egregiously erred in rejecting the importance of knowledge and repudiating the impact of society.

The rest of the *Spirit of the Educational Method of Pestalozzi* is occupied by treatment of the nine remaining "principles," twelve "distinctive characteristics," and an account of the several subdivisions of Pestalozzi's school, including an institute for girls, who are to be brought up to be intelligent advisers and companions for men, good mothers, skilled household managers, and mistresses of private life.

Pestalozzi's school ran into difficulties, one of which was disagreement between him and his coworkers, some of whom went off to set up schools elsewhere, in one case at Naples and in another at Philadelphia, where Joseph Neef founded the "Pestalozzian movement" in the United States. Jullien withdrew his sons from Pestalozzi's school in 1816, perhaps because of its internal troubles, and perhaps because he had concluded that Pestalozzi's teaching methods were best suited only for younger children.

He also at this time met and admired P. E. Fellenberg, another former associate of Pestalozzi's, who had established his own school at Hofwyl, also in Switzerland. With Fellenberg and others he helped to establish a Society for Elementary Instruction in Paris, which sponsored a new periodical, the *Journal d'Éducation*. For this journal, Jullien wrote a series of articles, in which he saw Fellenberg's establishment at Hofwyl as an improvement on Pestalozzi's at Yverdon. Fellenberg, he thought, more than Pestalozzi, shared a belief that Jullien had expressed in his *General Essay* of 1808, that for a productive and stable society it was best for different social classes to have different kinds of schools. He remained seriously concerned for the education of manual workers, but was most interested in producing future leaders in all useful spheres of society.

> The establishment formed by M. Fellenberg, at Hofwyl near Berne, which has now existed for more than ten years, is composed of three distinct schools:
>
> **1.** A *school of industry for the children of the agricultural and laboring classes*, who are to be carefully shaped to habits of work, sobriety, and economy, to make them better and more happy in the position in which they are destined to live.
>
> **2.** An *institute of education for the children of the upper and middle classes of society*, to which are brought all the resources for a liberal and complete education.
>
> **3.** A *school of theoretical and practical agriculture* for educated farm owners, capable of making the most of the rural properties whose exploitation will later be entrusted to them.
>
> In the organization and direction of these three establishments M. Fellenberg has proposed four political objectives of the highest importance:

1. To make the condition of the lower and laboring classes of society more pleasant and happy by assisting in their acquisition of knowledge favorable to the development and progress of industry; thus gradually to advance civilization without compromising public tranquillity and social order, by neutralizing the corrosive passions of ambition and envy, which have played a great part in our political upheavals.

2. To bring together, under the influence of a shared education, and to make them have a deep feeling of good will and love of humanity, a certain number of the children of leading families of different nations who will later help to cement union and peace among their respective countries.

3. To raise up the condition of agricultural workers and artisans and strengthen the social structure; uproot the seeds of corruption; introduce and propagate improvements in agriculture and the mechanical arts; elevate the profession of teaching, whose lack of recognition is bad for education itself; and finally, as the estimable Pestalozzi would wish, to arouse in individuals of all social classes the sentiment of human dignity, the prime source of all morality. . . .

4. To prepare good teachers for the primary schools, able professors for the higher and scientific schools, good elementary books for all branches of human knowledge, and in short a complete system . . . with appropriate modifications for the particular and special needs of the different classes of society.

In the school for the laboring classes the pupils are to learn reading, writing, and arithmetic "by the method of mutual teaching" in which older children teach the younger (called the Lancastrian system at this time in England and the United States); some elementary geometry; mechanical drawing; history and geography; and singing and music. They will also receive religious and moral instruction throughout, and learn to swim. The French government or philanthropic private persons, says Jullien, should do what the governments of Russia, Poland, Prussia, and other German states are already doing—that is, send young men to work with either Fellenberg or Pestalozzi to prepare themselves as teachers in rural and elementary schools.

This measure, which seems of great importance, especially after our long and disastrous revolutions that have loosened all religious, moral and social ties, deserves the attention of a minister who is a statesman and a man of good will.

Fellenberg's school "for children of rich or well-to-do families" consisted of twenty-two teachers for about sixty students from seven to twenty years old, drawn from several European countries. It was a model for an elite boarding school:

> Discipline is mild, fatherly and benevolent. Penalties and rewards are useless and unknown. The only punishments are mild reproaches. M. de Fellenberg, like M. Pestalozzi and for the same reasons, has banished the use of competitive compositions and the emulation which is thought necessary in other institutions but is often corrupting and dangerous.
>
> There is no rivalry or distinction of ranks. Pupils do not compare themselves with their comrades; pride and vanity are not aroused. . . .
>
> The teaching of the ancient languages, Greek and Latin, and of the modern languages, German, French, Italian and English, is combined with the study of the geography and history of each country. History is taught along with languages and religious and moral instruction. The languages are taught solidly and completely, as so many methods of analysis invented by the human mind. Almost nothing is learned by heart; historical facts and other pieces of knowledge are so presented as to arouse interest, gain attention, develop the mind, form the judgment, penetrate the heart and engrave every newly acquired notion in the understanding.
>
> Calculation and mathematics are taught by Pestalozzi's method, first of all by exercises in the head to strengthen the faculty of thought, then by the use of written numerals and algebraic signs, all shown in relation to logic. The professor takes the pupils separately in small groups, according to their level of progress, so that each in a way builds up the science for himself.
>
> Perspective drawing is connected with geometry and mathematics, and also with historical studies and natural history.
>
> Lessons in natural history, most often given in the open country, are of lively interest to the students.
>
> Singing and music have a moral objective. Every Sunday the pupils of the two schools are assembled and sing together. It is the only connection that exists between the two schools.

To summarize, and to justify the use of such diverse and separate schools as models for a general reform of education:

> We must start at the point where we are, take men, things and the state of society as they now exist, and give no reasonable ground for alarm to those who oppose innovations. Methods, schools and levels of instruction should meet the present needs of each class of which society is composed. The distinction between rich classes and poor

classes, a necessary consequence of social life, should be considered in education. Only, however, with the proviso that any individual privileged and endowed by nature with a superior merit should find an easy access to a higher condition than that in which he is born. The preeminence given to virtues, talents and services rendered to society is a matter of justice and is in the true interest of society itself. It therefore appears unfounded to reproach M. de Fellenberg for an oligarchic tendency in the differential organization of his two great schools.

Jullien undoubtedly believed in the desirability of upward social mobility, careers open to talents, and an "easy access," in his words, for gifted poor youths to rise into higher positions. But he has nothing to say, and quotes nothing from Fellenberg, about the means by which such access might be provided. A system of scholarships for boys needing financial assistance had existed in France before the Revolution, was much discussed during the Revolution, and was incorporated into Napoleon's university. Jullien never proposed any such system.

He spent most of the year 1816 in Switzerland, after the elections of 1815 made life less comfortable in France for persons with his political antecedents. During this time he not only became acquainted with Fellenberg and his school at Hofwyl but also wrote the fifth and last of his more memorable works on education. It was a short book, or pamphlet, published shortly after his return to Paris in 1817, and entitled *A Sketch and Preliminary View of a Work on Comparative Education.* The diversity among schools in the cantons of Switzerland, differing as they did in language, religion, and degree of urbanization, gave him the idea for a vast comparative survey that might be extended to all Europe. It would take the form of a detailed questionnaire to be sent to all governments willing to participate. Since Russia, Prussia, and others had already sent official visitors to Pestalozzi's school, he assumed that many or most states might join in such a common project. He even hoped for support by the Holy Alliance, which, recently formed to oppose Napoleonic and Revolutionary sentiment, was not yet seen by liberals as a reactionary coalition. Indeed, our liberal was now himself a "reactionary" against events of the past twenty-odd years.

The questionnaire was to be administered by a proposed international commission. The replies to it would be digested into a huge system of tables, by which each country could see the strengths and weaknesses of its own educational institutions, and so have a guide to what was feasible in planning for improvements. Jullien proposed six categories of questions: elementary education; secondary and classical education; higher and scientific education; normal schools to train teachers; girls' schools; and the relation of education to the laws and institutions of each country. He offered as an example 120 questions in the first category on elementary schools, and 146 questions in the second category for the secondary level. He said that he would soon provide questions for the remaining four categories, but he never did so.

He prefaced his numbered list of questions with a twenty-page explanation of his purpose. It opened with a statement in which educational reformers before and since 1817 might hear a congenial voice:

> Any sensible man observing the moral state of the different countries of Europe will see with regret that the education given today, whether in the family or in public schools, is all too often incomplete, defective, and without continuity or connection among the various levels through which it must pass, without consistency within itself in the *physical*, *moral* and *intellectual* spheres in which pupils should be guided in the same spirit toward the same goal; in short, without proportion to the real needs of children and young people, to their place in society, or to the public needs of nations and governments.
>
> An interesting and instructive book could be written from all the complaints, unfortunately too well grounded, made by men of superior understanding from Montaigne and Bacon to Rollin, Franklin and Basedow. Such a work would not be a simple, sterile and aimless compilation, but a well-organized collection of observations and experience on a matter of interest to everyone. It is always useful to point out the obstacles to private happiness and the prosperity of states. But a work that showed actual results, more immediately useful and important, would be a comparative table of the principal educational establishments that exist today in the various countries of Europe. . . .
>
> It is ignorance, forgetfulness and violation of all duties, the loosening and dissolution of all religions, moral and social bonds, the extreme corruption and degradation of hearts and minds, that have produced the cruelly prolonged revolutions and wars whose frightful consequences have desolated all the countries of Europe.
>
> It is by extirpating this corruption . . . by a return to religion and morality in their true sense. . .and by a wisely conducted reform of public education . . . that new troubles and recurring calamities can be prevented. . . .

Education, like all other arts and sciences, is composed of facts and observations. It thus seems necessary to produce for this science, as has been done for the other branches of knowledge, collections of facts and observations arranged in analytical tables, so that these facts and observations can be compared and certain principles and definite rules deduced from them, so that education may become an almost positive science. . . .

He goes on to say that so wide-ranging a project needs the sponsorship of the enlightened princes of Europe, that meanwhile he will first attempt to employ it in Switzerland as a microcosm of religious and linguistic differences, and that national prejudices against foreigners must be overcome. He surmises that there may be some hesitation to take advice from a Frenchman, since "France became, by an inconceivable chain of circumstances, the main instrument of the misfortunes of Europe, and of its own ruin."

But being a foreigner is a kind of guarantee of independence and impartiality. . . .

When a Frenchman, whose mind is old by experience but still young in energy and purity of feeling, and who is already known for several philosophical works on *The Employment of Time*, on *Physical, Moral and Intellectual Education*, and on *The Educational Method of Pestalozzi*, now presents the first sketch for a good and useful work on *comparative education*, which may be extended and applied to all European nations, why should there be any refusal to examine his views and assist in their application, if they seem in conformity to reason and inspired by a true love of humanity?

He then gives a description of the six categories and a formulation of the questions. These consist of 120 questions in Series "A" on elementary education, and 146 questions in Series "B" on secondary education. They are impressive in their wide range and concreteness of detail. They ask for information on numbers of schools, pupils, and teachers in proportion to population, the selection and qualification of teachers, the school hours per day and days per year, length of vacations, books used in teaching, content and frequency of examinations, methods of grading, moral education, health and the use of vaccination, discipline and penalties, and incentives and awards. A sampling must suffice to convey their tone. In Series "A" on elementary schools:

94. How are the lessons given? To all pupils together, or in small sections according to their comparative abilities and development of their intelligence?

95. Is some particular simplified and improved method used in teaching? To what branches of elementary knowledge is it applied? What does it consist in?

96. Is the new method of mutual instruction originating in England, and known by the names of its inventors Bell and Lancaster, applied generally in your country, or only in some places?

97. Is use made of the method of computation practiced successfully by M. Pestalozzi in his institute, or of other methods of the same kind, either in arithmetic or other parts of instruction?

98. Is use made of the analytic method of the Abbé Gaultier, which is ingenious, instructive and amusing for teaching grammar, geography, etc.?

99. What are the first elementary books placed in the hands of children?

100. Are children taught to learn their lessons by heart, and if so are they made to repeat what they have learned mechanically; or are they taught to explain what they have retained? Is the attempt made to *fix things in their understanding rather than words in their memory*?

101. What effort is made to develop and train in the children, gradually and insensibly, first the faculty of *attention*, which is the primary faculty that generates all others; then the faculty of making *comparisons*; and finally *reasoning* (which are the three essential and fundamental faculties of the human mind, in the distinction established by M. la Romiguière in his *Lessons in Philosophy*)?

102. What is the duration of class meetings, during the day, and for how many months a year? How are classes allocated by hours in winter and summer?

103. Between classes with their teachers do the children have one or more hours of private study to go over the lessons received?

And for the Series "B" on secondary education:

102. Do the children, before entering a secondary school or college, take a preliminary examination on the results of their primary studies, and if so what knowledge is required of them?

105. How far do the secondary schools carry the study of *ancient and modern languages, drawing, geography, history, physics*, and the various branches of *natural history*?

107. Is care taken to adapt methods of education and instruction to the character of youth in general, and to the capacities and dispositions of individual pupils?

111. Are pupils examined individually and carefully at certain times of the year? How are these examinations given? May they sometimes discourage those who work hard but are not favored by

nature, and often see themselves surpassed by others who are less studious but have greater natural abilities?

112. Is the *memory* trained, and how? Is a *reasoned memory* formed, rather than a *mechanical memory*? (See question No. 100 in Series A above.)

113. Is care taken to train the judgment, and by what means? (Question No. 101 of the preceding series may be reproduced here.)

114. What is done to cultivate the *imagination*? Is there an attempt to arouse it in pupils who have little of it, and to regulate it in those in whom it is too lively and ardent?

121. Is there an attempt to make study attractive and agreeable to the students; and by what means? (But knowledge must not be provided only in connection with amusement. For they would form the habit and feel the need of being always amused, and neglect or turn against serious studies and occupations.)

124. Has there been an attempt to reduce the time given to study of Latin and Greek, or even to remove it entirely from secondary education and replace it with studies more in keeping with the needs of each individual, in view of the social, commercial, military or other career for which he appears to be destined? If so, what good or bad consequences have resulted?

125. Are pupils made to write letters to friends and distant parents? Do they learn the usefulness of forming an *epistolary style*?

126. Are they taught *bookkeeping* in single and double entry?

One comes away from such a barrage of questions with a feeling that Jullien really knew what the problems of schooling were, that he was no mere *philosophe* or *homme de lettres* with opinions on the subject, and that he really meant to be helpful and useful to those who had the power to set changes into motion. It is equally evident that the project was impractical. The replies to his questions, if any had ever been made, would have been so voluminous, tentative and qualified, and if extended to several countries, so various and confusing, as to be irreducible to the analytic tabulation that he had in mind. The questionnaire was never put into effect anywhere, and was soon forgotten. Barely or rarely mentioned in the nineteenth-century literature on education, it remained to be truly rediscovered in the 1940s, as already noted, by educators with a broad outlook at Columbia University, the United Nations, and the International Bureau of Education.

After 1817 Jullien wrote nothing more of importance on education, except for new editions or adaptations of his previous work. He was busy with other things, addressing advice to the electoral colleges and hoping for election himself to the Chamber of Deputies, and taking part with others in founding a journal, *Le Constitutionnel*, which became a leading organ of liberal thinking during the Restoration. Mainly, from 1819 to 1830, he was engaged in editing the *Revue Encyclopédique*.

It seems fitting to close this chapter with a few words by Thomas Jefferson. Beginning with the *General Essay* of 1808, Jullien sent copies of eight of his writings to Jefferson, whom he admired as president and ex-president of the United States. Only two of these actually reached Jefferson, and Jefferson's acknowledgments never reached Jullien. This more than usual uncertainty of "transmission across the Atlantic," as Jefferson called it, may symbolize the oblivion into which most of Jullien's efforts fell. Jefferson did receive, however, a copy of the *Sketch of a Work on Comparative Education*, which he acknowledged in a letter of July 1818. Jefferson of course fully agreed with Jullien on the importance, necessity, and beneficent effects of education for social improvement. He described Jullien's work on comparative education as "an additional proof of his useful assiduities on this interesting subject."

NINE

APOSTLE OF CIVILIZATION

"CIVILIZATION" was a new word in both French and English at the beginning of the nineteenth century, and Marc-Antoine Jullien was one of the first to use it as an important and recurrent term in his own thinking. Derived from the older "civil" and "civility," it denoted a condition of society in which scientific knowledge, ingenious inventions, productive labor, and humane feeling all combined to constitute a desirable way of life. Like the English word "progress," it could be used in Jullien's time only in the singular. There was no plurality of civilizations, but different societies differed in the level of civilization that they had achieved. The opposite of civilization was barbarism. There were various intermediate levels.

Jullien had used the words "progress of civilization" in his advice to Bonaparte in 1799. In 1808, on the title page of his *General Essay on Education*, he announced its purpose as the promotion of "civilization and prosperity." In 1810 he called Napoleon the "arbiter of the civilized world." In 1813 "the rebirth of European civilization" depended on Napoleon's defeat. However else he might change his mind, the idea of civilization was a constant.

He closed the *General Essay* of 1808 with several pages on the meaning of the word, which he reproduced verbatim in later editions of the *Employment of Time*. He stressed both material and moral aspects.

> ... Whatever may be said by the enemies of civilization, who nevertheless enjoy all its advantages and may be accused of ingratitude to the society that clothes, houses and feeds them and provides them with well-being, utility, convenience and pleasure, it is still true to say that moral ideas develop and spread, and that they mature and improve, with the progress of enlightenment.
>
> Barbarous and brutish nations, and those not yet arrived at a certain social level, engage in acts of cruelty unknown to civilized peoples (*les peuples policés*). This truth is confirmed by a comparative history of different ages of the world and different countries of the earth, by ancient and modern annals, and by travelers' reports.

He goes on to condemn the barbarism of the vaunted Romans and Spartans, with their gladiators, slaves, and helots. And he announces, in 1808, that he will someday produce an *Essay on the philosophy of the sciences* with "some conjectures on the further probable and possible progress of civilization."

Diverted for several years by sojourns in Italy and Switzerland, and by his attention to schools and politics, he waited until 1819 to publish the promised work on the philosophy of the sciences. It then appeared only as a "sketch," a plan for a vast project of classification of all knowledge. Science was taken to mean mental activity of all kinds, including applied technology, political and economic treatises, imaginative literature, and the fine arts. Jullien was well aware of his predecessors in his enterprise, frequently referring to Francis Bacon, d'Alembert's introduction to Diderot's *Encyclopedia* and Destutt de Tracy's *Elements of Ideology*, but in his proposed procedure he followed the plan for his survey of comparative education. There was to be an international organization through which learned persons of many countries would contribute their findings for final consolidation in a vast table. But the *Sketch for an Essay on the philosophy of the sciences* looked also to the future. It was published by the same printing house in Paris, and in the same year, 1819, as the prospectus and first number of the *Revue Encyclopédique*. This review, with its many collaborators and correspondents under Jullien's editorship, would be for a dozen years, in effect, the great network of coworkers that Jullien had envisaged for his previous projects.

He begins the *Sketch for an Essay* with a preface, declaring that his purpose is

> to make a successful orderly classification of our branches of knowledge as a whole, as if on a vast world map . . . or in statistical tables, if one may so call them, showing the advantages and support that human industry and genius can use for the benefit of civilization.

Our author then says that he had begun to think about this subject as long ago as 1800, but had been repeatedly frustrated by a series of misfortunes which he details at length; that his *Employment of Time* and other works on education had foreshadowed it; and that there were other relevant matters, such as religion and the role of women. The latter was purely auxiliary. It was to judge and admire the work of men.

> We do not separate the philosophy of the sciences from moral philosophy and religious sentiments, which elevate, ennoble and purify our understanding. These sentiments, by offering man the most sublime model of a sovereign author of the universe, animate our thinking by

the universal benevolence that becomes our moral law and directs our thought toward the good of humanity, the work most agreeable to the Creator.

And I dare appeal to women, you who are companions in our destinies, for the support of your influence and your honorable concurrence. Your insight by a kind of instinct, your deep and keen sensibility that so powerfully affects our minds, your fine and delicate tact and exquisite judgment should pronounce on all products of thought. What you say and how you look at us have inspired heroes, knights, troubadours, poets and great writers; your hands have distributed the palms of glory. How could you refuse to encourage, animate and reward with your approval the men of learning, philosophers and their young disciples who are launched on an immense and difficult enterprise, in which the imagination and genius of new Columbuses are to create or at least discover new worlds?

The great work should not take very long to accomplish:

The task is to produce, in *ten or fifteen years*, by more effectively bringing together men engaged in the observation of nature and cultivation of the sciences, using a simplified means of exchange among them, the advantageous results and improvements which, in the natural and ordinary course of things, would be obtained, in the sciences, only after *a whole century* of work.

Further discussion is summarized in the promised table, measuring ten by fourteen inches and folded into the format of the book. A condensed version (table 1) appears on the following page.

The first number of the *Revue Encyclopédique* appeared early in 1819. Its title page carried no editor's name, but presented the work as a collaborative undertaking "by a combination of members of the Institute and other men of letters." In the following years many persons contributed articles, reports, book reviews and notes, both signed and unsigned, and Jullien was both one of these contributors and the chief editor. He himself contributed about 300 items, ranging from short notices to more extended discussions. The monthly numbers were combined into four volumes for each year, each volume containing from 600 to 1000 pages, so that there were over 30,000 pages for the twelve years of Jullien's editorship. Even an alphabetical index compiled for the first ten years of the *Revue* runs to 1,109 pages of fine print. Such a quantity of material by many writers on many subjects invites to a computerized statistical study, in the absence of which the following can give only a sporadic sample.

TABLE 1

Synoptic Table of Human Knowledge According to a New Method of Classification By Marc-Antoine Jullien, of Paris

Orders

First Order	*Second Order*
Physical sciences, relative to material bodies	Metaphysical, moral and intellectual sciences, relative to the mind
A. Positive, concerning facts	A. Positive, concerning facts
B. Instrumental, concerning methods and instruments	B. Instrumental, concerning methods and instruments

Categories

I. Descriptive and observational sciences

Cosmography, geography, etc.	History, etc.

II. Descriptive and classificatory sciences

Natural history, etc.	Psychology, grammar, etc.

III. Speculative, rational, and investigative sciences, applied to the search for causes

Physics, chemistry, astronomy, physiology	Natural theology, metaphysics, doctrine of perfectibility, and means for regulating the employment of time and the improvement of man

IV. Practical and applied sciences

Agriculture, mining, engineering, healing	Political economy Statistics Education Practical morality Liberal arts Fine arts

[N.B. The subjects in each category are also subdivided into A and B, Positive and Instrumental.]

The very first article of the first number, signed by Jullien, somewhat paradoxically affirms both the leadership of France and its laggard status.

France has lacked, if one may dare say so, a journal such as the one for which we here indicate the PLAN, SPIRIT, AND AIM. Our new journal should therefore meet one of the needs of our time.

Its object is to set forth, accurately and faithfully, the march and continuing progress of human knowledge in relation to the social order and its improvement which constitute true civilization. . . .

Other journals of this kind, successfully published in foreign countries, will serve us as our guides and often supply us with valuable materials.

France is rightly considered to be in some ways, by its geographical position and its distinctive spirit of sociability, the hearth and center of European civilization. The French language, purified and perfected by our great writers, has come to enjoy a universal and classical use. . . .

Our *Revue Encyclopédique*, established on the plan of certain English and German journals of wide repute, will occupy a place hitherto vacant in France and fill a void that several alert minds have noticed. There now exist in France a great many journals and collections devoted to particular and special branches of the sciences, natural history, physics, chemistry, medicine, pharmacy, mathematics, rural economy, the industrial arts, commerce, religion, philosophy, education, legislation, jurisprudence, politics, languages, bibliography, erudition, fine arts, military arts and sciences, etc.

But these journals, designed for a particular class of readers and treating only predetermined subjects, cannot present the whole product of human thought in all its mutual relationships and instructive interconnections.

Far from competing with these kinds of writings, we shall be able, by following our own goal, to extend their reputation and give them a more general and easy circulation, for we plan to publish, at intervals, summaries of their most substantial offerings or even analyses of matters they have treated. We shall thus inspire a desire to consult them and facilitate their researches.

We will not ourselves treat the sciences in a technical or didactic manner for those who wish to go into them more deeply, but will take a more general point of view, almost moral and philosophical. . . .

This enterprise, of interest both to the highly educated and to those whose instruction is still superficial and incomplete, should be essentially useful to all ages.

A need for readings and solid studies is generally felt. Our public schools, more numerous and with more students than ever before, attest to the commendable interest of our younger contemporaries. The zeal of enlightened teachers that they eagerly seek out shows a noble ardor for the sciences. But too many obstacles stand in the way of communication. . . .

The object of the *Revue Encyclopédique* is to remove these obstacles and make these barriers gradually disappear. . . .

Paris, a vast center of enlightenment, is one of the capitals of Europe that has the greatest resources for instruction, and proportionally the greatest number of men engaged in the pursuit of sciences and letters. . . .

We invite literary and learned persons to communicate to us, for insertion in this journal, any extracts or analyses that they wish to send in. . . . They will thus become our collaborators without being diverted from their own reflections and habitual studies.

Some idea of these collaborators may be obtained from the index, already mentioned, for the first forty volumes of the *Revue*, or the years 1819 through 1828. An appended list of initials for "anonymous collaborators and correspondents" indicates about four hundred persons. In so huge an index those who signed their contributions are hard to count, since the index gives the names of far more persons as subjects than as authors. That is, the number of persons whose work is noted or reported on is far greater than the number of those writing the notes and reports. In the natural sciences, the work of Georges Cuvier and J. B. Fourier receives much attention, but Cuvier is not listed as a collaborator, and Fourier is listed only once. The historians Mignet, Thierry, and Thiers, the poet Lamartine, and the painters Delacroix and Géricault are reported on, but submitted nothing themselves. The social philosopher Saint-Simon is noted, but not as a contributor. Benjamin Constant, Victor Cousin and François Guizot figure frequently as subjects, but Constant and Guizot each appear only once as a contributor, and Cousin not at all. On the other hand, among frequent contributors, as well as subjects, we find the Swiss publicist J.C.L. Sismondi, the French economist J. B. Say, and the septuagenarian Abbé Grégoire, who had been prominent in the Revolution and was still active in the 1820s. In general it seems that Jullien, as editor, managed to report on a wide range of scientific, literary, and artistic work, but relied on a relatively small number of persons, including himself, for the bulk of the contents of the *Revue*.

Jullien occasionally included in the *Revue* a "letter" to its collaborators and correspondents, of which one in 1823 is of interest. He noted that their journal, now in its fifth year, was "circulated through all countries of the civilized world and had a growing number of readers. . . ."

. . . It is not enough for us to be *encyclopedists*; we aspire especially to be *cosmopolites*. We would not think our task fulfilled unless each of our numbers presented, in the most complete and accurate way, the state of the sciences, letters, arts, intellectual labors and moral improvement throughout the surface of the globe. Judge for yourselves, Messieurs, what we owe to the voluntary contributions of observers in places with which we have not hitherto been able to have any direct or continuous relations.

Our *Revue* is the first and only work to have executed, by periodical publication, the great *Baconian* idea of the *unity of the sciences*, brought together in such a form as to resemble a *universal Congress*, in an *alliance* truly *holy* for advancement of the human mind toward the same moral and philosophical goal in the infinitely varied spheres where it is destined to operate. . . .

And finally, our *Revue Encyclopédique* is a kind of intermediate agent and common bond, not only among the enlightened men of different nations, but within each country among the *learned* who explore nature and expand the sciences, the *practical men* who apply the discoveries of the learned, and the *public*, or those of various conditions who wish to know the *theories* of the former and to benefit from the *applications* of the latter.

The learned societies of all countries were an obvious source of information for the *Revue*, and Jullien from time to time published a survey of such societies. In 1820:

Foreign Learned Societies

The institution of learned societies characterizes a time when the development of human knowledge invites those who pursue it to classify it, make orderly reports on it, and guide its application. . . .

It is in the spirit of this journal to follow and make known the progress of these useful institutions, whose history is so essentially linked to that of the human mind. Hence we shall devote a few articles to a kind of literary statistics of various countries of the civilized world. The documents we publish will be most often provided by persons of the nation concerned, or at least by those who maintain close ties with the countries on which they contribute news.

America
United States

The United States of America will first receive our attention. Its civilization, already very advanced in many ways, offers a spectacle worthy of study. It is the only modern society established from the outset on a reasonable basis, with no need to compromise with vicious antecedents, and which consequently marches directly toward a certain degree of perfection without having to pass through the dreadful ordeal of revolutions. In a young nation enjoying growing prosperity, with a population not yet numerous but extended over an immense territory, human activity must be mainly engaged in agriculture, commerce and administration. The speculative sciences and the arts of enjoyment cannot be generally cultivated. Hence the formation of learned societies in the United States is of recent date.

We know, up to now, of seven scientific, literary or philosophical societies established in the principal cities of the United States. We shall have occasion later to offer a summary of their most important work.

1. The Society at Philadelphia has already published six volumes in quarto entitled *Transactions of the American Philosophical Society, held at Philadelphia for promoting useful knowledge*. The first volume appeared in 1771, the latest in 1818.

2. The *American Academy of Arts and Sciences*, established at Boston in 1780, has published four volumes in quarto, of which the fourth was in 1818.

He lists five others at New Orleans, Charleston, Washington, New York, and Hartford, which had published very little and none of which was to enjoy the success and longevity of the first two. Then follow a large number for Europe and Asia, including the Asiatic Society in Calcutta, with twelve volumes of publications since its founding by the British in 1784.

To illustrate its globe-encircling program, the *Revue* published a table in January 1827, classifying 2,452 items appearing in its twelve monthly numbers for 1826 according to the country concerned. Of these, 1,790 were only very short notices or book reviews. The remaining 662 more substantial articles were distributed as follows in table 2. It is natural that even a cosmopolitan journal published in Paris should be heavily weighted toward France; it is more surprising that, in the conditions of the 1820s, Great Britain rates no higher than the Netherlands and that so much attention is given to the Americas. Here the United States rates almost as high as Britain, and Latin America with the Caribbean even higher than the United States. Writers for the *Revue* were repeatedly drawn to a consideration of Haiti, where black slaves had rebelled and set up their own republic, which Jullien and his *encyclopédistes* viewed with approval and high hopes, since they detested American slavery.

The dozen years of the *Revue* stood on the eve of the great nineteenth-century revolution in transport and communication. Canal-building was at its height. Within thirty years the railroad, steamship, and electric telegraph would be commonly used. Suspension bridges would soar above inaccessible gorges, and at lower levels connect

TABLE 2

Classification By Nation and Region of Articles in the *Revue Encyclopédique* for 1826

America	
United States, "and a few other parts of North America"	38
Republic of Haiti	15
Mexico	2
Other Latin American	27
Asia	
China, Persia, etc.	4
British colonies [mainly India]	13
Australia and Oceania	1
Africa	
Egypt and European colonies	11
Europe	
Italy	47
Netherlands [then including Belgium]	45
Great Britain	42
German states	41
Russia	40
Switzerland	29
Scandinavian states	29
Other European	16
France: Departments	46
France: Paris	216
	662

the land without interfering with shipping on the waterways below. Lithography would bring new visual images and copies of famous paintings to a wide audience. Gas lighting would illuminate public buildings, streets, and homes. All these were prefigured in the *Revue*. The volumes for the very first year, 1819, carried three notable news items:

> *Lithography*. Dr. Foerster, professor at the school of artillery and engineering at Berlin, is the first to have applied the art of lithography to the printing of books. He has written on stone with his own hand a new work entitled *Introduction to Geodesy*. His effort was perfectly successful, and shows that lithography has great advantages over typography for mathematical works, where it is more agreeable to see the drawing or figure alongside the text than to look for it on a special plate at the end of the book.

Beginning in 1824 each volume of the *Revue* carried as its frontispiece a lithographed portrait (often made from an earlier painting) of a notable person who had died during the preceding year. The first so honored was "Edward Jenner, inventor of vaccination." The following years portrayed notable scientists, the British jurist Lord Erskine, the painter David, and various others.

But even more portentous, in 1819:

England

Arrival in Europe of the first steamship to cross the ocean. The city of Liverpool, on last 20 June, saw the arrival of an American vessel of 360 tons after a 24-day crossing from Savannah. For 18 days it used a steam engine with wheels attached to the two sides of the ship, which, when the sea was too high for them to be used, could be hoisted on board as rapidly as the time needed to set the sails. This ship, the first to cross the ocean by steam, also has masts and sails to be used as needed, as on other ships, and its construction is the same. It had previously made the 300-league passage from New York to Savannah.

Steam navigation on rivers had preceded this Atlantic crossing, and the *Revue* is full of notices of such development on many rivers of Europe, but we find a curious item concerning America for the same year 1819:

United States. *Navigation by steamboat.* On 28 May the steamboat *Independence* arrived at Franklin on the Missouri River [about fifty miles above St. Louis]. It is the first ship of this kind to have ascended this river. It was saluted on its arrival with numerous salvos of artillery. The inhabitants know that easy communications are necessary for increase of their own wealth.

... Steamboats surely contribute much to the rapid progress of civilization in the interior of North America. To give an idea of the importance of navigation at present on the Mississippi, we can report that the steamboat *St. Louis*, arriving on 25 June at New Orleans in eight days from St. Louis, passed thirteen similar ships moving upstream.

In these years of canal-building the *Revue* reported on a great many canals connecting the rivers of Europe, and even on two projects for joining the Atlantic and Pacific oceans, but we note here only the case of the Erie Canal. In 1822 the *Revue* published a digest, written by the notable economist J. B. Say, of documents concerning the canal published by the state of New York. Say's digest is in form a long essay on the United States. Not foreseeing the magnitude of migration into the upper Middle West that the canal would make possible, Say notes that it will enable shipping to proceed from New York through Lake Erie to New Orleans by way of a shortcut through eastern Ohio.

The United States of America were at first only a nation extending along the coasts of a vast continent covered with forests. Now that they have pushed their settlements to the Mississippi they form a vast empire almost as wide as long, and mainly agricultural. But the eastern and western parts of this empire communicate with difficulty; they are separated by the chain of the Alleghenies, which intercepts all navigation between the waters emptying into the ocean and those flowing into the Mississippi.

The necessary relations between the two halves of so large a country have brought about, by land, an active communication between Philadelphia on the ocean and Pittsburgh on the Ohio, at the point where this river becomes easily navigable. But, to give an idea of the difficulty in this mountainous connection by land, though it is the shortest possible between east and west, it burdens the transported merchandise with a cost of at least 30 francs per hundred pounds of weight. Almost no agricultural product can support such an expense, so that the products of half the states in the Union must find their outlet by way of the Mississippi and New Orleans, and obtain returning goods by the same route.

Internal navigation can and soon will join the two halves of the American confederation. The Alleghenies that separate them become lower and disappear as they approach the immense lakes that flow into the St. Lawrence River. Hence a canal can be opened running from the Hudson River near Albany to Lake Erie. Then, by a canal only two leagues long [six miles] which presents no difficulty, Lake Erie can communicate with the Cuyahoga, Muskingum and Ohio rivers. The Ohio is the great artery of the west. . . . The essential segment, establishing communication between New York City and Lake Erie, begun in 1817, will be finished in 1823.

. . . An excellent memoir, first published in 1816, led to appointment of a commission, which took the trouble to traverse the 160 leagues over which the Erie canal had to pass. Specifications were drawn up, mile by mile, with costs of construction according to various features of the terrain, and it was only after a thorough investigation that the state of New York adopted the project and put it into execution. . . . We presume, from what we have read here, that within three years a steamboat will be able to leave New York, pass from the Hudson River into Lake Erie, gain the Ohio, and reach New Orleans after descending the Mississippi.

For all their emphasis on agriculture, the writers for the *Revue Encyclopédique* did not think of the United States as a rural country. In 1827 they received information from Philadelphia on prizes to be awarded for technical achievements by the Franklin Institute in that city.

Philadelphia. Industrial statistics. Prizes proposed by the Franklin Institute. These prizes will be awarded next October; it is thus too late to call the program to the attention of those who might wish to compete. But in the long list of proposed subjects we find a kind of statistics of American industry. We see that the production of artificial soda has crossed the Atlantic, that the mulberry tree is cultivated in Pennsylvania and nourishes silkworms whose product is put to use locally. We have no doubt that work is in progress on the improvement of steam engines and ways to prevent the explosion of boilers. It seems that the processing of iron with coke and coal needs encouragement, since a gold medal is decreed for it, while all other kinds of manufacture are to receive only silver medals. There is much activity on means to heat apartments with coal, although wood is not yet as rare in Pennsylvania as in several parts of Europe that are less foresighted. Pigskins are now being tanned. An appeal is made to all who may have useful ideas on the building of roads. Manufacture of woollen and cotton cloth seems very advanced. Local production of ceramics is surpassed only by the most famous manufactures in Europe. Production of molten steel has apparently not yet been attempted. Hunting guns are still imported, but some gunsmiths are trying to compete with the best that European industry produces. A country that two generations of men have been able to raise to this degree of manufacturing prosperity, and whose territory reaches two oceans and contains the entire course of the Mississippi, is called to high destinies—may it achieve them, for the happiness of mankind!

Since the American union did not yet reach two oceans in 1827, the *Revue* was premature, or prophetic, in thus sensing its "high destinies."

With the building of canals and development of internal waterways there was more need for bridges, which with improvements in metalworking were increasingly made of iron. Suspension bridges were among the oldest of human constructions, having been made even in Neolithic times with ropes thrown over gullies to hold a walkway; by 1820 a roadway might hang from chains of iron links or segments of bar iron. The modern suspension bridge, hung from cables consisting of strands of iron wire twisted together, was announced in the *Revue*

Encyclopédique in 1822. The Seguin brothers, a well-known family of manufacturers related to the Montgolfiers who had invented the balloon, had built a small bridge hung from cables across a stream near their factory. It was only eighteen meters long, but was intended as a model for a much larger bridge over the Rhône that they already had in mind. This was built in 1825, and was reported on in 1826 by Jullien's son Adolphe, who later became known as a railway builder himself. The oldest of the Seguin brothers, said Adolphe Jullien,

> . . . is the first to have had the happy idea of making the chains for suspension bridges out of cables, or bundles of iron wires. He has built a suspension bridge over the Rhône between Tain and Tournon, and this bridge, formed by two spans each 85 meters wide, has passed all the tests made to find whether it could be delivered to the public without danger. One span was loaded with a weight of 69,150 kilograms, a weight heavier than if its surface had been covered with people, and the masonry of the abutments to which the suspending cables are attached showed no signs of dislocation; the wire within the cables held perfectly; and there was noticed only a momentary deformation of the curve of the cables, which had been foreseen in advance.
>
> These tests, in the presence of engineers from the department of the Ardèche and neighboring departments, together with the passage of large vehicles over the bridge since it was opened for traffic, leave no doubt as to its solidity. . . . M. Seguin has rendered a true service to science in proposing to replace bar iron with iron wires in the chains of suspension bridges, and by demonstrating the usefulness of this innovation by numerous trials and experiments.

The words "railway" and "telegraph," *chemin de fer* and *télégraphe*, existed before the devices with which they were later associated. Rails had been laid for the easier movement of loaded horse-drawn carts, and "telegraphy" meant both signaling by ships at sea and a system of land communication initiated in France during the Revolution. By this system a series of tall semaphores had been installed at high points, at distances such that each could be seen by telescope from one station to the next, for rapid communication between Paris and Lille in connection with the war against the First Coalition. A news item on telegraphy signed by Jullien himself appeared in the *Revue* in 1821. He did not foresee the Morse electric telegraph that came hardly twenty years later. It may be noted parenthetically that, although the kilometer had also been introduced during the Revolution, it was still customary to measure distance by the league, equivalent to about three English miles.

General telegraphy, nautical and commercial. In our number for last May we expressed a wish that *Telegraphy* might be applied to commercial and individual relations. . . . We dared not hope that our wish would be so promptly realized. We have learned that a French vice-admiral, baron de Saint-Haouen, has presented the government with a new telegraphic system that promises great advantages. Experiments at Le Havre, by land and sea, and by day and night, by order of the government, have proved that even in very bad weather signals by day can be distinguished and exactly repeated at a distance of three or four leagues, and by night at four or five leagues even when the horizon is lit by the moon. . . .

Despite lighting by 113 lighthouses the wreck of 1,026 commercial vessels on the coasts of France in the last six years, and of 2,190 on the coasts of England, shows the inadequacy of lighting and pilotage, at present, for the safety of navigation. Certain French business interests have offered to pay the expense of a telegraphic establishment by day and night according to the system proposed by M. de Saint-Haouen.

But the great breakthrough of the 1820s came with the steam locomotive and the railroad, called in England the railway because "rail ways" already existed. In 1829 the *Revue* carried a long description of this climactic event.

Contest of steam vehicles. The company formed to build a railway from Manchester to Liverpool had offered a prize of £ 500 (about 13,000 francs) for the best steam-powered vehicle to be presented to it. The terms were that (1) the machines admitted to the contest must not weigh more than 6,000 kilograms; (2) they must have the power to pull, over a distance of about eleven leagues, not counting provision for necessary water and fuel, a train of transport vehicles with a weight of three times the machine itself; (3) they must go at a speed of ten English miles an hour (three and a half leagues); (4) the steam pressure in the boiler must not exceed 50 pounds per square inch; (5) the height of the machine from ground to chimney top must not be over fifteen feet; and finally (6) the machine must burn its smoke. On the new railway between Liverpool and Manchester, at a place where the route is perfectly flat, a segment about a league long was chosen where the machines, by reversing direction several times, could make the trajectory of eleven leagues required by the program.

On last 6 October, the date set for the opening of the contest, a crowd of learned men, engineers, and the merely curious arrived from all parts of England and gathered on the road to Liverpool to witness these interesting experiments, which were to last for twelve days.

Ten contestants had registered, but whether because of breakdown in their machines or because they were not quite ready, only five were able to compete.

Three of these were eliminated during their operation, leaving a contest between two called the *Novelty* and the *Rocket*.

The lightness of the *Novelty*, its small size and the elegance and finish of its workmanship, aroused the general admiration of the spectators. Its weight was about 3,000 kilograms. Its fire was lighted; and in less than forty minutes and with the use of about fifteen pounds of coke the steam pressure rose to fifty pounds per square inch. First it was made to go alone, that is, only carrying its fuel and water and the men operating it. It reached a speed of twenty-eight miles (nine and a half leagues) an hour, and in fact made one league in the short space of five minutes. If the whole way from Liverpool to Manchester had been completed, this machine would have covered the distance of eleven leagues in less than an hour. Despite this surprising speed the motion of the vehicle was uniform, sure and regular; it entirely consumed its own smoke, not the least amount of which could be seen coming out of its chimney. A load of three times its weight, or almost 11,000 kilograms, was then attached to it. It pulled this load with facility, maintaining a speed of *seven leagues an hour*. When steam began to leak from a small tube it was stopped for repairs. . . . When the test was resumed the *Novelty*, with its load behind it, had already gone three leagues at five leagues an hour when the material filling the joints in the boiler began to melt, and it was necessary to suspend the experiment until a later time.

Mr. *Robert* STEPHENSON presented another vehicle, called the *Rocket*. This machine is large and solidly built. Its weight with the boiler full of water was 4,000 kilograms. Drawing after it a load of about 13,000 kilograms, it proceeded for thirty-five miles (almost twelve leagues) in three hours and ten minutes, including the stops and delays needed for each turnaround. In a second test it did the same in two hours and forty-five minutes, which was more than four leagues an hour including the stops. Another time the *Rocket*, relieved of the load it had pulled, covered a space of over ten leagues in an hour. It was noticed that this machine let a little smoke escape, and that its movement was sometimes uneven, varying between four-and-a-half and five leagues an hour. Nevertheless it seemed well established that it could easily move at five leagues an hour while pulling a load of 13,000 kilograms. The consumption of coke in one run of twenty-four leagues was about five hundred kilograms.

It was this vehicle that the committee in charge of the contest chose for the prize of 13,000 francs.

In this same year (1829) we find a more disconcerting case of busy experimentation during this first Industrial Revolution. It was an attempt to propel a coach by steam on ordinary roads and streets, which had to await the internal combustion engine long afterward for success. The news was from London:

> *London. Steam coach.* This coach, invented by Mr. Gurney, and which all the English journals were talking about and praising a year ago, has been put again into action and departed from Bath to London, carrying Mr. Gurney with two friends, and, among others, two persons who had invested considerable sums in it for a speculation. The trip passed without incident as far as Melksham [about ten miles from Bath], where the coach arrived about eight o'clock in the evening. It was passing through the town and rolling along very well, when a crowd gathered in the street and pelted it with a hail of stones that broke its windows, injured several passengers, and forced it to stop. Its occupants managed to get it into a shed, not without difficulty. Without intervention by the magistrates it would have been demolished. The wrath of the crowd, it is said, came from the hatred of the inhabitants for any kind of machine. They see in such machines the ruin of the country and the poverty of the population formerly employed in manufactures.

It was not only such Luddites that interfered with what Jullien saw as civilization and progress. From a more literary quarter there came Mary Shelley's *Frankenstein*, which was translated and published in Paris in three volumes in 1821. Along with its horrors it conveyed the message that the pursuit of knowledge might have very bad consequences. Jullien, shocked and disgusted, summarized its story and expressed his opinion in a signed article.

Frankenstein, or The Modern Prometheus . . .
by Mary Shelley . . .

This bizarre production of a sick imagination makes one regret that the author has not applied her talent to a more reasonable and interesting production. It is especially to be wished that a work by a woman would offer more pleasing and gracious scenes, instead of tales and subjects that are always hideous and revolting. A man from

Geneva, named Frankenstein, goes to study at Ingolstadt, where he takes courses in natural philosophy and alchemy. Drawing on the reveries of Cornelius Agrippa, Paracelsus and Albertus Magnus, he succeeds in stealing from nature the mysterious causes of generation and life. He is finally able even to animate inert matter; but he gives existence to a frightful being, gigantic in form, with a human face, half human, half demon, at the sight of which he himself feels an invincible horror, and of which he becomes the redoubtable and desperate enemy because he refuses to give him a female companion. This monster kills the brother, friend, fiancée and father of the unfortunate Frankenstein, who pursues him, to save the human race, to the very ice of the arctic pole, where he is found by an English ship and ends his sad career worn out by fatigue and suffering. The horrible creature that has ruined his life dies after him by plunging into an abyss in the glacial sea.

There remains in the reader's mind only a painful sense of disgust after devouring this tissue of improbable and absurd adventures in which the characters inspire no interest, and after reading about extravagant inventions that have no moral purpose and can neither enlighten the mind, nor uplift the soul, nor instruct, nor amuse. Let us hope that in another work, on another subject, the author will offer more agreeable images, more interesting characters and more useful relationships, and will apply the precepts of the great masters. Common sense and reason should be the main guides of a writer in whatever kind of work.

In addition to the notices and short pieces cited above, the *Revue* also published longer articles containing more considered discussion, of which only three can be excerpted here: one on America by the Swiss economist and historian Sismondi; and two by Jullien himself, one on German idealist philosophy, and one on Robert Owen's famous socialized cotton mill (or company town) at New Lanark in Scotland.

For Sismondi, as for other contributors, "America" always meant the two continents. Interest in Spanish America was high because the revolutions for independence from Spain were barely ending. Sismondi hoped to read signs for the future, which he admitted to be nearly impossible, but he clearly identified the great difference between Europe and both Americas, namely the coexistence in America of different races and the inequalities between them, reaching the point of abject chattel slavery, especially in the United States. For all writers in the *Revue* a generally favorable attitude to the United States was always clouded by this malignant reality.

Sismondi begins with an expression of wonder at the ease of modern communications, which a later time would find overstated:

America

The world today is rich for us in great spectacles. Since all communications between men have become so easy and the dangers, delays and difficulties of travel have almost disappeared, and since trade brings all climates, industries and products of the world so rapidly into connection and our written thoughts circulate even more rapidly . . . our interest falls upon the entire human race. . . .

Among the spectacles provided by our time, which posterity will wonder at, and on which it will ask us for our observations as witnesses, there is one that has perhaps not received enough attention, but in less than a century will doubtless seem the most wonderful of all those in modern history. We are present at the birth of great nations that may some day hold the scepter of power, wealth and intelligence. We see them being born not in isolation but together, with means of growth and prosperity not given to any other people at its origin . . . . On all sides America is bringing forth republics, confederations and states demanding independence. Beholding so great a movement, one would wish to consult the future on the destiny of so many new peoples. . . .

The population, it is true, of these vast regions is far from proportional to their great extent. The United States have over ten million inhabitants, Mexico over six, Colombia three. . . . The population of the United States may continue to double every twenty-five years for a century, and so reach 160,000,000, a figure that the newer and less populous republics might reach in two centuries.

But is it probable that this prosperity will continue? . . .

He refrains from attempting an answer, noting that conditions in the former Spanish possessions are unknown or unstable, with boundaries fluctuating, and fighting still going on against the Spanish remnants, among revolutionary leaders themselves, and between social classes. He devotes the last third of his article to his thoughts on class, race, and slavery.

History teaches us that the greatest dangers to which human societies can be exposed come from oppression of the lower classes of the people. The man whose enforced labor produces wealth is irritated by suffering and brutalized by ignorance. Having nothing to lose, he has no respect for the established order. . . . On the other hand, the well-being of the poor man, the esteem that is shown for him, and the protection that he enjoys, guarantee the security of the rich man and the peace of states.

But America is so constituted that the lowest class of society, reduced to slavery, is more unfortunate than in any other part of the world. This slavery is more cruel than that of the Russian or Polish serf, or of feudal times, or among the Greeks and Romans, because it is aggravated by the hatred and scorn for the black race that have been instilled in the whites, so that even emancipation cannot restore equality between oppressed and oppressor after several generations. . . .

Four colors are mingled in America, and they never forget their differences—whites from Europe, blacks from Africa, red indigenous Americans, and yellow arising from mixture of the others.

In the United States in 1820, in a population of nine and a half millions, the black slaves numbered 1,538,118, free persons of color 235,557, and red Indians 4,631. Almost all the slaves are in ten states with a white population of 2,685,081 and a black slave population of 1,496,285. . . .

Sismondi's figures here, though obviously absurd to the seventh digit, correspond fairly closely to those reported by the United States census of 1820. He goes on to offer similar figures for half a dozen Spanish American states and Brazil, where hardly more than rough estimates were then possible.

Such is the information we have today on the mixture of races. Such is the ulcer eating away at America, beside which the serfdom and feudalism of old Europe are hardly worth mentioning. If the lawmakers of America do not work steadily to restore bonds of fraternity among men on whom nature has imprinted such fateful distinctions, if they do not work to persuade them of the equality of their origin and let them enjoy an equality of rights, then any progress in America will augment the danger, and a frightful civil war, or war of extermination, will sooner or later replunge America into barbarism.

Surely the republicans of the United States, as those who have possessed liberty, enlightenment and a religion of brotherhood for the longest time, should be the ones to give an example of liberality and humanity. They have done exactly the contrary; slavery is more rigorous among them than in any other of the independent American peoples. The violent prejudice against persons of color is more offensive, more cruel and more shameful among them than among the Spaniards. . . .

Would anyone believe that in this land of liberty and equality they will not allow a free Negro, or a colored man no matter how slight his admixture of Negro blood, to sit at a table with a white man, share in his pleasures and holidays, join in an assembly with him, or even receive the paid services of the same barber? . . .

The Negroes, they say, are of an inferior race; they are not the equals of whites. I do not believe it. They are only a race that you have degraded. . . .

To destroy this pernicious and shameful prejudice all enlightened, humane and religious persons must work in all the Americas. It is their duty to testify by example that they recognize men of all colors as their brothers, capable of becoming their equals in virtue and talents. . . .

The white man must see himself as sometimes bound to respect and obey the black man; some men of color must be introduced into the highest dignities of the republic, as living examples to remind the citizens of the equality of races. When a few free blacks will be elected to Congress, when they sit on the bench as judges, are professors in universities, or preachers in the pulpit, then the plague of America will begin to be relieved, and the fearful storm menacing these republics will be averted.

Another idea of freedom was being developed at this time in Germany as a branch of the metaphysics of Immanuel Kant. Jullien undertook to explain it to the French. Not knowing German himself, he says that he had learned about it from conversations with a German professor during his travels in Germany and Switzerland. The following translation, which simply turns Jullien's *liberté*, *raison*, and *éducation* into their English counterparts, may do less than justice to the German *Freiheit*, *Verstand*, and *Bildung*. Jullien, like others, is awed and puzzled by these German profundities. But he finds in them a parallel to his own ideas.

Some Views on the Natural and Progressive Development
of the Human Mind and of Civilization

The famous German philosopher FICHTE, who may be considered as the successor and in some ways the continuator of KANT, has expressed his fundamental ideas on man, his nature, destiny and duties, as well as on education, morality and politics, in works that are highly esteemed in Germany, where he has numerous disciples. The fundamental idea of *Education*, taken in its widest and most complete sense, is connected, according to him, with a progressive development of the human faculties, which should be cultivated harmoniously, according to their nature and with all relationships kept in view. He first examines the moral force of man. He distinguishes *instinctive morality*, good in principle but weak and inadequate, from *reasoned morality* which is positive and practical, and which man appropriates for himself by the formation of character, by reflection and habit and especially by control of his passions and the force of his will.

Since the works of Fichte are little known in France [none had yet been translated] the reader may be interested in what follows. I fear that I have been unable to remove entirely the obscurity for which German philosophy has been reproached.

Jullien finds in Fichte's thought "five great epochs" or stages of social advancement, involving an interplay of reason, law, force, and liberty. The first two stages are primitive. In the third stage Turkey and the France of 1793 and 1794 are much alike, since in Turkey there is no liberty because of despotism, and in France only a "false appearance" of it, because of the revolutionary crisis. In the fourth stage liberty and reason begin to come together; liberty submits to law, and reason "begins to preside over the social order." This is the era of "greater improvement of the human race" and of "the commercial and industrial nations."

Finally, there is the fifth and last epoch, which can be called the apogee of improvement of the human race. Liberty and law are combined in a kind of fusion; penetrating each other and no longer acting separately, they become elements of one identical whole. There is no liberty without law, and no law without liberty. In this fifth stage, unfortunately not yet reached among any people, reason becomes both a science and a practical art; it gradually produces the highest perfection accessible to human nature; it is the epoch of the free and entire development of our faculties.

After this "very imperfect sketch" Jullien compares Fichte's work to Condorcet's *Sketch of the progress of the human mind*, since both affirm that "the force of reason alone, disseminating its light by degrees, must suffice for resolving the problem of civilization."

But Jullien has his doubts about such philosophizing, and on the adequacy of the self-created morality favored by Fichte. He concludes:

Several German philosophers, however disposed to what they call *religiosity*, may be reproached for forgetting, among the means of human improvement, the need for a morality imposed on man by his nature, which always brings him back to laws and precepts of which the morality of the Gospel, properly understood and applied, will always be the most perfect type.

In any case we should recognize that purely metaphysical specula-
tions, isolated from the study of history and the positive facts that it
furnishes to the observant philosopher who travels in different ages
and among different peoples, are not enough to light the way to
civilization.

He restates the idea of a "pragmatic" history, which was going out of
date in the 1820s, and not only in Germany.

By consulting the annals of the human race attentively with patience
and sagacity, by observing and comparing nations in the successive
periods they have traversed, by plumbing the abysses that sometimes
separate these periods (such as the *middle ages*, an immense gap or
sort of sandy island between two fertile and cultivated countries), by
relying on history and its well-established facts and by seeking to
know better the nature of man—it is thus that we shall catch the mysterious connections between his organization and his intelligence,
and that a man of superior gifts will trace, with a bold and faithful
brush, a true picture of civilization and indicate the possible and future progress of the human race.

Jullien soon found a more congenial subject, actual and functioning
in the real world and apparently very practical, yet realizing his own
hopes for human improvement. He found it in the famous social experiment conducted by Robert Owen at New Lanark. Owen had not
yet moved on to what Karl Marx would call Utopian socialism; his
project was neither socialist nor social democratic, being rather a
showcase for benevolent proprietorship, or social planning at the level
of company management. Since Jullien's visit was brief, his report
may depend as much on what he was told in answer to his questions
as on what he really saw.

Notice
On the Industrial Colony at New Lanark in Scotland,
Founded By Mr. Robert Owen

Great Britain and especially Scotland are among the privileged countries in Europe where it is possible and allowable to work for human
happiness, where many individual ideas and public acts aim at the
welfare of all social classes, and where generous mortals who have a
similar purpose [such as M.-A. Jullien] are not obstructed, calumniated and persecuted but easily find auxiliaries and support. . . .

I myself in September 1822 visited the founder of the establishments at New Lanark. In conversation with him I probed the sentiments and principles that have guided him. I observed the labors of
his workers and the instruction, exercises and games of the children

whose upbringing he supervises. I passed a day, all too short and fleeting, in this obscure and picturesque village, this delicious retreat where labor, mutual good will, calm peace and happiness reign. . . .

I had heard much about the industrial colony founded by Mr. Robert OWEN, and I had read his publication called *An Institution to Improve the Moral Character of the People.* One of my objectives on my visit to England and Scotland in the summer of 1822 was to observe this institution more closely and judge whether it seemed to realize the benevolent views of its founder. On the way from Glasgow to New Lanark (a distance of 25 English miles) I passed through continuous fertile fields, smiling meadows, gardens and orchards made fruitful by careful and intelligent cultivation. I had as a traveling companion a Frenchman who had long lived in England. . . .

Half way up a slope we found a dwelling of very pleasing appearance, large and commodious but simple and elegant, surrounded by woods and meadows, from which we could see at the end of a long avenue planted with trees, and near the river, the buildings occupied by the colony and forming the village called New Lanark. Mr. Owen was among his work people and their children, and it was there that we hurried to meet him without being expected or announced.

Mr. Owen, 51 years old, seems hardly to be over 40. He has the gentle and calm expression of a benevolent, intelligent and happy man whose life is devoted to the happiness of his fellows. About 24 years ago he took over the management of this enterprise, where order, activity and happiness are now evident. It was then a large mill that had existed for about a dozen years, and where, as in most such establishments, only ignorance, disorder, immorality and poverty were to be found. In his first ten or twelve years he produced a complete metamorphosis, and the striking contrast between the old mill and the regenerated colony gives precious evidence of the primitive goodness of human nature. . . .

To favor the free development of man and his physical, moral and intellectual faculties—remove from him all corrupt influences that arouse vicious inclinations—eliminate the fears and hopes of self-interest . . . render useless and superfluous the rivalry, rewards and penalties that excite pride, ambition, envy and cupidity . . . see that good conduct becomes a habit..in short, make a love of work, order and good behavior come from their very attractiveness: such are the principles that the Scottish philanthropist has constantly professed and applied, and of which long and repeated experience has confirmed the good effect. . . .

I have mentioned the long avenue that leads from Mr. Owen's house to New Lanark. The external facade of the colony is regular, of a simple but elegant architecture, and the internal arrangements are perfectly appropriate to their use. On our left we saw several buildings at the foot of a hill; some contain rooms or separate apartments for one or two workers, or for husband and wife with two children, or for more numerous families; others have storage rooms on their upper floors for provisions needed by the colony, with shops below where at certain hours the workers or their wives come to buy what they need. Each single worker and each family has a line of credit, and can make purchases up to the amount of the monthly pay. Advances are sometimes granted under unusual circumstances, such as an unforeseen accident, an illness, the birth of a child, or short absence for family affairs. . . .

To the right of the avenue are, first, a large factory in six stories for the spinning machinery; then a fine building on a spacious court for the children of both sexes, containing their schoolrooms and places for exercise and prayers; and finally, a little further, by the canal that here joins the Clyde, a building still under construction where there are to be a common kitchen and refectory for unmarried single workers, or those not living with parents, or any residents who wish to use them.

An infirmary, with a doctor and surgeon in attendance, and where the children are vaccinated, now houses 38 patients out of the 2,300 persons (including 350 children) who compose the colony. About 1,800 work in the mill; the others are busy in kitchen gardens and housekeeping. There are a third more women than men. All are free to leave the establishment but are attached to it as to a family, and remain voluntarily because they find happiness there. About 250 non-residents come from the village of old Lanark to take part in the work. . . .

Most curious visitors to the colony, who have numbered about 1,800 this year, have been surprised that there are so few subjects of complaint in a workplace where so many persons are brought together and where the discipline is not severe. The men earn about 15 shillings a week, the women 8, 9 or 10, the young girls from 5 to 8 or 9 shillings according to their age and work assignment. Blacksmiths, carpenters, masons and others earn about two and a half shillings a day.

The mingling of the two sexes causes no disorder; indeed, it results in several marriages each year, and almost all these unions are happy because the partners are well matched.

Jullien goes on at length to describe the schools at New Lanark and Owen's views on the subject. And then to the mill itself:

... I should like now to conduct my reader into the rooms of the factory, which are all equally clean, well aired, and without unpleasant or unwholesome odors. I would point out to him the different kinds of work performed, and the air of contentment of the workers. He would see several ingenious procedures, some of them invented by Mr. Owen, for raising the raw cotton quickly to the upper floors and then making the spun cotton thread descend; and another for cleaning the cotton with a machine called the *devil*, which is attached to a ventilator that expels the dust through an opening in the wall, so that the workers are never troubled by dust but enjoy pure air and free respiration. We might also visit the foundry, the forge, and the shops of the carpenters, joiners, wood turners, painters and glass workers, for everything needed for the well-being and labors of members of the colony is made in the colony itself. About 30,000 pounds weight of cotton is produced each week. . . .

A large apparatus moved by water power keeps all the machines going; no steam engines are employed. Mr. Owen told me that, by mechanical inventions applied to spinning and other branches of the industry, 240,000 persons now do what would require the labor of 28 or 29 millions by the older methods. The constantly increasing progress of the mechanical and chemical sciences is changing the moral world. Production becomes much greater than consumption. The population should grow to an extent for which it is hard to assign any limits. . . .

All men of good will should strongly support Mr. Owen in the execution of his ideas. What he has already done proves what he can still do. His government, compatriots and foreigners, joined in affection for mankind, should assist in the noble work he has undertaken. We must gradually, and while harming no one, remove the causes of human misery and the disorders and vices that come from this misery, and bring it about that a better employment of men, a better direction of their labors, and a more equal distribution of knowledge among the poor and the working classes may contribute to the progress of civilization and virtue.

So concludes Jullien's account of the great experiment at New Lanark. With his phrase "the employment of men" he echoes what he had said in his books of 1808 and their subsequent reprintings, and with "progress," "civilization," "virtue," and "distribution of knowledge among the poor and the working classes," all requiring a "better direction of labor," he rings the bells of both the political economy and the liberalism of the time. The young Jacobin had come a long way. But the change was more in the means than in the end.

TEN

THE LATER YEARS

FOR ALL HIS CONFIDENCE in civilization and hopes for humanity, Jullien's sense of his own life became increasingly troubled as he grew older. He reflected more often on his own past. Unlike younger and more perceptive liberals of his time, such as Guizot and Mignet, he could never disentangle the history of France since 1789 from a story of his own personal tribulations.

Even his attempts to take part in politics under the constitutional monarchy turned him to introspection and self-justification. His advice to electors projected his image of himself. By 1830 he was writing less often for the *Revue Encyclopédique*, which, after passing into other hands, including those of his son Auguste, finally expired in 1833. His father, the former Conventionnel and regicide, died in 1821; his mother, who had been equally devoted to the Revolution, died in 1824; and his wife, the daughter of another Conventionnel who had voted for the death of Louis XVI, died in 1832 after a long illness. He could take some satisfaction in his children; three sons attended the École Polytechnique, one of whom later became an architect and another an engineer involved in the building of the Paris-Lyon Railway; but with his son Auguste he had painful disputes over the *Revue Encyclopédique*, and his young daughter wrote in her journal in 1830 that "there is no family so sad as the Julliens." (She did better when she later married the playwright Lockroy.) But Jullien as a theorist of education was probably a hard father to live with.

He never produced the memoirs that he said on several occasions he intended to write. But as already seen, he put a good deal of autobiographical material into print. At the time of the second Bourbon restoration he gave various of his manuscripts to Friedrich Schoell for publication, meaning to show that he had not been a follower of Napoleon. When he aspired to election to the Chamber of Deputies in 1815, 1817, and 1824, he told how he had been unappreciated and misunderstood. In 1821 he published an indignant protest against articles on himself in several new biographical dictionaries. When Louvet's memoirs appeared, he took pains to refute the charge that he had been responsible for the death of the Girondins at Bordeaux. When Gohier's were published, he denied that he had encouraged Bonaparte after the coup d'état of Brumaire. In 1825 he published a collection of his poems, called *My Regrets and my Hopes*, including the one composed in prison in 1794 quoted in chapter 3 above, along with others of which the general tenor was the sad plight of a virtuous man in a world of slander and intrigue. In 1828 a new edition appeared of Courtois's report to the Convention in 1795, and readers could again see the letters written by Jullien to Robespierre during the Terror. The *Revue Encyclopédique* warned its readers against "this arsenal of scandalous libels and odious calumnies."

There were two new biographical dictionaries containing articles on Jullien of which he could approve, and which indeed sound as if written by Jullien himself or by persons who interviewed and agreed with him. They are especially informative and have been drawn on for the present book. One, published in 1829, was reproduced verbatim by Jullien in the *Notice Biographique* that he published in 1831 to support another attempt at election to the Chamber of Deputies. It is reinforced by an appendix containing 63 documents dating as far back as 1792, which only Jullien could have supplied, and a list of his published works from which everything published before 1808 was omitted, that is, a list apparently supplied and expurgated by himself. The other, published in 1841, terminates with a list of 67 books, pamphlets, printed speeches, and poems of which Jullien was the author. It appears to be very complete as far back as 1796, but excludes the speeches and pamphlets printed during the height of the Revolution, with one exception, the speech delivered by the sixteen-year-old Jullien at the Jacobin Club of Paris in January 1792, advising against war unless France was actually attacked.

He had preserved the letters from his mother written to him during the Revolution, and which form the main content of the first chapter of this book. He read them over and pondered them, and in 1829 had them reproduced by a professional copyist. On these copies he made various marginal notes and excisions, as if preparing them for publication with many names to be omitted, including his mother's. Apparently he thought, rightly enough, that these letters would give the younger generation a vivid idea of what the great Revolution had been like. No doubt a rereading of the letters raised vivid memories and mixed feelings in his own mind. He gave up the project, and it was Jullien's grandson, Edouard Lockroy, who published the letters half a century later.

Jullien was soon disappointed by the Revolution of 1830, as by every regime that had preceded it. It was not only that he failed to get elected to the Chamber in 1831. The revolution seems also to have damaged his personal finances, though how and to what extent is unknown. In October 1831 he wrote a letter to his friend the Swiss educator Fellenberg. Its complex syntax exudes such woe as to arouse the suspicion of exaggeration. He said he was financially ruined, but a few years later, in 1839, he could still sign his name as a *propriétaire à Paris* and as both an *électeur* and an *éligible*. He wrote to Fellenberg in 1831:

> . . . I have suffered from cruel vicissitudes, and the revolution of July 1830, which has mistreated so many uncorrupted and disinterested men and made the fortune of so many ambitious intriguers who are prompt and adroit in exploiting events for their own profit, has entirely changed my situation and ruined the *Revue Encyclopédique*, on which for thirteen laborious years I expended all my efforts, heavy labors, and painful sacrifices of every kind; and it has also ruined me personally. Now at the age of fifty-six I must begin a new career and take up I know not what kind of work to support my numerous family of a wife and six children, only one of whom, an engineer for roads and bridges, is self-supporting with an honorable means of living. Fortunately, my health is good. . . . I have been the dupe, victim, and prey of several arrant rascals, one of them a notary who seemed to merit my confidence, but who profited from the fact that all my attention was absorbed by immense labors, so that he compromised my fortune, which though modest and honest was more than enough for the needs of my family, and was the fruit not only of what my father left me but of forty years of my public services and my savings, economies, privations and sacrifices. A vast and total shipwreck has swallowed up everything. I still have a small house and some land suitable for building, which was worth about 200,000 francs two years ago, but which since the July revolution and collapse of all property values, especially for building sites, no longer has and for a long time will not have any kind of value. In addition, the *Revue*, in succumbing, has left me with very onerous burdens and debts, for I tried to sustain it until the end. I shall honor all my engagements to the extent of the last property that I own, and I am left with the small house where I have come to live and puny assets that must be increased by intelligent and well-directed work. . . .

The work to which he refers, and in which he engaged for the rest of his life, could not have been very remunerative. It consisted in contributions to new and ephemeral journals and editorial projects, preparation of new editions of his books on education written twenty years before, occasional pamphlets on timely subjects of which more will be said, and a concern for, and attendance at, a large number of scientific and literary societies and associations for public improvements. The list made in 1841 names 66 such societies of which Jullien was a member, and of which 14 were in Paris, 24 in other parts of France, and 28 in foreign countries. Those in Paris were for various specialties from antiquities to vaccination. The other French societies were more comprehensive in their interests but local. The 28 foreign societies ranged over the European continent from Lisbon to Vilna; but the list named only one in Great Britain (a society for promoting peace), while including no less than five in the United States, of which the most famous was the American Philosophical Society in Philadelphia.

Jullien had long admired the United States, and knew several Americans who resided in Paris or often visited it. David Warden was a Protestant refugee from the United Irish uprising of 1798; he had become an American citizen and was the author of a three-volume description of the United States. He lived in Paris for years, and was a frequent contributor to the *Revue Encyclopédique*. Peter Du Ponceau, born in France but long an American citizen, wrote extensively on the American Indian languages. William Maclure, born in Scotland but also an American citizen, after making a fortune in business became a pioneer of North American geology and had many philanthropic interests, including Robert Owen's utopian colony at New Harmony, Indiana. On one of his trips to France he purchased a large collection of some 25,000 items printed during the Revolution—pamphlets, speeches, laws, newspapers, and other periodicals—which is now in the library of the University of Pennsylvania. It has been argued, with good evidence, that Maclure may have bought this collection from Jullien. But this seems doubtful, since there is no allusion to any such collection in Jullien's writings, and the collection lacks many items that one would expect to find in it if it had been his.

Warden, Du Ponceau, and Maclure all had their books reviewed at length in the *Revue Encyclopédique*. All three were members of the American Philosophical Society, as was Jullien's elderly acquaintance Lafayette, who had been a member since 1781. It was Du Ponceau who proposed Jullien for election to the Society in 1830. He wrote to its president:

> *Philadelphia*
> *20 August 1830*

Sir:

We beg leave to propose as a candidate for membership in this Society Marc-Antoine Jullien, of Paris, member of the Columbian Institute at Washington, of the Royal Academy of Sciences at Lisbon, of the Royal Society of Warsaw, of the Mineralogical Society of Jena, of the Society for Natural Sciences at Dresden, etc.

M. Jullien is the founder and principal editor of *La Revue Ency-clopédique*, a scientific and literary journal well known to the members of this Society. In this journal M. Jullien has also given a distinguished place to American works, and constantly exerted himself to make our literature favorably known to Europe and to the world at large, and he has never missed an opportunity to speak with praise of the learned men and literati of the United States and particularly of this Society. We think he will be, if elected, a deserving and useful member of our Association.

There is no reference in the letter to Jullien's activities during the Revolution and under Napoleon, or to his political ambitions under the restored monarchy, all of which must have been known at least vaguely to his American friends in Paris, who no doubt regarded them as irrelevant to membership in the American Philosophical Society.

Jullien was duly elected to the Society in October 1830. He never managed to visit the United States or appear in person for formal induction. But he soon had the pleasure of having preceded his own king in this honor, for King Louis-Philippe became a member in 1831, under the less royal name of Louis-Philippe d'Orléans.

In 1832 the Academy of Moral and Political Sciences was reconstituted in Paris as a component of the National Institute. Dating from 1795, it had been dissolved by Napoleon in 1802, and its revival was a sign of a revived liberalization after the revolution of 1830. It might be expected that Jullien, active in so many learned societies and editor of the *Revue Encyclopédique* in its best years, might qualify as a member. Several others who had been prominent in the Revolution, including the octogenarian Abbé Sieyès, who had voted for the death of Louis XVI, were included in the new Academy, but not Marc-Antoine Jullien. Former revolutionaries were now acceptable, but it was harder to honor one who could be remembered as the friend of Robespierre and the butcher of Bordeaux.

Turning to England to improve his prospects, Jullien visited that country in 1833, where he published a work in French, though with a London bookseller, called *A Letter to the English Nation*. The *Letter* was a curious and composite volume. It makes no reference to the agitation in England and Reform Act of 1832, which others saw as somehow analogous to the Revolution of 1830 in France. It begins with an epistle to "the generous English nation" on a project for a new journal, proceeds to a detailed description of his Biometer with a view to its sale in England, and concludes with an assortment of "a few poems and a discourse in verse" on famous British philosophers, scientists, poets, writers, and artists. The enormous opening sentence recalls his visit to England in 1792, but of course makes no mention of his eagerness, as expressed in a letter of 1794 to Prieur of the Marne, to take part in an invasion of England and an English revolution some forty years before.

May it be permitted to a Frenchman who from early youth, before his eighteenth birthday (in 1792), made a first visit to this classic land of liberty and was welcomed there by one of the illustrious heads of the opposition, Lord Stanhope, and by that modest but famous man of learning, Dr. Priestley, the friend of Franklin, Washington, and Jefferson; who since then on a second occasion (in 1822) visited your great capital, your principal commercial and industrial cities, and your Scotland so beautiful by its romantic and picturesque nature. . .; who for twelve years of a laborious life, suffering cruel vicissitudes, devoted all his time, abilities, and part of his fortune to promoting a better understanding, in the matter of literature and the sciences, between France and England, and reciprocally between England and France, in a journal (the *Revue Encyclopédique*) which he had founded in 1819. . . : may it be permitted, I say, to this Frenchman who is no stranger among you to offer you the tribute both of his own high and sincere admiration and that of his compatriots for the noble examples that you have given to the world. . . .

It was to your BACON, rightly called the father of modern philosophy, that the first inspiration for the *Revue Encyclopédique* was due; and it is to him also that I owe the thought of a REVUE COSMOPOLITE, or *comparative survey of Great Britain and France, and of other countries in their relations with these two peoples,* or a STATISTICAL AND PROGRESSIVE TABLE OF THE CIVILIZED WORLD. . . .

Our illustrious and learned CUVIER, whose recent death was a loss as keenly felt in England as in France, had rightly judged, in his lofty meditations, that only *comparative anatomy* and *comparative geology* could advance the sciences of anatomy and geology which remained so long in their infancy. Similarly, only *comparative civilization* can speedily advance our present civilization, which still preserves, despite its brilliant varnish and imposing wonders, the deep and afflicting traces of the old barbarism. . . .

The proposal was to found a journal to be concerned with all countries but "especially England and France, the two model nations of Europe which should march together at the head of civilization and consolidate the peace of the world, the primary necessary condition of every kind of progress." Interested persons, i.e., "the friends of humanity and of the union of peoples and civilization," were invited to participate as stockholders in launching the enterprise, or as initial subscribers, or as contributors and correspondents. The new journal would be called the *Revue Cosmopolite et Comparative des Nations*. From Jullien's detailed exposition of the proposed contents, it is clear that he had in mind a sequel to the defunct *Revue Encyclopédique*.

Changing the subject abruptly, Jullien went on in the *Letter* to explain to the English a device of his own invention, for which he credited the original idea also to Francis Bacon. It was his Biometer and it was the same as the concluding tabulation in his book on *The Employment of Time* dating from 1808. Nineteen columns, on physical, moral, intellectual, and social matters, were to be crossed by horizontal lines for each day in the week, producing squares in which the user was to record the hours spent each day in each of these various ways.

> ... Just as an *ordinary watch* helps to appreciate the rapid flight of hours and allows one to survey their use more exactly, I have thought it possible to imagine and execute a kind of *Moral Watch*, which I call the *Biometer*, as a measure or evaluation of life, designed to provide any individual who uses it with an easy and simple means for measuring his life by estimating the various uses of each interval in a twenty-four hour day. ...

After eight pages of further description we are told that the use of the Biometer will promote religious, philosophical, moral, and economic values—in a highly organized form:

> Use of the Biometer only applies to ordinary living the principles of *commercial accounting*, and to the inspection of our hours and days the *strictness of military reviews and inspections*, which establish and maintain discipline, order, regularity and simultaneity of movement for the assemblages of men called *companies, battalions* or *squadrons* and *regiments, divisions*, and *army corps*.
>
> Finally, to offer a less serious but no less truthful image to WOMEN, who are called upon to exercise so high and powerful an influence on the regeneration and improvement of the human species. ... I will say that the Biometer is like a harpsichord. The spaces in the Biometer, for recording the hours spent in diverse employments of one's life, are like the keys of the harpsichord that produce sounds of varying length, and more pleasing or less so, whose concord tends to make life into a sort of harmonious concert that can be renewed each day.

It is regrettable that Jullien had no sense of humor.

The whole second half of the *Letter to the English Nation* was made up of assorted poems, some of which were short elegiac pieces, such as "Meditations at Sea" while crossing the Channel, and the longest was literally a Discourse in Verse in three hundred rhymed twelve-syllable lines. The Discourse praised in turn a series of great men produced in England and Scotland, from Bacon, Locke, and Newton, including Shakespeare and Milton, along with David Hume and Adam Smith, to Jullien's contemporaries Sir Walter Scott and Lord Byron.

The *Letter to the English Nation*, published in French, found a cool reception in Great Britain. The proposed *Revue Cosmopolite* never materialized. A *Biometer* appeared in English in 1833, but its extreme rarity today suggests that it sold few copies. The poems, as French poetry, however laudatory of England, could hardly have been appreciated by English readers. Jullien's visit to England in 1833 resulted in another of his many disappointments.

Twice again, in 1837 and 1839, he offered himself as a candidate for the Chamber of Deputies and published advice to the electors. The advice given in 1839 extended to seventy numbered paragraphs. More than in his previous such efforts he now addressed specific issues, and he also urged reform in the electoral system. The country was unsettled, since several French cities had been disturbed by working-class uprisings, and there was also a fear of war, as France and the other European powers took opposing sides in disputes involving Egypt and the Ottoman Empire. The ministry, hard pressed, had dissolved the Chamber of Deputies and called for a general election. Jullien wrote:

... **10.** The problem is to reduce the chances of both war and revolution. A policy of timid concession to foreign powers and of division and corruption at home, in which the ministers have blindly persisted, has put France on a fast downward slope that leads to a precipice.

11. There is still time. A firm, dignified and moderate attitude may still prevent war. . . .

17. The Government is now consulting the *legal and official nation*, which is composed of about *180,000 electors* who constitutionally and in reality wield the powers of the 33,000,000 to whom they are responsible when they vote. This *legal nation* should clearly formulate, by its choice of deputies, what the *entire nation* expects of those who preside over its destinies. . . .

33. What do the great majority of the French really want? The reply to this question is naturally evident to any man of common sense and good faith who consults his conscience and takes account of the opinion of his fellow citizens.

34. France wants to preserve, improve and complete its institutions, which should be *cast in bronze* and not *molded in plaster*.

35. France, too often hoodwinked and exploited, wants to obtain the just and natural consequences of the Revolution of July. It does not want to remain *stuck in the mud*, the inevitable prelude to new struggles and commotions.

36. France wants *the reality of representative government*, or of *government by and for the country*, the SERIOUS AND SINCERE REALIZATION OF REPRESENTATIVE MONARCHY, that is, an effective control over the acts of government, to procure without violent upheaval a gradual reform of abuses, a reduction of taxes, an immediate diminution of public expenditures that are not of obvious and demonstrated necessity and utility; and furthermore, a better organization of labor and prompt improvement in the lot of the poor and suffering classes; and finally, the loyal and complete application of the principles of public law enshrined in its constitution.

37. France wants to strengthen its government to obtain order and liberty at home, and peace abroad. . . .

38. France wants to move forward with civilized nations on a track of social progress; it even takes a noble pride in believing that it can give useful direction, and that other nations have their eyes fixed on it and are inclined to follow its example.

39. Hence FRANCE is essentially and simultaneously CONSERVATIVE, wisely REFORMIST, and instinctively PROGRESSIVE.

40. Hence the Deputies of France, to be worthy and capable of representing it, must be simultaneously CONSERVATIVE, REFORMIST, PROGRESSIVE, and above all DISINTERESTED.

41. Hence, so far as possible, we must send to the national Chamber, along with honorable men who deserve to retain their seats, a certain number of *new men* to reinvigorate it, and most especially *men of conscience and experience, probity and honor*, without ambition, strangers to intrigues and coteries, independent by character and position, determined to attend usefully and seriously to the business of the country, and not to their own personal or family interests.

42. ELECTORAL REFORM has been widely demanded, and is a fundamental point. In the interest of the country and of the government itself we must not delay until it might be brought on with violence by the force of events, or go beyond certain limits within which it is best to hold it.

Jullien's proposals for electoral reform fell far short of popular government. In the 1790s he had spoken well of "democracy," and in 1799 had even suggested to Bonaparte that a touch of "democratization" might be desirable, but no form of the word "democracy" occurs in this tract of 1839. The Chamber of Deputies after 1831 was chosen by electors who were neither elected nor appointed by anybody, but automatically qualified by payment of at least two hundred francs a year in direct taxes, signifying an income from property of several thousands. They met in "colleges" to make their choices. Only about a thirtieth of adult male Frenchmen were electors.

For Jullien the main problem was not the narrowness of the suffrage but the fact the Chamber was actually controlled by the government, containing not only men of wealth but many salaried public officials, contractors, and others that the ministers in power could manipulate. To correct this evil his idea was simply to enlarge the districts within which the electors met. By the existing system they met in each *arrondissement*, one of the smaller areas into which each *département* was divided, and in each arrondissement they chose only one deputy to go to the Chamber. In some arrondissements the electors were very few, locally minded, and inclined to choose one of themselves. Jullien proposed that the electors should assemble in the chief town of each department, where being in larger numbers they would exchange ideas and acquire broader views, and choose not merely one but a number of deputies depending on the importance of the department. The constitution provided that a certain fraction of deputies need not be residents of the districts that sent them. Jullien thought that an electoral college meeting at the departmental level would be more likely to know of persons of national standing (such as himself) whom it might wish to include in its deputation to the Chamber.

45. Our electoral law is radically defective, not so much because it concentrates the choice of deputies in a small privileged circle or because it excludes a large number of able men from the right to be electors, as because it limits each arrondissement to the naming of only one deputy.

46. In one central departmental college each elector would take part in the choice of all deputies from the department. Members of the college could reach agreements and take concerted action to make combinations to reconcile local and national interests. If in one or two such elections a majority let itself be dominated by local and personal interests, at least in some others it could rise to considerations of a higher order and act with complete independence.

49. The need of transporting oneself to the chief town of the department in order to vote in the elections, far from being an inconvenience as some appear to have believed, would become a real advantage and means of political education for the electors. The expense of

the journey would hardly come more often than once every four or five years. Such movement, by taking the elector out of his own locality and habitual sphere, would broaden his horizon ... and enable him to make better choices from eminently patriotic motives.

He did suggest, but only in passing, the possibility of extending the suffrage in the future, through a procedure in which the electors should be themselves elected by a larger body of original voters:

53. The time may come to examine carefully the question of whether an electoral system in two steps, as adopted by the Constituent Assembly in 1791 and consistently practiced until 1814, could not be restored with advantage, because it would allow the greatest number of citizens to participate in the choice of the electors, who would then be charged with naming the mandatories of the country.

But it is more important to broaden the views of the existing electors:

66. If there are men long tried by our political troubles, relentlessly pursued by unfair prejudices and the odious calumnies of party spirit, hatred and envy ... such men [i.e., Jullien] ... should be brought to the attention of the electoral colleges, even though they might hesitate to present themselves, out of modesty or lack of ambition.

67. Even candidates living farthest away from the seat of the electoral college should obtain a majority of its votes, if their names have been made known in advance and if no competitor has the same claim to public confidence.

The seventieth and final paragraph of this advice warns against "self-interest, an antisocial vice," and is followed by a long postscript in which Jullien, overcoming his modesty, rehearses his credentials for election: his writings on education, editorship of the *Revue Encyclopédique*, and authorship of the Declaration of the Chamber of Representatives in defiance of the Allied invaders of 1815. And then:

Already old in years (63) and in the misfortunes of all kinds that have devastated his life, but still young at heart and in the purity and energy of his feelings; a wounded athlete, but still vigorous and strengthened by the political storms he has traversed; knowing in advance that at the national tribune, if he is called to it, he will speak no word not inspired by his conscience and not deserving the approval of good citizens and good men; wanting nothing for himself but everything for his country; strongly moved, without exaggerated pride and without false modesty, by the deep and intimate conviction that he can render his country real service, he would offer himself with confidence to the suffrage of electors who might agree with what he has written here.

THE STYLE IS THE MAN, said Buffon. ELECTORS! In the preceding pages is reflected the wholly French soul of their author.

Whatever impact this style and these arguments may have had, Jullien again failed to be elected in any of the electoral colleges.

A few weeks later he wrote another of his very long letters to Fellenberg in Switzerland. It expressed, with incessant repetition, both disgust with the electoral system and dissatisfaction with the state of publishing and the book trade. It was also another exercise in self-pity. But Jullien's contemporaries Tocqueville, Marx, and the caricaturist Daumier, had they been able to read it, would have welcomed its denunciation of the money power.

> ... Today it is the power of money that obtains announcements, critical reviews or praises for new books, whether good or bad, and the best writer, if he is poor, will either be unable to print his works himself or will see them printed but perish in dust and oblivion because he cannot pay for the advertising. There is venality in public offices that are given to the highest bidder whatever his morals or education. The same corrupt influence enters into the election of deputies; there is an open traffic in jobs; and we have the ignoble and lying spectacle of an entirely false national representation, which can only impress people who live far away or are poorly informed on our electoral operations and the immoral use of millions in secret funds to bring into the so-called national chamber immoral, corrupt and servile men, groveling mediocrities, passive instruments and purchased loyalties. The sad results of the total absence of religious and moral sense that is the scourge of our society! ...

> My old age is afflicted by the sad sight of complete demoralization and frightening dissolution of the social and political body. In my first youth I smiled at the prospect of a wholly different future. In my long career I have been a *living martyr*, faithful to the sacred cause of truth, country and humanity, always unhonored, ill treated, persecuted, calumniated, imprisoned, exiled and overwhelmed by humiliations, outrages, animosities and misfortunes of every kind, all for having tried to oppose, with moderation but with firmness and perseverance, the invasion of vices, corrupt elements and ruin brought on in France in turn by the National Convention, the Directory, the First Consul Bonaparte, the Emperor Napoleon, and the three kings Louis XVIII, Charles X, and Louis-Philippe. ...

You have read in our newspapers of our long ministerial interregnum, our shameful and manipulated elections, our sad combinations ostensibly formed to organize a parliamentary government to satisfy different shades of opinion. There is no thought but of personal interests, never of the public interest. Jobs are searched for or created for certain privileged men; there is no search for men who are honest, moral, intelligent, conscientious, experienced and suited for the functions they are to discharge. . . . God knows where so many deplorable follies will lead. . . .

When the election brought in a new ministry not very different from the old, Jullien returned to the political fray, publishing a tract called *The Voice of France* in 1840. By its subtitle it also offered "reflections" on what the new ministry should do. And we find here the word "democracy" on the title page (though nowhere else), in an assertion quoted from Montesquieu: "True representative government is the democracy of enlightened reason." Jullien published this tract anonymously, but anyone familiar with his style could easily have identified the author.

Preamble
The author of these reflections, written under the inspiration of the grave circumstances that surround us, is a sincere man now old in experience and misfortune even more than in years, but still young in the purity and strength of his sentiments. He has traversed the whole long period of our revolutions since 1789, always fulfilling, without hesitation and in the most stormy crises, the duties of a good citizen outside all parties and coteries. . . .

He names in turn all groups and persons who had attempted to govern since 1789:

All were beguiled by illusions and false hopes, and were plunged, until the last hour when power escaped them, in a profound ignorance of the immense and imminent dangers that were to bring on their inevitable ruin.

He would save the present government from the same fate. But he has always been "misunderstood, calumniated, persecuted, incarcerated, exiled, proscribed under all governments and by all parties. . . ." He has been a veritable

Cassandra, revealing on the walls of Troy to her blind and short-sighted fellow citizens the great evils about to fall upon their heads, which they might have conjured away and prevented. . . . May she no longer be rejected!

The author would not be averse to signing his name to what he writes, for he has never had to disavow his acts or writings. But since his name might perhaps revive the unjust and inveterate prejudices against him propagated by his political adversaries under all regimes . . . . he prefers to preserve anonymity.

With his taste for figures he then offers his advice in 52 numbered paragraphs. The first 21 only restate the general principles and altruistic ideas he had often expressed before, together with his proposal of 1839 for electoral reform. There is no mention of widening the suffrage or of "democracy." But the remainder of the *Voice of France* is impressive, and is unique among his writings, for the variety of immediate practical problems that it addresses:

22. The question of RAILROADS is the one most in need of prompt resolution. We have already lost precious time through serious errors, wrong specifications and inconceivable delays. We remain very much behind several other great states in these new means of communication. . . .

The government should not itself descend into the arena in competition with private interests. It should preserve its higher position as arbiter and final judge, to oversee and inspect, and to protect the public interest. . . .

23. The RESTRUCTURING OF THE PUBLIC DEBT should be prudently arranged in such a way as not to undermine the public faith and the sanctity of engagements contracted by the State, and not to leave to arbitrary ministerial decision the timing and execution of measures so vital to private interests and the national credit, to reduction of the interest rate, and to making capital available to agriculture and industry. . . .

24. For the same reasons *a reform of the law of mortgages* is desirable, since the law now makes the transfer of property too difficult and handicaps transactions.

25. There must be an examination and solution, with similar views, of questions concerning extension of the privilege of the BANK OF FRANCE, and the founding of INDUSTRIAL AND AGRICULTURAL BANKS, some in the departments and some in local communities, as so frequently demanded in several parts of the kingdom.

26. The same urgent need of opening new and larger markets for our products . . . should suggest important modifications in our TARIFF LEGISLATION. . . . There is the same need to speed up the organization of *transatlantic navigation* with active, regular and frequent com-

munication by large steam-powered vessels to multiply and improve long-distance voyages and provide a merchant marine as a useful auxiliary to the navy.

27. The SUGAR LAW needs conscientious attention [to accommodate the interests of French beet farmers, colonial sugar growers, manufacturers, and consumers.]

28. A law, often promised, on SECONDARY EDUCATION, should adjust our public education, still so defective, to the needs of our time and give a true *preparation of youth for the various occupations in our social life.*

29. A law on the PRISON SYSTEM, to instil habits of work and morality in our houses of detention. . . .

30. The legislators should also give thought to establishing a BETTER ORGANIZATION OF WORK, to find an effective remedy for the latent but desperate struggle which, under the specious name of *free competition*, produces in the heart of our society a veritable war between men of the same occupation who find it in their interest to mutually injure instead of helping each other. . . .

Here our liberal joins forces with the socialist Louis Blanc, whose book, *The Organization of Work*, appeared in this same year 1840.

35. Inviolable respect for INDIVIDUAL LIBERTY is not sufficiently assured by our legislation. . . .

36. The express demand made by Benjamin CONSTANT shortly after 1830 should be reiterated and consecrated in a special PRESS CODE, to produce a general revision of laws on the licensing of printers, public criers and press offenses. The press having become one of the public powers, this code should give it a regular organization and make it liable to jurisdiction by a jury, and so assure its independence of action and protection against oppressive and arbitrary interference. The code should also guarantee citizens and public servants against violent and unjust attacks, defamations and calumnies, and protect the public morality against the excesses and vagaries of an unbridled freedom. . . .

37. Thorough work on the REDUCTION AND BETTER APPORTIONMENT OF TAXES, and a *strict control over their use*, are among the needs of our time.

38. It would be well to meet the wishes and needs of the country by a certain EXTENSION OF MUNICIPAL POWERS, which were often respected even by absolute kings, and which within proper limits are more suited than the central power to direct local affairs with intelligence, economy and dispatch.

Here we hear the concern, familiar to all readers of Alexis de Tocqueville, with the growing and overgrown centralization of government.

39. An INDUSTRIAL ORGANIZATION OF THE ARMY, employing it in part on public works, and preserving it from the dangerous idleness of garrison life, will make it possible to realize several works of public utility in a few years, and to arouse a wholesome emulation and redoubled activity on the territory of France.

40. An organization of FREE PRIMARY EDUCATION, widely distributed through all the communes of France, as a foremost and sacred debt of the country and government to its citizens, will be easily reconciled with a reasonable FREEDOM FOR PRIVATE SCHOOLS, with regulations demanded by public morality and the interest of families.

A few paragraphs follow on what was then called the Eastern Question, involving at the time a separation of Egypt from the Ottoman Empire, and steps to be taken for civil government and French colonization in Algeria, which France had recently occupied. Then:

47. Renew activity in public works and large undertakings, now almost all suspended, and you will provide employment to millions of workers who are in need of work and bread.

48. If the suffering laboring classes see that attention is paid to their problems, they will cease to feel the anxiety, irritation and hostile attitudes which too often lead to dangerous explosions. If the government no longer feels it has to distrust a discontented population and arm itself against it, it will see its domestic strength and power greatly increased, and be able to exercise in foreign policy a salutary influence on the great powers . . . contribute to the peace of the world . . . and obtain a *proportional reduction in the military forces of different States. . . .*

49. We must finally emerge from the critical, uncertain and precarious condition in which we have tossed for ten years. We shall emerge either by violence or by wisdom, either by revolutions or by regular peaceful methods, either by a solidly grounded peace or by a general war.

50. Ministers of France, if you are wise and skillful enough to understand and fulfill your mission, you can strengthen the throne, allay passions, pacify the country. . . .

If on the other hand you follow in the course of your predecessors, who have been lacking in frankness, wisdom and firmness, you will show again to France and to the world, after a few months of an un-

easy, agitated and ephemeral existence, the scandal of another rema-
nipulation of ministries, which . . . will make people feel the painful
necessity . . . of shaking and perhaps overthrowing our political and
social edifice, to obtain by a complete renovation the end of evils of all
kinds which our so-called statesmen have so far only made worse.

So Jullien, in a characteristic cloud of words, anticipates (or predicts?)
the coming revolution of 1848.

51. Between these two roles, Ministers of France and of the king,
you must CHOOSE. Your destiny and that of France for several years
depends on the choice you make.

52. It is not the form or even the personnel of government that is
most important to the country. It is the way in which government
fulfills its task, which is to be occupied USEFULLY AND ACTIVELY WITH
THE WELL-BEING OF THE GREATEST NUMBER.

Napoleon III might have agreed with this final flourish. Jullien did not
live to see the Second Empire, under which some of what he called for,
except for peace, would be advanced.

More immediately, an issue soon arose that confirmed Jullien's belief in the incompetence of the government. After the war scare of
1840, and with memories of the invasion of France and occupation of
Paris by foreign armies in 1814 and 1815, it was proposed to build a
massive defensive wall around the city. Jullien advised against it in a
series of three pamphlets called the *Fortifications of Paris*, issued in
February and March 1841. But the wall was in fact built in the following years, and the last remnants of it did not disappear until the 1920s.
In the Franco-Prussian war of 1870 the wall proved to be useless, or
indeed wholly counterproductive, when Paris was besieged for three
months like a walled city of the Middle Ages. It suffered worse than a
medieval city, for it was bombarded by the modernized long-range
German artillery, and being cut off from the rest of France it endured
deprivations of food and supplies unparalleled for so large a city until
the siege of Leningrad in the Second World War.

In his *Fortifications of Paris* Jullien foresaw these consequences. Of all
his many writings, this was the one in which he most carefully argued
the case of a concrete problem. He quoted at length from French military men, who also advised against enclosing the city in such a wall.
Ironically, since the proposal had already been adopted by the Chamber of Deputies, he addressed his tract to the Chamber of Peers, a body
of which he had generally disapproved. He appealed to the Peers to
bring about the formation of a special National Commission of Inquiry

to examine the project in all its ramifications. Its report, he said, should consist of three volumes and be circulated in 60,000 copies for public discussion.

Fortifications of Paris

21 February 1841

The Chamber of Peers is constituted in our political organization to furnish a salutary counterweight to the Chamber of Deputies on important and difficult occasions. . . .

The members of this Chamber, which includes so many illustrious men in military, administrative and political affairs, have never had so favorable an opportunity to save the country by their practical observations and long personal experience. . . .

The general principle is incontestable that *Paris must be sheltered from attack and another military occupation of the city be prevented.* . . . The question is how to reach an understanding on the choice of means and on a defensive system suited to our time, to the true function of the capital, the French character, our military and civil organization, and the sentiments, interests and needs of the nation. Above all, the defense of Paris must not be taken in isolation, but joined with the general defense of national unity and independence. We must not add to the centralization in the capital, already perhaps excessive, another more absolute kind of centralization by making it an armed center of unique importance, which the enemy need only capture in order to dictate his will for France. Instead, we should make it the center of a very wide circle of defenses, supported by a few fortified points, and served by railways over an extensive area. Such a deployment will cover the capital without exposing it to the horrors of blockade and siege, and will preserve for it a free and easy access for provisions and a large breathing space in which neighboring departments can assist in its defense, and the Government and the two Chambers will have freedom of action in taking measures for the public safety. . . .

Paris should be an "open city," that is, not militarily defended, and Jullien quotes several French generals who are of this opinion. He even cites Napoleon: "To want to convert a great capital today into a fortress is an anachronism, a retrograde idea, antisocial and barbarous; it is to misunderstand our time." And he notes that Carnot, who in 1793 and 1794 had organized the victorious resistance of France to the European coalition, had "openly opposed the idea of fortifying Paris."

In fact, the progress of civilization, the present political circumstances of France and Europe, the new system of war and new means of attack and defense in which the attack has an unquestionable superiority, have brought notable changes in the respective position of States and the means of security that they should adopt toward one another. . . .

Two great principles divide Europe today: *absolutism, or the aristocratic and oligarchic principle*; and the *constitutional* or *democratic principle*.

We note here the reentry of the word "democratic" into Jullien's vocabulary. Was his liberalism slipping? No liberal would equate absolutism with aristocracy, or believe that constitutional government had to be democratic. He was thinking, however, about the Great Revolution.

The struggle between these two principles, begun or rather openly engaged in 1789, has not yet ended. On any day an unforeseen event might become a cause of war; a small spark can ignite a great conflagration. . . .

Two great powers, ENGLAND and RUSSIA, are truly independent and virtually secure from attack on their own territory, and they dominate Europe. One is protected by the natural rampart of the Ocean that surrounds it. The other is defended by its perpetual ice and rigorous climate. These two alone can move freely and easily as they wish; they make the whole world feel their preponderant influence. The Russian government is antipathetic to the nature and principle of our institutions. The British government, whose institutions are almost the same as ours and should incline it toward us, cannot give up the old spirit of jealousy in which it opposes the growth of the French naval power and increase of our prosperity.

FRANCE, almost isolated and left to itself, may in the visible future have to contend with these two great powers and with some formidable coalition that they might assemble. It must think of its defense. . . .

But our France is nevertheless stronger than these two States for withstanding the blows of Europe. Its geographical position on the European continent, with over 40 million inhabitants in a compact territory, the homogeneity of its population, the universality of its language and religion, its acknowledged superiority in enlightenment and intellectual activity, the patriotism and courage of its people, in a word its *great national unity*, give it advantages and qualifications to make it victorious over its enemies, if only those who preside over its destinies can and will understand its eminently socializing and civilizing influence and know how to use its potential for success.

As sources of strength for France, Jullien perhaps put too much faith in its "civilizing influence"; he surely put too much faith in its internal unity, as too many episodes in its later history would reveal. But in his thinking that national unity was more important than fortification of Paris for defense in some future war it is easier to agree with him:

It is then in the GREAT FRENCH NATIONAL UNITY, and not in the capital city ... that we must find the means of resistance in a general and unanimous uprising, organized well in advance, against any new coalition that anyone might dare to form against us. . . .

By defending France, Paris is defended; by defending Paris, France is not adequately protected. . . .

The true defense of France consists simultaneously in a good strong military organization, a rectification of our present law on recruitment, the formation of a strong reserve force, prompt and easy mobilization of national guards frequently trained in military evolutions and maneuvers, an enlargement of our cavalry, the suppression of many now useless forts and their replacement by ten or twelve new ones properly located and equipped, entrenched camps protected by rivers and waterways and served by railroads, where even troops with little training can oppose the enemy and impede his movements from point to point, and from one obstacle to another, and so give time for a great national uprising to mature and multiply into terrible explosions, all directed by a central motive power. Thus each such defensive point will become a breeding ground for popular insurrection, a place for manufacture of arms, a new center of coordinated resistance. . . .

If our fathers in 1792 and 1793 knew how to improvise a new system of attack to repel a Europe allied against them, their sons . . . should know how to use a new system of defense worthy of their country and their time. Steam engines and railroads, allowing transport between distant points within a few hours of troops, arms, munitions, provisions, news, and orders, must not be overlooked. . . .

After thus arguing that a wall around Paris would be useless in time of war, Jullien went on to demonstrate that it would be actually deleterious in time of peace. Even if war should never come, or come only many years later, the wall would inhibit and abort the growth of the city. Productive workers of all classes, and productive enterprises of many kinds, would avoid the uncertainty and anxiety of living in such a place.

This disastrous project of turning Paris into a fortress or a bastille, of converting a large, populous and magnificent city, the ornament and pride of France and almost of Europe and the civilized world, into a gigantic place of war, a veritable fortress, will tend to reduce our capital from its high position as the metropolis of modern civilization, the intellectual center and the hotel of nations. For Paris is no longer just a city of consumption, pleasure and luxury; it is also a city of production, industry and commerce, and the uncontested capital of the arts and sciences.

Does anyone really wish to bring on a progressive and inevitable diminution of its population, its wealth, and its social and political prominence?. . .

The successive governments of France since the beginning of this century have spent over a billion francs on improvement of the royal highways, which all converge upon Paris and bring ever increasing numbers of travelers of all classes, both those active and hard-working in industry and idle consumers. More than 500,000,000 francs have been spent on canals, all converging on Paris. . .and facilitating the arrival of raw materials for all kinds of work and needs. Paris has become a vast manufacturing center to which all countries resort for thousands of varied products. A continuous surrounding wall and network of separate forts will gradually restrict and destroy, to the great detriment of our capital and kingdom, all that has been done for fifty years to augment its work force, wealth and influence.

The manufactures, textile plants, distilleries and workshops that exist and tend to multiply on the outskirts of Paris will depart for more distant places from year to year rather than to remain exposed to the dangers of being neighbors to a huge fortress. . . .

The capital, if changed into a fortified place, subject to military experimentations and threatened by the possibility of siege and bombardment, must inevitably, and we cannot too often repeat it, see its population diminish at a rapidly decreasing rate. Disturbance of private fortunes, depreciation of property values, disappearance of great industrial plants, will be for Paris the immediate consequences of adoption of this project.

Fortification of Paris will sooner or later mean the transfer of the seat of representative government to another location. The national Chambers could not long remain confined in a city surrounded by fortified walls and cannon, dependent on the action and supremacy of military authority, which would constantly offer, even though involuntarily, a possible threat to the independence of their deliberations.

And finally, he countered the argument, which he said was felt by some but seldom expressed, that the projected wall would protect Paris from strikes and riots and latent revolutionary sentiment. Such arguments he dismissed as specious. Strikes and riots, if brought on only by activists and minorities, could be controlled by the national guards, reinforced by a few regular soldiers. If more widespread, if there should be truly mass upheaval, the discontent would be shared by the army, composed of citizen soldiers; the army would be useless for repression, and a more extensive change of government would be needed. In either case the wall was irrelevant.

In the following years Jullien published nothing new of any significance, with one exception. It was now his habit to attend scientific congresses and at one such, at Angers in 1843, he caught another glimpse of the future of civilization. A Peruvian, a certain Don Pazos, "a descendant of the Incas," had appeared at the Angers meeting, where he had dwelt on the vast possibilities presented by the Amazon River, which with its many tributaries reached from the Atlantic across the continent to Peru, Ecuador, and Bolivia. Shortly after the congress Jullien published a short tract, *Transatlantic Steam Navigation*, on the advantages of European penetration of the Amazon basin. It is free of the self-righteous and disapproving tone of so many of his other writings. Our near-septuagenarian has recovered his youthful capacity for excitement. He enthusiastically anticipates the arguments heard fifty years later at the height of European imperialism. A passing reference to Calcutta implies his belief that the British were already engaged in similar activities in India.

Immediate Application of
Transatlantic Steam Navigation
for Exploration of the Amazon and Its Tributaries

. . . The key to this immense concentration of wealth is in the hands of France with its possession of French Guyana. This colony, our outpost in this part of the world, provides us with a favorable base and transfer point not far from the mouth of the Amazon, and allows us in the near future to meet the hopes and wishes of far-away populations that now call on and await us.

France and Europe need new markets for their agriculture and industrial products, and should establish new relations with the huge states of the two Americas which have varied and abundant riches to exchange for our wares. Another need, generally felt, is to open advantageous careers for our young men, who no longer find adequate outlets for their activity at home. Another and urgent need, which can stir generous hearts and ardent imaginations, is to enlarge and extend the bounds of general knowledge by multiplying the subjects and methods of observation and experience. In short, we should wish to satisfy not only the physical and material needs of our country, but also its moral needs and high sense of its dignity, honor and mission, which calls on it to work effectively for the progress of universal civilization.

The era in which we live, with its greater facility of communication, its railroads, steam navigation, taste for travel, need of nourishing and exercising the mind, and rapid growth of populations that aspire to know, instruct and aid one another, all impel us to explore a new world almost unknown until now. . . .

So! Let us establish a *free port* in French Guyana. It will offer a common meeting place for all peoples who take part in world trade. *Before ten years* our France will have its *Calcutta*. It will be enough to have a few naval vessels, accompanied by commercial shipping, to proceed up the Amazon and some of its tributaries to establish exchange with the nations living along these rivers. We will undertake exploration of all kinds there to the advantage of the natural sciences and our industry. We will set up French consular agents with an understanding of commercial interests, who will expand and solidify our relations there, and who will soon grow in numbers. The reports of travelers in those countries, and the assertions of the honorable Don Pazos, show the existence in these countries of a general sympathy for France and an instinctive willingness to receive its products.

At this same free port where European ships will begin communication with the peoples of South America we can establish a great university, whose faculties can study the natural and medical sciences, the historical and geographical sciences, archaeology, philology, international law, industry, trade, and the practical arts.

The elite of American youth will come down the great river and its tributaries to devour the solid and varied instruction for which they thirst. And these young students from different countries, receiving the same education, will develop from an early age the friendly relationships and intimacy that will later lead to the reciprocal union of the nations to which they belong! A great South American federation will be formed under the auspices of France and Europe, to tighten the bonds of a general alliance of peoples and consolidate universal peace! And our French youth, inspired by our capable professors, will go and diffuse in the Franco-American university the benefits of the education they have received in France! And many American families, visiting their children in this university, and finding that a crossing to France takes only fifteen days, will not hesitate to embark on a voyage that will complement the instruction that we will have

offered them! And these multiple relations, as valuable for the progress of science as for the progress of industry, will infinitely expand
the benefits of exchanges and of an increasingly improved social advancement! And this influence of our own country and the other
European nations, an influence wholly pacific, wholly scientific, intellectual and industrial, will be to the advantage of Europe itself, of
America, and the entire world!

This pleasing picture of a not distant future is no vain seductive
utopia. Its realization lies in our hands if we strongly will it. It will be
a potent remedy for the sufferings of our laboring classes. . . .

The lessons of the past, the imperious needs of the present, the
demands of the future, all invite us to seize the magnificent gift now
offered to us, A NEW WORLD TO BE EXPLOITED not by war and conquest
but by the sciences, the arts of peace, and by industry and commerce.

North America in 1789 imported our products to a value of *two
million* francs; today it imports over *200 millions*. The vast regions
of South America before long, by the means we have indicated,
will expand our exchanges with them in very different proportions.
This prodigious result will require less sacrifice from us than our
recent establishment in the Marquesas Islands, and certainly less than
the unfortunate fortifications of Paris. A few naval and commercial
ships will suffice for the proposed explorations. What a fine and useful application of transatlantic steam navigation, sanctioned by our
laws and consigned to the intelligent activity of government and
commerce!

> M.-A. Jullien (of Paris)
> Vice-president of the scientific congress

Nothing came of this Amazonian dream. France in the 1840s was pre-
occupied with a very different kind of expansion in Algeria.

Little can be known of Jullien's state of mind or activities during the
next few years. There is no evidence that he was in touch with the
republican and revolutionary underground. But with his low opinion
of the July Monarchy he was probably not surprised by the sudden
eruption of revolution in 1848.

On 22 February of that year disturbances in Paris brought about,
within three days, the abdication of Louis-Philippe, his flight to
England, the proclamation of the Republic, and the installation of a
provisional government. Activists throughout the city began to meet
in improvised neighborhood assemblies. They evoked memories of
the "popular societies" or local Jacobin clubs of the Great Revolution
fifty-odd years before. One of them met in the first arrondissement in
the city center a few days after the February Revolution. It called itself

a *réunion*, or meeting, since the word *assemblée* suggested an official body. Among those attending it was Marc-Antoine Jullien, who in fact soon became its chairman or "president."

Thus Jullien, after many years as a liberal who had warned against republicans as a radical minority which, if in power, would produce general disorder and risk intervention by monarchist Europe, emerged in the last year of his life as a republican himself, as he had been in the 1790s. Disgusted with the July Monarchy, he may have come forward on his own initiative. Or the republicans may have sought him out and urged him to join them, wanting an older man of some prominence who had revolutionary credentials from the distant past. Our only evidence is his signature to a placard issued by the unofficial assembly of the first arrondissement, intended to be posted throughout the neighborhood with a view to attracting more members.

This placard, or poster, listed fourteen principles. Jullien signed it, but we cannot tell whether he wrote it or whether he only consented to sign a paper put before him by others. Probably he at least took part in the discussions from which it emerged. Twelve of the fourteen principles were such that he might have favored them as a mere liberal. Only the first two were strictly revolutionary: the first, announcing the sovereignty of the people through direct universal (male) suffrage; and the second, pronouncing the new regime to be a republic. Here is the poster:

French Republic
Democratic Meeting of the First Arrondissement

The glorious victory just won by the people is only the outburst of a universal feeling of revulsion, of rejection of a system based on continuous acts of internal corruption, humiliation abroad, and flagrant violation of the rights and interests of the Nation.

The Republic is the only remedy for such great evils. . . .

This Democratic Meeting adopts as principles:

1. The sovereignty of the people exercised by direct and universal suffrage.

2. The unity and indivisibility of the French Republic.

3. Primary education in free public schools, or in private schools, and in either case obligatory for all; the existence of private secondary education under supervision exclusively by the State [i.e., not by the church].

4. Freedom of religion.

5. Absolute freedom of association.

6. Individual freedom strongly guaranteed.

7. Freedom of the press and of all modes of manifestation of thought, subject to restraints legitimated by a jury.

8. Progressive organization of agricultural and industrial labor.

9. Abolition of slavery in all French possessions.

10. Establishment of a progressive and proportionate system of taxation.

11. Serious accountability of all agents of the executive power.

12. Incorporation of every Citizen in the National Guard.

13. Judicial proceedings without cost.

14. Democratic organization of local government, and the principle of election generally introduced wherever it may be applied.

Sessions of the Democratic Meeting of the First Arrondissement, in view of the inadequacy of its first location, will take place beginning next Tuesday, 21 March, at the Saint-Hyacinthe Chapel in the rue Neuve de Luxembourg.

The day and hour of meeting will still be Tuesday, Thursday and Saturday at 8 o'clock in the evening.

Citizens newly responding to this call will receive definitive admission cards at the meeting place.

The Citizen President
JULLIEN of Paris

It would be gratifying to conclude that at the close of his life Jullien saw the dreams of his youth finally realized. He was not so fortunate. He lived only until the following October. It was long enough for him to see the high hopes of February exploded, the new revolutionaries divided by conflicting class interests, the insurrection in Paris and class war of June, its severe repression, and the drafting of a new republican constitution that provided for a strong presidential power. Had he lived six weeks longer he would have seen the election, by an overwhelming majority in a universal male suffrage, of Louis-Napoleon Bonaparte as president of the republic. He might have been so appalled by the violence of the June Days, on the part of both the rioters and the authorities, as to vote for a strong president. He is less likely to have wanted another Bonaparte. If he had lived until 1852 he would have seen the new Bonaparte proclaim himself Emperor. A cycle seemed to be repeating itself for France, and for Marc-Antoine Jullien his long cycle of hopes and disappointments would have been renewed.

He had accepted every regime since leaving school in 1792, and had also accepted the fall of every regime in turn. He had worked for the government during the Terror, indirectly under the Directory, and for Bonaparte as First Consul and Emperor, and he had attempted repeatedly, though without success, to sit in the Chamber of Deputies under the restored Bourbons and under the July Monarchy. He was marginal to every successive regime. Feeling excluded, he fell into a mood of chronic self-pity and self-justification; probably he had an exaggerated idea of his own abilities and his own importance. He was marginal also to the educational theorists and practitioners of his day, and to the sciences that he greatly admired. But he was more than a marginal man, and certainly not a nonentity. He was an intelligent expositor and publicist for the work of others. To be such is a useful social role; leaders must have followers, and can be judged by the quality of followership that they attract, and which they can also lose.

He had begun as a revolutionary, but hardly of the kind that would start a revolution. As a terrorist in 1794 he had believed himself to be defending a revolution launched five years before, and in 1797, in his advice to Italians on how to revolutionize Italy, he had urged them to act prudently, gradually, and with circumspection. Thereafter, in both his political and educational writings, his concern was to prevent future "commotions." He signed his name to the placard of 1848 after the revolution had occurred.

He represented several though not all of the long strands in the nineteenth-century history of France, and indeed of Europe. He favored the advance of science and technology, the spread of knowledge to widening segments of the population, and what came to be called industrialization in a capitalistic economy. He was deaf to socialism, romanticism, and the kind of nationalism in which nations were pitted against each other. He continued to assert the sovereignty of the nation as a means of securing equality of civil rights and liberty of thought and action, with appropriate considerations for the preservation of law and order. On such matters he gave essentially the same advice, derived from these principles of 1789, to Bonaparte in 1799 and 1804 and again during the Hundred Days, to the restored Bourbon monarchy in 1815, in the confused situation in July 1830, and again in the *Voice of France* in 1840. Could he have returned to earth toward the close of the twentieth century he would have been glad to see these ideas still alive.

REFERENCES

IN ADDITION to works noted for each chapter in the present volume, there have been three books on the career of Marc-Antoine Jullien as a whole. The three are very different.

Helmut Goetz, *Marc-Antoine Jullien de Paris (1775–1848): Der geistige Werdegang eines Revolutionärs. Ein Beitrag zur Geschichte der Vorläufer internationaler Organisationen des 20 Jahrhunderts.* Druck Hugo Mayer, Dornbirn (Switzerland), 1954. This book originated as a doctoral dissertation at the University of Zurich. Goetz was a native of Leipzig and a refugee from the communist takeover in East Germany. He later became connected with the International Bureau of Education at Geneva, and presented Jullien as a precursor to that Bureau, to UNESCO, and to organizations concerned with comparative education. Three-fourths of his book is devoted to the fifty-four years of Jullien's life after the fall of Robespierre. Throughout, however, he is concerned to show how the French Revolution anticipated the totalitarianism and communism of the twentieth century. The book is thoroughly researched, but suffers from the author's own preoccupations and from his habit of mixing statements made by Jullien at very different periods of his life. The bibliography is very extensive and highly useful. There are 892 numbered reference notes. Goetz's book was translated into French by C. Cuénot and published by the Institut pédagogique national in Paris in 1962: *Marc-Antoine Jullien de Paris (1775–1848): L'évolution spirituelle d'un révolutionnaire.* The translator says that he has made slight adaptations; he has also made a few additions to Goetz's already large bibliography and arranged it more conveniently. He lists in chronological sequence no less than 357 pamphlets, books, open letters, speeches, announcements, articles, reports, book reviews, and poems published by Jullien from 1792 until his death in 1848.

Pierre Gascar, *L'Ombre de Robespierre*, Gallimard, Paris, 1979. Gascar, a French man of letters, is the author of novels, essays, and television and film scripts, and is a chevalier of the Legion of Honor. His method is narrative and dramatic, and he evokes a sense of the human reality of his subject. He has a sympathetic and judicious understanding of the Revolution, on which his readings have been extensive. Nine-tenths of his book is on the period before the fall of Robespierre; only a tenth is on the later years on which Goetz is expansive. Presenting Jullien as "Robespierre's shadow," Gascar naturally personalizes their relationship and highlights Robespierre as an individual distinct from the Committee of Public Safety. He sees the Rousseauism that suffused Jullien's family (as in the love of virtue, the good and sovereign people, etc.); he is critical, but does not see the Revolution as an early phase in a process unfolding into later totalitarianism. He provides no notes or references whatever. In such a work numbered notes and precise references would be incongruous and distracting, but their absence is frustrating to a historian, even one who admires the author's literary skill. It is hard to see what sources Gascar has used. It appears that he has drawn heavily but by no means exclusively on Jullien's recollections as expressed by himself or told to others many years later.

Carlo Pancera, *Una vita tra politica e pedagogia: M. A. Jullien de Paris (1775–1848)*, announced for early publication in Italy. I am indebted to M. Dominique Julia of Paris, and to M. Pancera himself, for the opportunity to see the page proofs of this comprehensive study before its publication. Pancera's work is thoroughly annotated, and draws on sources unknown to Goetz and Gascar. It is especially informative on Jullien's activities in Italy in 1797–1799, on his sojourns in Switzerland and Italy after 1810, and on his continuing relations with the Swiss educators J. H. Pestalozzi and P. E. Fellenberg and their then famous schools at Yverdon and Hofwyl. Pancera achieves a better balance than Goetz or Gascar in his treatment of Jullien as a political figure, educational writer, and publicist for science.

There are articles on Jullien in several biographical dictionaries published in the later years of his life. One is an article in the *Biographie universelle et portative des contemporains*, Paris, 1829–30. This article was reprinted as *Notice biographique de Marc-Antoine Jullien, de Paris*, Paris, June 1831, where it is supplemented by a preface signed by Jullien and by 58 pages of documents provided by Jullien for the years since 1792. Even more valuable is an article by G. Sarrut and B. Saint-Edme in their *Biographie des hommes du jour*, 6 vols., Paris, 1835–41. This article was also published separately as *Biographie de M. Jullien de Paris . . . par MM. G. Sarrut et B. Saint-Edme*, Paris, 1842, in 46 pages. The authors interviewed Jullien, who provided them with a good many documents from his past, which they added as a supplement to their biographical sketch. Indeed, much of this article reads as if it had been written by Jullien himself.

Jullien left a considerable corpus of family papers, from which his grandson, Edouard Lockroy, produced two books, published in 1881 and 1893, as explained in the notes to chapters 1 and 2 below. Some of these papers were given by the heirs in the 1920s, on the advice of the French historian Georges Bourgin, to the Marx-Lenin Institute in Moscow, where they were used by Victor Dalin, as explained in the note to chapter 3 below. Others remain in the Archives Nationales in Paris under the call number 39AP, and were used by Barbara Corrado Pope for an unpublished doctoral dissertation at Columbia University in 1981 entitled "Mothers and Daughters in Early Nineteenth-Century France." I am indebted to Professor Isser Woloch of Columbia University for information about this dissertation, which is valuable for the Jullien family after about 1810. Copies also exist, made by Jullien in 1829, of letters to him from his mother from 1785 to 1793; these copies were used by Gascar for his book of 1979, as explained in the note to chapter 10 below.

CHAPTER ONE
A Boy and His Parents in the French Revolution

For particulars on Marc-Antoine Jullien's father and family see the usual biographical dictionaries, and especially J. Brun-Durand, ed., *Dictionnaire biographique . . . de la Drôme*, 2 vols. Grenoble, 1900 (reprinted 1970), vol. 2, pp. 27–29. Since father and son had the same given names they eventually came to be distinguished as Jullien de la Drôme (the father) and Jullien de Paris, the subject of the present book. They were sometimes confused in the older biographical dictionaries. On the financial circumstances of the elder Jullien see "La fortune de Jullien de la Drôme," a document of 1795 published by Albert Mathiez in his *Annales révolutionnaires* 13 (1921), pp. 150–51.

All translated excerpts in this first chapter, with two exceptions, are from letters written by Marc-Antoine's mother, with a few from his father, as published by Edouard Lockroy, ed., *Journal d'une bourgeoise pendant la Révolution, 1791–1793*, Paris, 1881. Lockroy had married the daughter of Marc-Antoine Jullien and so was a grandson of Marc-Antoine and a great-grandson of Rosalie Jullien, whose letters he found among the family papers to which he had access. Lockroy was himself a prominent figure among the Radical Republicans of the early Third Republic. His book of over 300 pages consists entirely of Rosalie Jullien's letters to her son and husband, with a few from her husband to their son. A complete translation into English appeared immediately: *The Great French Revolution of 1785–1793, narrated by the letters of Madame J— of the Jacobin party, edited by her grandson, M. Edouard Lockroy, from the French by Miss Martin and an American collaborator*, London, 1881. I have been unable to learn the identity of Miss Martin or her collaborator. I have selected and newly translated only about a tenth of the contents of Lockroy's volume.

The two exceptions, noted above, are Jullien's speech at the Jacobin club of January 1792 and his letter to Condorcet of August 1792. The speech was published at the time with the full title, *Discours d'un jeune citoyen patriote sur les mesures à prendre dans les circonstances actuelles, prononcé à la Société Fraternelle des Jacobins de la rue Saint-Honoré, le Dimanche 22 Janvier 1792, l'an quatrième de la liberté*. The letter to Condorcet was found by Alphonse Aulard in the archives of the French foreign office, and published in his journal, *La Révolution française* 12 (1887), pp. 639–41.

CHAPTER TWO
Young Agent of the Terror

The materials for this chapter come mostly from two sources. One is a volume published by the same Edouard Lockroy, *Une mission en Vendée*, Paris, 1893. It contains copies made by Jullien or an assistant of letters sent by him to the Committee of Public Safety and to Robespierre and others, as well as notes and the text of speeches made by Jullien while on his mission in western France. The other main source is the volume published by the National Convention in 1795, containing the report of a committee appointed to examine the papers found in the lodgings of Robespierre and a few others who had been overthrown on 9 Thermidor of the Year II (27 July 1794). The purpose of the Convention was to find evidence to prove the existence of a Robespierrist conspiracy. The chairman of the committee was E. B. Courtois, who reported to the Convention in January 1795 in a four-hour speech which was "frequently interrupted by the most lively applause." The report was ordered printed by the Convention as *Rapport de la commission chargée de l'examen des papiers trouvés chez Robespierre et ses complices*, par E. B. Courtois, Paris An III. An amplified new edition was published in 1828 as *Papiers inédits trouvés chez Robespierre, Saint-Just, Payan, etc.*, 3 vols., Paris, 1828. Fifteen letters written by Jullien are identical in the two editions; only one was added in 1828 despite the editor's claim to publish *inédits*.

Courtois had access to the original letters addressed to Robespierre and others, but not to those addressed to the Committee of Public Safety. The originals seen by Courtois were subsequently destroyed or lost. Lockroy of course had only the copies made by Jullien. Those published by Courtois are virtually identical with the copies published by Lockroy, with occasional variations of a few words perhaps intended by Courtois to make his case against Robespierre. As between the two sources, the greater value of Courtois is that he included Jullien's letters from Bordeaux, which Lockroy did not include since his subject was Jullien's mission to the Vendée, and the greater value of Lockroy is his inclusion of letters to the Committee of Public Safety, Barère, Prieur of the Marne, and others, which were not available to Courtois. The interested reader can locate any letter in either of these sources according to its date.

In 1926 Georges Michon published his *Correspondance de Maximilien et Augustin Robespierre*, containing many items unknown until then, but for the letters translated in the present volume he was content simply to cite the relevant pages in Courtois and in Lockroy's *Mission en Vendée*. Michon had access to the family papers which Lockroy had seen, some of which were later sent to Moscow, as noted above. Michon's acceptance of Lockroy's publication of Jullien's copies gives additional assurance of their reliability. The present volume contains only one item from Michon not found in Courtois or Lockroy; it is a paragraph from a letter to Robespierre under date of 10 Pluviôse.

The few orders of the Committee translated here are from Alphonse Aulard et al., eds., *Recueil des actes du Comité du salut public avec la correspondance des représentants en mission*, 28 vols., Paris, 1889–1951. These, too, can be easily located by their date. The *Actes* contain nothing received by the Committee from Jullien, since he was not a *représentant en mission*. Jullien's speech at the Paris Jacobin club is in Aulard, *La Société des Jacobins*, 6 vols., Paris, 1889–1897, vol. 6, pp. 131–32.

Further information on Jullien's activities at Bordeaux is furnished by Pierre Bécamps, *La Révolution à Bordeaux, 1789–1794*, Bordeaux and Paris, 1953. Bécamps used the papers of the local authorities and political clubs preserved in the local archives. On Bordeaux see also Alan Forrest, *Society and Politics in Revolutionary Bordeaux*, Oxford, 1975.

The phrase about liberty lying on mattresses for corpses, often held against Jullien in later years, is quoted from his *Discours sur les dangers du modérantisme et les moyens de former la conscience politique*, as printed at Bordeaux in 1794, p. 24. The same words are quoted by Goetz, who saw the first edition, in his *Werdegang eines Revolutionärs*, p. 40. The statements by Gascar, in *Ombre de Robespierre*, p. 231, and by Dalin in *Annales historiques de la Révolution française* 36 (1964), p. 162, to the effect that Jullien was only citing Raynal and Mirabeau, seem to derive from what Jullien said in self-extenuation in 1823. See his letter to the editors of *Mémoires de Louvet*, printed in the second edition of these memoirs, Paris, 1823, pp. 391–98, and reprinted by Jullien in his *Notice Bibliographique*, Paris, 1831, pp. 19–26 (especially p. 25).

For Jullien's suspicions of Robespierre on 15 Thermidor, as quoted at the end of this chapter, see *Marc-Antoine Jullien à ses frères et amis de la société populaire de La Rochelle; Rochefort, ce 15 thermidor, an second de la République française une et indivisible*, pp. 2 and 6–7. For the speech prefixed with an *avis* concerning the "execrable Robespierre" see *Adresse du Club National de Bordeaux aux sociétés populaires affiliées . . . du 21 germinal, l'an deuxième de la République par M. A. Jullien, fils, agent du Comité de Salut public. . . .*, n.p.n.d., but with a note at the end showing a printer's name at Bordeaux.

CHAPTER THREE
Democrat among the "Anarchists"

The session of the Convention on 11 Thermidor at which Jullien was denounced was reported in the *Moniteur universel* for 13 Thermidor. His report to the Committee of Public Safety was printed as *Marc-Antoine Jullien aux Représentants du Peuple composant le Comité de Salut public*, Paris, n.d., but the text gives the date 24 Thermidor. The quoted verses, written in prison, are from "Mes adieux à ma patrie (1794)" included in *La France en 1825, ou mes regrets et mes espérances, discours en vers . . . . seconde édition, suivie de quelques autres poésies detachées . . . .*, Paris, 1825.

Jullien's letter of 21 October to the Club National at Bordeaux was found by Pierre Bécamps in the departmental archives of the Gironde and quoted at length in his article, "M. A. Jullien agent du Comité de Salut public a't-il servi ou trahi Robespierre?" in *Revue historique de Bordeaux et du département de la Gironde*, n.s. 3 (1953), pp. 205–10. Bécamps concluded that Jullien's claim to have suspected Robespierre before 9 Thermidor was probably false, being special pleading after Robespierre's death. He cited other evidence but seems not to have known of the letter sent from Rochefort on 15 Thermidor or the speech of 21 Germinal published after Robespierre's death, both cited in the reference to chapter 2 above, or of Jullien's own report to the Committee of Public Safety dated 24 Thermidor.

For the rest of this chapter 3 the sources are the Jullien papers at the Marx-Lenin Institute in Moscow, used in three excellent articles by Victor Dalin in the *Annales historiques de la Révolution française*, "Marc-Antoine Jullien après le 9 thermidor," *A.H.R.F.* 36 (1964), pp. 159–73; 37 (1965), pp. 187–203; and 38 (1966), pp. 390–412. Dalin provides many quotations from Jullien's memoranda and journal written during his imprisonment. Jullien began to write his "prison journal" on 7 September 1795, so that it is not a true day-to-day journal but a retrospective reflection on his captivity and on what he had heard of events outside the prison during the past year; see Dalin, *A.H.R.F.* 36 (1964), pp. 163ff.

For Jullien's writings in the *Orateur plébéien* see its numbers for 5, 7, and 21 Frimaire An IV. Babeuf's comments on these writings are from Dalin, *A.H.R.F.* 37 (1965), pp. 195–96.

CHAPTER FOUR
Bonaparte—Italy—Egypt—Naples

A connected account of the period treated in this chapter is given by V. M. Dalin, with quotations from the Jullien papers at the Marx-Lenin Institute in Moscow. See his "Marc-Antoine Jullien après le 9 thermidor," in *Annales historiques de la Révolution française* 38 (1966), pp. 390–412. For the revolutionary republics set up in Italy from 1796 to 1799 see my *Age of the Democratic Revolution*, vol. 2, Princeton, 1964, chapters 9–12, pp. 263–391, and also 559–61.

The letter of Jullien to Bonaparte is printed in full by Dalin, *A.H.R.F.* 37 (1965), pp. 201–3. For Prudhomme and Mme Jullien see L. M. Prudhomme, *Histoire générale et impartiale des erreurs des fautes et des crimes commis pendant la Révolution française* 5 vols., Paris, An V, vol. 5, pp. 456 and 463–66; and in the second edition of 1824, vol. 9, pp. 278, 282, 286–89. The letters from Marshal Augereau and General Bon were published from copies in his possession by Jullien in his *Notice biographique . . . suivie de documents inédits . . .* , Paris, 1831, pp. 37-40. Only one copy of the *Quelques conseils aux patriotes cisalpins* is known; it is in the Archives Nationales; but its full text was published by G. Vaccarino in *I patrioti "anarchistes" e l'idea dell'unità italiana*, Einaudi 1955, pp. 113–24. The *Courrier de l'armée d'Italie* is also rare; its prospectus was published by Georges Bourgin in *Revue des études napoléoniennes* 18 (1922), pp. 225–31. For a few unimportant papers and his claim to have written a lost journal of his trip to Egypt see the *Notice biographique* of 1831, pp. 41–43. The quotation with which this chapter ends is from Dalin, *A.H.R.F.* (1966), p. 404.

CHAPTER FIVE
For and Against Napoleon

The *Political Colloquy* was published as *Entretien politique sur la situation actuelle en France et sur les plans du nouveau gouvernement*, Paris, Frimaire an VIII (November 1799). The pamphlet of 1801 is *Appel aux véritables amis de la patrie, de la liberté et de la paix, ou Tableau des principaux résultats de l'administrations des consuls et des resources actuelles de la République française*, Paris, Germinal an IX (March–April 1801). An Italian translation appeared at Milan, also in 1801.

The published General Essay is *Essai général de l'éducation physique, morale et intellectuelle, suivi d'un plan d'éducation pratique pour l'enfance, l'adolescence et la jeunesse, ou Recherches sur les principes et les bases de l'Education à donner aux enfants des premières familles de l'Etat, pour accélérer la marche de la Nation vers la civilisation et la prosperité.* Par M.-A.J., Paris, 1808. The selection translated is from pp. vii and viii.

Other materials contained in this chapter, written by Jullien between 1800 and 1814 but not published at the time, were made public by Jullien after Napoleon's abdication in the work of M. S. Friedrich Schoell, *Recueil des pièces officielles destinées à détromper les Français sur les événements qui se sont passés depuis quelques années,* 9 vols., Paris, 1814–1816. Schoell was a bilingual native of Saarbrücken on the Franco-German border who took part in the Revolution at Strasbourg until 1792, then emigrated to Germany, and was active in publishing at Paris from 1803 to 1814. Turning against Napoleon, as Jullien did, he was employed by the Prussian envoy, Hardenburg, at the Congress of Vienna. Published in preparation for the Congress, the *Recueil* was a compilation mainly of official documents designed to disabuse those of the French who still had any confidence in Napoleon. It is possible that Jullien and Schoell became acquainted during the years in Paris. In any case Jullien provided him in 1814 and 1815 with various of his manuscript writings of the preceding years. These fill about half of Schoell's ninth and final volume, and are introduced by three short prefaces signed by "Le chevalier A. de Clendi," a pseudonym that Jullien adopted briefly and only for this purpose. He thus preserved his anonymity during the difficulties of the Bourbon restoration, but he claimed authorship a few years later, and French bibliographers concur in attributing these writings to Jullien.

In the three short prefaces he explained why he was making these materials public by way of the final volume of Schoell's compilation. His purpose was to make himself acceptable to the new Bourbon régime by showing that he had tried in vain to give Bonaparte good advice, that he had long believed that Bonaparte had betrayed his own followers, and that he had long anticipated the collapse of the Napoleonic system. The first preface, dated June 1814 (Schoell, pp. 5–8), written during the first Bourbon restoration of March 1814, introduces Jullien's diatribe against Napoleon of October 1813. The other two prefaces, both dated September 1815, after Waterloo and the second Restoration (Schoell, pp. 145–54), introduce his private notes and his advice to Bonaparte from 1800 through 1805. In this volume of Schoell's work, appearing early in 1816, Jullien carefully refrained from mentioning what he had done or published during the Hundred Days, March–June 1815, when he had briefly taken Napoleon's side.

The Memoir of 1800 on Italy, submitted to Bonaparte, is "Mémoire sur l'organisation fédérative et indépendante de l'Italie," in Schoell, pp. 155–63. The private memo of January 1804 is "Coup d'oeil sur quelques-unes des institutions de la France au commencement de l'an 12," in Schoell, pp. 164–69. The memo submitted to Bonaparte in May 1804 is "Mémoire soumis au Général Bonaparte premier consul de la République française sur la situation politique de la France au mois de floréal an 12 (mai 1804) et sur quelques-unes des bases de la nouvelle forme de gouvernement qu'il paratrait convenable d'adopter" (Schoell, pp. 112–44). The private memo of 1805 is "Fragment sur la situation morale et politique de la France et sur la situation générale de l'Europe au mois de mai 1805," in Schoell, pp. 171–82. The *Preserver of Europe* of October 1813 is "Le conservateur de l'Europe, ou considérations sur la situation actuelle de l'Europe et sur les moyens d'y rétablir l'équilibre politique des différents états, et une paix générale solidement affermie," in Schoell, pp. 9–82.

CHAPTER SIX
The Hundred Days

The sources of this chapter are *Profession de foi d'un militaire français*, Paris, mai 1815; *Le Conciliateur, ou La septième époque, appel à tous les Français; considérations impartiales sur la situation politique et les vrais intérêts de la France à l'époque du 1ere mai 1815, par un Français, ami de la patrie et membre d'un collège electoral*, Paris, mai 1815; and *De la Représentation nationale dans les journées des 21 et 22 juin 1815*, Paris, 25 juin 1815.

Shortly after the revolution of 1830 Jullien published as item No. 62 among the documents appended to *Notice biographique sur Marc-Antoine Jullien*, Paris, 1831, his text of the "Déclaration de la Chambre des Représentants, séance du 5 juillet 1815," together with another document, item 61, a letter of 1828 from Antoine Jay to Jullien attesting to Jullien's authorship of the Declaration of 5 July. Jay had been a member of the Chamber of Representatives in 1815, was a well-known liberal of the 1820s, and lived until 1854. The texts of both declarations adopted by the Chamber of Representatives on 5 July 1815 were published later in *Archives parlementaires*, second series, vol. 14 (1860), pp. 609–10, together with a brief account of the debate. The texts of the second declaration, as given in the *Archives parlementaires* and by Jullien in 1831, are identical. No historian seems to have known or mentioned this second and more significant declaration of the moribund Chamber.

CHAPTER SEVEN
Constitutional Monarchist

The first of the two tracts published soon after the second Restoration is *Des élections qui vont avoir lieu pour former une nouvelle Chambre de Députés . . . à l'époque du 1ᵉʳ* août 1815 par un membre d'un collège électoral, Paris, 1815. The second is *Quelques réflexions sur l'esprit qui doit . . . diriger les membres des collèges électoraux . . . par Marc-Antoine Jullien, propriétaire à Paris, membre d'un collège électoral et de la Légion d'Honneur . . .* , Paris, 12 août 1815. For the papers published by Schoell see the references for chapter 5 above.

Further advice to electors is in the anonymous *Manuel électoral à l'usage de MM. les électeurs des départements de France*, Paris, 1817, a work of over a hundred pages containing excerpts from the constitutional charter and the laws concerning elections, and lists of qualified electors; reprinted under the same title but adding *par M.-A. Jullien, de Paris, électeur éligible du département de la Seine*, seconde édition, Paris, 1818. Next comes *Directions pour la conscience d'un électeur, par un électeur éligible . . .* , Paris, 1824; my short quotation is from pp. 50–51.

Jullien defends his reputation in *Réponse provisoire à quelques articles des répertoires de mensonges, de diffamations et de calomnies, intitulés Biographie des hommes vivants, Biographie moderne, Nouvelle biographie, etc. . . . par M.-A. Jullien, de Paris*, Paris, 1821; it was first published in the *Annales encyclopédiques* of December 1818, and reprinted in the *Notice biographique* of 1831 cited below. Jullien's letter of protest to the editors of Louvet's memoirs was published by them in their second edition, Paris, 1823, and reprinted in the *Notice biographique* cited below. On Gohier see the signed review by Jullien of the *Mémoires de Louis-Jerome Gohier président du Directoire au 18 brumaire*, Paris, 1824, in the *Revue encyclopédique* of May 1824, pp. 432–36.

For Jullien on the Revolution of 1830 see *Le bon sens national*, par Marc-Antoine Jullien, de Paris, 6 août 1830. The publication of 1831 is *Notice biographique sur Marc-Antoine Jullien, de Paris . . . précédée d'un coup d'oeil sur la situation politique . . . et suivie de documents inédits, de letters et de pièces justificatives*, Paris, juin 1831. The biography included here was first published in *Biographie universelle et portative des contemporains*, Paris, 1829–1830.

CHAPTER EIGHT
Theorist of Education

On the renewed interest in Jullien as an educational theorist see I. L. Kandel, of Teachers College, Columbia University, "International cooperation in education: an early nineteenth-century aspiration," in

Educational Forum 7 (1942); P. Rosello, *M. A. Jullien de Paris, père de l'éducation comparée*, Geneva, 1943; and for the centennial publication by the Musée Pédagogique in Paris and the French Ministry of National Education, *La pédagogie comparée: Un précurseur, M. A. Jullien de Paris*, Paris, 1949. More thorough scholarly studies followed later: H. Goetz, *Marc-Antoine Jullien de Paris (1775–1848). Der geistige Werdegang eines Revolutionärs. Ein Beitrag zur Geschichte der Vorläufer internationaler Organisationen des 20. Jahrhunderts*, Dornbirn (Switzerland), 1954, with a French translation by C. Cuénot, Paris, 1962; S. Fraser, *Jullien's plan for comparative education, 1816–1817*, New York, 1964; C. Pancera, *Una vita tra politica e pedagogia*, 1991. More generally, for educational plans and reforms in France from about 1760 to 1815 reference may be made to my *Improvement of Humanity: Education and the French Revolution*, Princeton, 1985; and my book on the College of Louis-le-Grand from 1762 to 1814, *The School of the French Revolution*, Princeton, 1975.

For Jullien's advice to the Italian patriots in 1797 and to Bonaparte in 1799, and for his pamphlet of 1801, see the references to chapters 4 and 5 above. For his contacts with Gall and phrenology see Pancera, pp. 111–12, and the *Biographie des hommes du jour*, vol. 6, pp. 358 and 364.

Jullien's books on education excerpted in this chapter are as follows. The wording of title pages is given at length, since it so explicitly conveys content and purposes.

1. *Essai sur l'emploi du temps, ou Méthode qui a pour objet de bien régler sa vie, premier moyen d'être heureux, destinée spécialement à l'usage des jeunes gens, par Marc-Antoine Jullien, de Paris, chevalier de la Légion d'Honneur, Membre de . . . . troisième edition entièrement refondue et très augmentée*, Paris, 1824, but first published in 1808. I have used the edition of 1824. For the numerous reprintings and translations derived from this work, the *Biomètre*, the *Montre morale*, and others, see the catalogues of the Bibliothèque Nationale and the British Library; the *Biographie des hommes du jour*, vol. 6, pp. 364–65; and the bibliography appended to Goetz's book cited above.

2. *Essai géneral d'éducation physique, morale et intellectuelle, suivi d'un plan d'éducation pratique pour l'enfance, l'adolescence et la jeunesse, ou Recherches sur les principes et les bases de l'éducation à donner aux enfants des premières familles de l'Etat, pour accélérer la marche de la Nation vers la civilisation et la prospérité. Par M.-A.J.* Paris, 1808. A second edition followed in 1835.

3. *Esprit de la Méthode d'éducation de Pestalozzi, suivie et pratiquée dans l'Institut d'Éducation d'Yverdon, en Suisse, par M. Marc-Antoine Jullien, Chevalier de la Légion d'Honneur, membre de . . . .* 2 vols., Milan,

de l'Imprimerie royale, 1812. The *imprimerie royale* was the printer for the short-lived Napoleonic Kingdom of Italy under Eugène de Beauharnais as viceroy. There was a second edition at Paris, 1842.

4. *Précis sur les instituts d'éducation de M. de Fellenberg établis à Hofwyl auprès de Berne, extrait du Journal d'Éducation*, Paris, 1817. The passages translated here may be found in the *Journal d'Éducation* III (1817), pp. 77–91. There is an extensive and useful treatment of Jullien's connections with both Pestalozzi and Fellenberg in Pancera, pp. 155–57 and 182–216.

5. *Esquisse et vues préliminaires d'un ouvrage sur l'éducation comparée, entrepris d'abord pour les vingt-deux cantons de la Suisse, et pour quelques parties de l'Allemagne et de l'Italie, et qui doit comprendre successivement, d'après le même plan, tous les états de l'Europe, et Séries de questions sur l'éducation . . . . par M.M.A. Jullien, de Paris, Chevalier de l'ordre royal de la Légion d'Honneur, membre de . . . .* Paris, 1817. A complete translation of this work was made by Stewart Fraser in his *Jullien's Plan for Comparative Education* (see above), together with an extended discussion of its place in the history of educational thought. I have, however, made my own translations. Jefferson's letter of 1818 to Jullien is in the *Writings of Thomas Jefferson*, 20 vols., Washington, 1903, vol. 15, pp. 171–74.

CHAPTER NINE
Apostle of Civilization

For the first excerpt see "Sur la marche et les effets de la civilisation" in *Essai général d'éducation*, Paris, 1808, pp. 296–98. In the *Esquisse d'un essai sur la philosophie des sciences*, Paris, 1819, see especially pp. iv, 14–15, and the large unnumbered "Tableau synoptique des connaissances humaines." Jullien included a reproduction of this table in the *Revue Encyclopédique*, vol. 33 (1827), p. 782.

The ten-year index for the years 1819 through 1828 appeared in two volumes in 1831 under the name of its compiler, F.A.M. Miger, *Table décennale de la Revue encyclopédique, ou Repertoire général . . . quarante premiers volumes de ce recueil*, Paris, 1831. The *Revue* extended to sixty volumes before its expiration in 1833. The two volumes of the index have no volume numbers within the series, and some collections of the *Revue* lack the index, which, however, is included with the set at the Princeton University Library.

All the following translated passages in the present chapter are from the *Revue Encyclopédique*, identified by the first three words of the English translation:

"France has lacked": *RE* I (1819), pp. 5–17.
"It is not": *RE* XVII (1823), pp. 5–15.
"Foreign learned societies": *RE* V (1820), pp. 14–17.

"Classification by Nations": *RE* XXXIII (1827), p. 16.
"Lithography. Dr. Foerster": *RE* II (1819), p. 536.
"England. Arrival in": *RE* III (1819), p. 355.
"United States. Navigation": *RE* III (1819), p. 563.
"The United States": *RE* XIII (1822), pp. 385–87.
"Philadelphia. Industrial Statistics": *RE* XXXV (1827), pp. 764–65.
". . . is the first": *RE* XVI (1822), p. 408, and XXIX (1826), p. 512.
"General telegraphy, nautical": *RE* IX (1821), pp. 214–15.
"Contest of steam": *RE* XLIV (1829), pp. 503–5.
"The lightness of": ibid.
"London. Steam coach": *RE* XLIII (1829), pp. 489–90.
"Frankenstein, or the": *RE* XI (1821), pp. 191–92.
"America. The world": *RE* XXXIII (1827), pp. 17–18, 22–40.
"Some views on": *RE* XX (1823), pp. 5–10, 14.
"Notice on the": *RE* XVIII (1823), pp. 7–25.

CHAPTER TEN
The Later Years

For particulars on Jullien's family life in the 1820s see the dissertation by Barbara Corrado Pope noted in the General References above. For the quotation from his daughter's journal I am indebted to the late Professor Victor Dalin of Moscow, who included it in our correspondence noted in the references to chapter 3 above. For Jullien's self-justifications summarized at the beginning of the present chapter see the references to chapters 5 and 7 above, and the *Revue Encyclopédique*, vol. 40 (1828), pp. 479–80. The two biographical dictionaries of 1829 and 1841 are *Biographie universelle et portative des contemporains*, eds. A. Rabbe and V. de Boisjolin, Paris, 1829–1830; and *Biographie des hommes du jour, industriels, conseillers d'état . . . écrivains . . . savants*, eds. G. Sarrut and B. Saint-Edme, 6 vols., Paris, 1835–1841. In both these cases the articles on Jullien were also separately printed in pamphlet form. For the full title of Jullien's *Notice biographique* of 1831 see the references to chapter 7 above.

For Jullien's having his mother's letters professionally copied, with a view to their publication, see Pierre Gascar, *L'Ombre de Robespierre*, Paris, 1979, pp. 7–10, 310–13, and 321–25. The letter of 1831 to Fellenberg is quoted at length by Carlo Pancera, *Una vita tra politica e pedagogia: M. A. Jullien de Paris (1775–1848)*, pp. 244–45; the later letter to Fellenberg of 1839 is ibid., pp. 247–49.

The learned societies of which Jullien was a member are listed in the two biographical articles of 1829 and 1841. The three Americans known by Jullien in Paris are all in the *Dictionary of American Biography*. For the collection at the University of Pennsylvania see the published guide to its contents, *The Maclure Collection of French Revolutionary Materials*, Philadelphia, 1966; and for the possibility that Maclure may have bought the collection from Jullien see the preface by John H. Jensen, one of the editors of this guide, pp. xvii–xxiii. The letter from Du Ponceau proposing Jullien for membership is in the collections at the American Philosophical Society. For names of all members of the Institut de France before 1895, from which Jullien is conspicuously missing, see Comte de Franqueville, *Le premier siècle de l'Institut de France*, 1795–1895, 2 vols., Paris, 1895. The five persons elected in 1832 to the Academy of Moral and Political Sciences, who had supported the Revolution between 1789 and 1794, were Sieyès, Garat, Daunou, Roederer, and Talleyrand. Of these, only Sieyès had voted for the death of Louis XVI.

The writings of Jullien excerpted in the remainder of this chapter are:

Lettre à la nation anglaise sur l'union des peuples et la civilisation comparée, sur . . . le Biomètre, ou Montre Morale, suivie de quelques poésies et d'un Discours en Vers . . . , Londres, 15 septembre, 1833.

Biometer, or Moral Watch, serving to indicate the number of hours devoted every day to . . . , by Marc-Antoine Jullien, de Paris, chevalier de la Légion d'Honneur, author of the Essay on the Employment of Time, London, 1833. The table is at pp. 92–93. There is a copy of this work in the library of the American Philosophical Society, to which Jullien sent copies of some of his writings, sometimes inscribed in his own hand, both before and after his election to the Society. The rarity of the *Biometer* in English is indicated by its absence from the printed catalogues of the British Library, the Bibliothèque Nationale, and the Library of Congress Union Catalogue.

Appel au bons sens national et à la conscience politique sur la crise actuelle et sur les prochaines élections . . . , Paris, 1839.

La Voix de la France. Réflexions sur notre situation intérieure et extérieure . . . , Paris, 1840.

Fortifications de Paris, Première note sur la nécessité de repousser le projet de loi . . . adressée à . . . la Chambre de Pairs, Paris, 1841. This *Première note* is dated 24 February; the second and third with identical titles are dated 6 March and 24 March, respectively.

Application immédiate de la NAVIGATION TRANSATLANTIQUE à la vapeur à l'exploration des vastes et riches contrées que baignent le FLEUVE DES AMAZONES et ses nombreux affluents, Paris, 1843.

Réunion démocratique du 1ᵉ arrondissement. This placard bears no place or date, but internal evidence shows a date between 1 and 21 March 1848; and it is clearly Paris.

INDEX

Adams, John Quincy, 156
American Academy of Arts and Sciences, 182
American Philosophical Society, 182, 203–4
Augereau, 80–81

Babeuf, 24, 63, 68, 70–72, 74–75, 79, 83, 90, 102
Bacon, Francis, 112, 170, 176, 181, 205, 206, 207
Barbaroux, 35, 58, 60, 64
Barère, 33, 40, 42, 47, 59, 63, 131
Basedow, 170
Beauharnais, Eugène de, 110, 111, 113–114, 162
Bécamps, Pierre, 231
Bentham, 154
Bernadotte, 128, 143
Blanc, Louis, 214
Blücher, 130
Bon, General, 81–82
Bonaparte, 38, 71, 76–78, 80–81, 93–106. For dates after 1803 see Napoleon.
Bordeaux, 48–52, 54–60, 62–65, 66–67, 78, 134, 141–42, 149, 204
Bourbons, 119–22, 128–30, 134
Brissot, 9, 11, 22, 23, 25, 50, 65
Brissotins, 22, 23, 25
Brune, General, 89, 91
Buffon, 211
Buonarroti, 79
Burke, Edmund, 19, 102
Buzot, 23, 34, 58, 60, 64
Byron, Lord, 139, 207

Caen, 35
Caesar, Julius, 161
Campo Formio, 89
Carnot, 63, 124, 217
Carrier, J. B., 36, 40, 42–44, 63, 79, 141
Catholic and Royal Army, 36, 39
Cerise, Guglielmo, 79
Championnet, J. A., 90–91
Charette, 43
Charlemagne, 108, 110

Charles X, 144, 147
Cherbourg, 34
Cisalpine Republic, 82–87, 103, 151–52
Collot D'Herbois, 63
Commission on Public Instruction, 52–54, 151
Committee of Public Safety, 30–65, 95, 124, 131
Condorcet, 9, 11, 22, 154, 195
Constant, Benjamin, 124, 180, 214
Courtois, E. B., 68, 79, 201, 230–31
Cousin, Victor, 180
Cuénot, C., 227
Cuvier, Georges, 180, 205

d'Alembert, 176
Dalin, Victor, 228, 232–33, 239
Danton, 50, 51, 56
Daumier, 211
David, 184
Delacroix, 180
Destutt de Tracy, 176
Dumouriez, 9, 11, 22, 28, 65
Du Ponceau, Peter, 203

Egypt, 90
Erie Canal, 185
Erskine, Lord, 184

Fellenberg, P. E., 166–69, 202, 211
Feuillants, 17–18, 69
Fichte, J. G., 194–96
Forrest, Alan, 231
Fourier, J. B., 180
Franklin, Benjamin, 158, 170, 205
Franklin Institute, 186
Fraser, Stewart, 237, 238
Frederick the Great, 161

Gall, Joseph, 155
Garnier de Saintes, 60
Gascar, Pierre, 227
Gaultier, Abbé, 172
George III, 19–20, 41
Girondins, 9, 19, 22, 25–26, 28, 30, 48, 58–60, 63, 68–69, 72, 78, 141, 149, 204

Garat, 11
Géricault, 180
Gillray, 19
Goetz, Helmut, 227
Gohier, 141–43, 200
Grégoire, Abbé, 180
Gaudet, 23, 53, 60, 64, 141
Guizot, 180, 200

Hébert, 56
Hofwyl, 166–69
Hume, 207

Jacobin club of Paris, 7, 9–10, 13, 36, 52–53, 67, 154, 201
Jacobin clubs (popular societies), 24, 26, 32–35, 45, 48, 51, 223
"Jacobins" (loose sense), 102, 115, 152
Jefferson, Thomas, 110, 174, 205
Jenner, Edward, 184
Jensen, John H., 240
Julia, Dominique, 228
Jullien, Adolphe (son of M.A.J.), 187
Jullien, Auguste (son of M.A.J.), 200
Jullien, Marc-Antoine (father of M.A.J.), 3–4, 11, 22, 24–25, 26, 63, 93, 139
Jullien, Rosalie (mother of M.A.J.), 3–30, 63, 78–79, 93, 200–201
Jullien, Sophie (wife of M.A.J.), 93, 200

Kandel, I. L., 236
Kant, Immanuel, 194
Kosciuszko, 139

Lafayette, 5, 6, 7, 12–13, 133, 139, 143, 144, 150, 203
Lamartine, 180
Lancastrian system, 167, 172
La Rochelle, 45, 47–48, 51, 52, 61, 64, 142
La Romiguière, 172
Lebatteux, 37, 68
Legion of Honor, 105, 108, 111
Le Havre, 33
Leoben, 80
Le Peletier de Saint-Fargeau, 27
Lindet, 35
Locke, John, 207
Lockroy, Edouard, 201, 228, 229–31
Lorient, 36, 38, 52, 64
Louis XVI, 6, 9–10, 13, 19, 24, 26, 65
Louis XVIII, 68, 73, 76, 118–20, 122, 133, 137

Louis-Philippe, 144, 146, 204
Louvet, 141, 200
Lunéville, 102
Lyon, 49

Mably, Abbé, 3
Maclure, William, 203
Malesherbes, 140
Marat, 50, 52
Marengo, 100, 102
Marie-Antoinette, 6, 10
Marie-Louise, 113
Marx, 63, 196, 211
Masséna, 91
Mignet, 180, 200
Milton, 207
Mirabeau, 46, 142
Montagnards, 22, 23, 25–27
Montaigne, 170
Montesquieu, 212
Morbihan, 36–37, 39
Muscadins, 32, 34, 50

Nantes, 42–44
Napoleon I, 107–32, 136, 142–43. For dates before 1804 see Bonaparte.
Napoleon II, 129–30
Navarre College, 4
New Lanark, 196–99
Newton, Isaac, 207

Orateur plébéien, 63, 72–74
Owen, Robert, 196–99, 203

Pancera, Carlo, 228
Pantheon Club, 71, 72, 74
Pazos, Don, 221
Pestalozzi, 113, 137, 162–66, 168
Peter the Great, 116
Pétion, 9, 19, 58, 64
Pitt, William, 19, 39, 41, 45
Plessis Prison, 66
Pope, Barbara Corrado, 229
Priestley, Joseph, 11, 205
Prieur, C. A., 63
Prieur of the Marne, 31–32, 36, 38, 41, 205
Prudhomme, L. M., 79

Quimper, 39

Raynal, 46
Revue Encyclopédique, 133, 176–99, 202

Richelieu, 109
Robespierre, 9, 13, 22, 23, 27–28, 29–31, 34,
    40, 44, 50–54, 59–62, 64, 65, 67, 68, 85,
    134, 201, 204
Rochefort, 61, 62, 64
Rollin, 159, 170
Rosello, P., 237
Rosetta Stone, 90
Rousseau, 7, 17, 29, 159

Saint-André, Jeanbon, 31–32
Saint-Emilion, 58, 141
Saint-Haouen, baron de, 188
Saint-Just, 31, 57, 60
Saint-Malo, 34, 52
Saint-Simon, marquis de, 159, 180
Saliceti, 78
Say, J. B., 180, 184–85
Schoell, Friedrich, 137, 200, 234–35
Scott, Sir Walter, 207
Seguin brothers, 187
Servan, 22
Shakespeare, 207
Shelley, Mary, 190–91
Sieyès, Abbe, 204
Sismondi, 180, 191–94
Smith, Adam, 207
Socrates, 140
Stanhope, Lord, 11, 12, 205
Stephenson, Robert, 189

Supreme Being, 52–54, 68, 83, 85

Talleyrand, 11, 12, 154
Tallien, 50, 63, 141, 149
Theophilanthropy, 83
Thierry, 180
Thiers, 180
Tippoo-Saib, 12
Tocqueville, 211
Toulon, 32, 38
Tréhouard, 36, 37, 40
Tribun du peuple, 72
Tuileries, 15–16, 65, 103

Valmy, 22
Varennes, 7
Varlet, 68
Vendée, 32, 36, 78
Venice, 80, 82, 89, 101
Verdun, 20
Verona, 68, 76

Warden, David, 203
Washington, 146, 205
Wellington, 130
Woloch, Isser, 227

Ysabeau, 49–52, 54–56, 61–62, 66, 79,
    141
Yverdon, 162